PURE GOLD

PURE GOLD
EMBRACING GOD'S GRACE

PAM DAVIS

Authentic

COLORADO SPRINGS · MILTON KEYNES · HYDERABAD

Authentic Publishing
We welcome your questions and comments.

USA   1820 Jet Stream Drive, Colorado Springs, CO 80921
        www.authenticbooks.com
UK   9 Holdom Avenue, Bletchley, Milton Keynes, Bucks, MK1 1QR
        www.authenticmedia.co.uk
India   Logos Bhavan, Medchal Road, Jeedimetla Village, Secunderabad
        500 055, A.P.

Pure Gold
ISBN-13: 978-1-934068-64-9
ISBN-10: 1-934068-64-0

Library of Congress Cataloging-in-Publication Data

Davis, Pamula (Pamula Ann), 1965-
  Pure gold : embracing God's grace / Pam Davis.
    p. cm.
  Includes bibliographical references.
  ISBN-13: 978-1-934068-64-9
  ISBN-10: 1-934068-64-0
  1. Grace (Theology) 2. Spiritual life--Christianity. I. Title.

BT761.3.D38 2008
234--dc22
                                2008026245

Interior design: www.projectluz.com
Editorial team: Brad Lewis, Bette Smyth, Dan Johnson, Betsy Weinrich

Printed in the United States of America

Contents

Acknowledgments

Before we embark on the adventure of seeking God's treasure of grace, I must express my gratitude to those who have encouraged and enabled the writing of this book. First, to Jesus, for being the Good News and for making himself known and enabling and empowering me to write this message. To my husband, Steven, and children Alese, Rhett, and Rhys, along with my mom and dad, who minimized the risk with their unconditional love. To my brothers, Mike, Ken, and Steve, and their wives, who each uniquely reflect Christ so as to light my way. To the myriad of friends who encouraged me with their time, treasure, and talent and helped birth this book through prayer. To Brad Lewis and Bette Smyth, editors who challenged each word for clarity and accuracy. To the good people at IBS-STL who with great integrity are committed to communicate the good news of God's grace. Like strings on a harp, together we all desire to bring relief to tormented hearts and sound the praise of our God. To him alone be the glory and to his Son, Jesus Christ, the sole radiance of his glory. Thank you!

Dedication

To Steven, my beloved husband, for sharing with me
the cherished moments of a lifetime . . . I love you!

Introduction

When news of the discovery of gold near San Francisco in 1848 spread around the world, hundreds of thousands of people left their families to travel by ship and covered wagon to California. These gold seekers faced incredible hardships as they traveled to seek their fortunes. Over the next several years, the California gold rush yielded gold worth billions in today's dollars. While this led to great wealth for a few, many returned home with little more than they started with.[1]

What do you picture when you think about the type of people who rushed to California to get rich quick? Most of us see these miners as adventurous and, perhaps, somewhat crazed for leaving loved ones to search for a brilliant and shimmering rock. Surely, they had their reasons, and greed probably ranked high on the list.

However, let's suppose we live in a turbulent country where war has rendered our currency worthless. The standard of trade is reduced to a bartering system. While we try to keep our families alive, our basic needs—food, clothing, and shelter— become nearly impossible to provide. Yet the world agrees that one commodity is valuable: gold. Our own survival and the continued existence of our families depend on our finding and possessing this precious commodity. In this case, survival, not greed, would drive us to leave family and friends to seek after gold.

In the spiritual world today, we truly are at war. We have a real enemy. And we don't have the means for spiritual survival. The only valuable commodity is a brilliant and shimmering Rock—our only means to barter for life. Our spiritual lives depend on our finding it.

Your response might be, "Hey, I'm spiritually surviving. I see the Rock there in the mountain of Scripture. But isn't leaving family and friends to possess this spiritual commodity extreme?" If that's your response, then I'd say that you're disoriented. You're confused. You're leading your spiritual life and your family's spiritual future toward extinction. Jesus warns, "The thief comes only to steal and kill and destroy; I have come that [you] may have life, and have it to the full" (John 10:10).

Spiritual prospectors throughout the ages have dared to pursue the spiritual adventure now before you. Daily I hear of the wealth being mined and deposited in ordinary lives like yours and mine. Has this rich vein of gold been discovered in your life?

I hope so. Even if you've staked a claim to Jesus Christ as your savior, this book will help you discover a mountain of treasure awaiting you as you pick and shovel the Scriptures and discover more of the Rock of Jesus Christ for yourself. You can join those who shout from the pages of Scripture, "Good news—we've struck gold!"

The stories of gold and grace are similar. Both commodities are as old as civilization itself. Both are commodities of kingdoms. History and the world's marketplace give us a clear picture of one, and the Bible and God's kingdom give us a clear picture of the other. I am thrilled that you are joining me as we together explore why Jesus implored his church, "I counsel you to buy from me gold refined in the fire, so you can become rich" (Revelation 3:18).

God's Grace

What is this grace that the apostle Peter implores his readers to receive "in abundance" (2 Peter 1:2)? What is this grace that the apostle Paul writes about in every one of his letters (e.g., Romans 1:5; 1 Corinthians 1:3; Colossians 1:2; Titus 1:4)? As you read on, this is the question we will dig deeply to answer.

The title of this book, *Pure Gold: Embracing God's Grace*, comes from a definition of gold as something universally valued as a standard of highest worth and greatest value. This book is all about God's grace: God's unmerited favor and love offered to all through Christ. And God's grace is truly *pure gold!*

No Risk, No Gain

Receiving grace can be risky business. We risk moving from *self-rule* to *God's rule*. Prospectors of gold had to count the cost physically before searching for their treasure—realizing that many lost their lives in the pursuit. In the same way, Christians must count the cost spiritually before mining for grace—realizing that through the ages many have also sacrificed their lives in its pursuit. Jesus didn't mince words about the cost of following him: "Whoever wants to save his life will lose it, but whoever loses his life for me will save it. What good is it for a man to gain the whole world, and yet lose or forfeit his very self?" (Luke 9:24–25).

However, if you're serious about finding God's gold—if you're willing to abandon your life to truly become a disciple of Jesus Christ—then let's start the spiritual adventure to seek and mine grace: God's pure gold.

1

Gold and Grace

I remember a time in college when I headed to the beaches in Fort Lauderdale, Florida, for spring break. No, I wasn't there for something honorable, such as being part of a missionary team doing beach evangelism. In fact, I was more like the prodigal son in the company of swine about to come to my senses.

I sat in my car, thinking, *I can't find you, God. I've tried everywhere, good places and bad, but I can't find you. I've tried church, seminars, books, even Bible college.*

Then I said out loud, "Running in circles, where to start?" And in my heart, an answer followed: "The answer lies within your heart."

Hmmm. So I put my hands on the steering wheel and continued out loud, "Running in circles, where to begin?"

And again in my heart I heard, "Quit seeking outside and seek within."

This was such a novel thought. As a child, I had asked Jesus into my heart to save my sinful soul. So where did I expect to find him, except in my heart? As a confused college student, I suddenly realized the extent of my disorientation. Looking for God and his grace *out there* was like driving the wrong way on a highway. I'm doing everything right—foot on the gas, hands on the wheel, eyes on the road. And yet something's terribly wrong—I'm causing one crash after another, and I have the dings and dents to show for it. Not to mention the fact that my anxiety is off the charts.

This reminds me of the story of a woman driving down the highway when her cell phone rings. It's her husband, and frantically he shouts, "I just heard on the radio that a car is driving the wrong way on the highway you're on. Please be careful!"

"Dear, it's not one car," the woman responds. "It's hundreds of cars!"

We can easily be like that—disoriented. We can easily be disoriented from the truth that if we're saved by God's grace—through Christ Jesus—then he's not merely out there as a transcendent reality. But he also lives immanently, within our spiritual hearts, guiding and equipping us from within. Maybe we become disoriented so easily because we live in a culture so foreign to this biblical truth of a God-within reality. So that there is no confusion as to the term *God-within reality*, let me quote the words of Bible teacher Arthur W. Pink: "The great mistake made by most of the Lord's people is in the hoping to discover *in themselves* that which is to be found in Christ alone."[1] If you have been born again by the Spirit of God, then indeed within you is Christ's nature, and within him is the *God-within reality.*

Whether you're driving on a highway or trying to find God, disorientation can be deadly. Jesus knew this. He sent a messenger to a group of Christians to point out their disorientation and to reorient them. No wonder these believers were disoriented. Look at the foreign environment where they lived. Their society focused on freedom so much that they named their city "Rights of the People." They built their city in honor of a woman; so if a statue stood at the edge of town, it would have been a woman. These people, richest among their neighbors, established an elaborate banking system. Their textile industry made their citizens among the most finely dressed of their era. Their sophisticated medical school boasted advanced treatments.

No, this isn't a city in your country! It was Laodicea, the home of a church Jesus sent a messenger to. Listen to his words: "You say, 'I am rich; I have acquired wealth and do not need a thing.' But you do not realize that you are wretched, pitiful, poor, blind and naked. I counsel you to buy from me gold refined in the fire, so you can become rich" (Revelation 3:17–18).

Could Jesus be talking to us? Could our environment be so similar to that of the Laodicean Christians that we've also become disoriented, claiming we do not need a thing? His words are addressed to the "church." Could we—the church—be in a state of spiritual bankruptcy even though we're saved? If so, what did Jesus mean that we can buy gold from him and become rich?

Let's find out together—just in case we're the ones driving the wrong way.

The Commodity: Grace That Yields Life

My friend Laura[2] was a worker ant, or so it seemed. When she got up each morning, she organized her day, her husband's day, and their four children's day. Efficient, organized, and with a mind that worked at lightning speed, she was a vital member of her church, Parent-Teacher Association, and her husband's business. I felt tired just listening to her schedule, and I often sighed in amazement at all she seemed to accomplish every twenty-four hours.

Yet this worker ant, who was part of God's kingdom, grew unresponsive spiritually. Instead of the once-glowing and enthusiastic woman I loved to laugh with, my friend grew uniform and almost militant in her pursuit of productivity. Her spiritual life seemed to exist in a hole that she dug deeper and deeper away from the light. I remember praying, "God, she doesn't have to be a worker ant. You recreated her to be a queen—one who has wings and can leave the hole she's digging herself into to visit the heavens. You've transformed her and made her capable of breeding spiritual life."

An opportunity arose in God's divine timing. One day Laura came over for coffee and noticed a sticky note on my refrigerator that reads, "If you want to make God laugh, make plans." As she read it, she became deeply irritated and cried out, "If I don't plan things, they won't happen!" I countered, "Then what? You fail?"

After a moment, tears spilled from the corners of her eyes. Happiness, satisfaction, and joy had subtly been linked to productivity instead of to a relationship with Christ. That was okay for a worker ant. But not for a queen.

As we worked our way through a box of tissues together,

we talked about the "have to's" of life: *have to* take care of her family, *have to* fulfill what she felt God wanted to do through her in her church, *have to* be a helpmate in her husband's business. Then the challenge surfaced: If she didn't plan, how would she accomplish all the have to's? What resource could she draw on?

I told Laura that God had been teaching me how his grace is a resource that yields life. We can accomplish our activities as a manifestation of that life. Each day we can experience joy instead of the slow death of a numbing routine. I knew because I had experienced it both ways. Like Laura, in my attempt to be an obedient Christian, I had somehow missed the message that we not only begin our salvation by grace but also live it out by grace. In fact, I had found a verse that said this perfectly: "Are you so foolish? After beginning with the Spirit, are you now trying to attain your goal by human effort?" (Galatians 3:3).

It took some time, but Laura began to yield to God. As she saw him working within her each day, his grace brought excitement and childlike anticipation to her life. Somehow, she still accomplished all the necessary tasks—not always in the order or the ways she anticipated—but they got done. This new way of living surfaced another, more powerful, force behind Laura's need for productivity: her desire to be in control. Slowly and intentionally she discovered that when she yielded her control to Christ, she experienced his divine grace—the spiritual sweat of God's diligent work in and through us.

In addition, like a queen ant, she hatched "eggs"—eggs of life. Because Laura possessed grace, other people she came into contact with were dusted effortlessly with life. The worker received grace by faith to be a queen.

Disgustingly Lukewarm Believers

Each of us must receive from the Holy Spirit the very real spiritual commodity of grace to live Christ's life deposited within us. Receiving this grace comes through faith—faith in God instead of faith in self. Jesus desires that we possess all his riches: "All that belongs to the Father is mine. That is why I said the Spirit will take from what is mine and make it known to you" (John 16:15).

However, most of us are like Laura used to be. We get so wrapped up in getting through each day in an orderly fashion that we forget to put our faith in God. As we gradually transfer faith in him to faith in ourselves, we become lukewarm.

Jesus addressed this phenomenon in his message to the Laodicean Christians: "These are the words of the Amen, the faithful and true witness, the ruler of God's creation. I know your deeds, that you are neither cold nor hot. I wish you were either one or the other! So, because you are lukewarm—neither hot nor cold—I am about to spit you out of my mouth" (Revelation 3:14–16).

Jesus used strong language with these followers. He said, "I am about to spit you out." Actually, that's a nice way of saying, "I want to vomit you out"! Why did these Christians sicken Jesus so much?

In the ancient world, the master of the feast served cold beverages to refresh and revive or hot beverages to soothe and comfort. However, a lukewarm beverage—like drinking warm salt water—can make you sick. The Laodicean Christians knew this well, because they piped their drinking water from a city a few miles to the north. So by the time it reached their city, it was often lukewarm and even sickening to drink.

Yet instead of vomiting out these apathetic believers, Jesus offered them gold! This isn't gold as we usually think of it. It wasn't a tangible treasure. In fact, the Laodicean Christians had that. They paid more than twenty pounds in gold to Rome for taxes each year, yet Jesus called them "wretched, pitiful, poor, blind and naked." Instead, Jesus offered gold that the Old Testament prophet Malachi described this way: "He will sit as a refiner and purifier of silver; he will purify the Levites and refine them like gold and silver. Then the LORD will have men who will bring offerings in righteousness" (Malachi 3:3).

God's pure gold is his grace. Only this kind of gold can make us truly rich. Instead of us being wretched and afflicted, his grace enables us to endure troubles. Instead of us being pitiful, God's grace supplies us with the power to perform. Instead of us being poor and empty in satisfaction, his grace gives us wealth of significance. Instead of us being blind, the Lord's grace enables us to perceive eternal reality. And instead of us being naked, impoverished morally, and dishonoring of our purpose for existence, God's grace allows us to be clothed in right standing with him and able to offer righteous acts that will revive and comfort our disoriented world. All this will happen as we buy gold from Jesus.

The word *buy* is interesting (Rev. 3:17–18). Isn't God's grace *free*? Should Jesus have said, "receive" instead of "buy"?

Jesus is specific and intentional, and he indeed does say, "Buy." Why? Because when you buy instead of receive, your heart moves toward what you desire *at a cost*. In essence, Jesus was saying to these Christians who lived in a materially abundant society, "Don't just desire to be rich in God's grace; take action at a cost to yourself to receive grace." Let's examine what that looks like.

Physical and Spiritual Gold

Even though God's grace is spiritual gold, we can understand it better by comparing it to physical gold. For example, we know from artifacts of ancient civilizations that physical gold has been treasured since the beginning of history.[3]

Grace—spiritual gold—has also been treasured since the beginning of history. Philo, a first-century Jewish philosopher asserted,

> The just man seeking to understand the nature of all existing things, makes this one most excellent discovery, that everything which exists, does so according to the grace of God, and that there is nothing ever given by, just as there is nothing possessed by, the things of creation. On which account also it is proper to acknowledge gratitude to the Creator alone. Accordingly, to those persons who seek to investigate what is the origin of creation, we may most correctly make answer, that it is the goodness and the grace of God, which he has bestowed on the human race; for all the things which are in the world, and the world itself, are the gift and benefaction and free grace of God.[4]

Physical gold is also rare and beautiful. Even primitive people greatly desired this precious metal. However, they didn't value gold for its beauty alone. They thought gold was divine—the sweat of the gods.[5] When the ancient Egyptians discovered gold nuggets in riverbeds, they concluded that the gods had been working in Egypt and that the nuggets of gold provided evidence of the gods' sweat. They also believed that this rare commodity held magical power to cure illness and give knowledge.

Grace, spiritual gold, is certainly rare and beautiful—so rare that we can only find it in one source: Jesus Christ. Grace is also mystical, because we can't explain how grace given by Jesus Christ can cure illness, give knowledge, and impart life. The apostle Paul expressed it this way: "For if the many died by the trespass of the one man, how much more did God's grace and the gift that came by the grace of the one man, Jesus Christ, overflow to the many! . . . For if, by the trespass of the one man, death reigned through that one man, how much more will those who receive God's abundant provision of grace and of the gift of righteousness reign in life through the one man, Jesus Christ" (Romans 5:15, 17).

Further, grace is truly divine. We could say that God's grace is the spiritual sweat of his diligent work. Jesus said, "My Father has worked [even] until now, [He has never ceased working; He is still working] and I, too, must be at [divine] work" (John 5:17 AMP).

I like this summary of God's grace: inexhaustible, unmerited benefits that give us joy, pleasure, goodwill, thanksgiving, and the essential benefit—spiritual life.

A God of Grace

Almost everyone knows the Old Testament account of Noah and the ark. But in the many retellings of these events, we often miss the point. God revealed his abiding presence, provision, and authority, showing himself to be a God of grace, to Noah and his entire family and to generations that followed.

When I think about the story of Noah, I envision it like this:

> In Noah's time, lust had replaced love. The lust for wealth led to murder. The lust for sex led to beastly unions. Noah tried to remind his friends and coworkers that they were fortunate to have life in their bodies, to have food in their bellies, and to have children in their arms. All this provided evidence of the goodness of their God. But they wouldn't listen. They didn't care. Their evil thoughts and actions vilely betrayed the love of their unseen God.
>
> Alone, with his eyes toward heaven, Noah searched for God's formless face. Silently, he declared his devotion to righteousness, knowing in the pit of his being that this pleased God. And God responded, "Noah, I'm going to put an end to all people, for the earth is filled with violence. All the people of earth have corrupted their ways. I am surely going to destroy both them and the earth." The words sent a shock through Noah's body. But before Noah could respond, God

added, "But you, Noah, have found *grace* in my sight."

Of course, the rest of Noah's story is well known. God instructed him to build the ark, to gather pairs of every kind of animal, and to prepare for the flood. Noah and his wife, and their sons and their wives, along with the animals, were the only survivors of the flood.

After the floodwaters subsided, Noah stood with the grass moist beneath his feet and his sun-kissed face toward heaven. He beamed as tears streamed down his cheeks. Birds fluttered overhead. The jackrabbit and kangaroo seemed to race. Horses galloped by as bears rolled in the grass, scratching their backs. With his hands clasped behind his back, Noah felt a fragile hand in his own. He turned and again was enraptured by his own mate's eyes. "God has made a new home for us," she whispered tenderly.

At that moment, voices they'd heard a thousand times registered in their ears: "Mom! Dad! Look!" Turning toward their children, Noah and his wife saw the heavens as a brilliant canvas cascading with vibrant colors. A new home, a new land, love, harmony, blessing. Fixed on the glorious sky, Noah declared, "This rainbow is a sign of God's grace toward all life on the earth." (author's summary of Genesis 6:9–9:17)

Eternal Drudgery or Eternal Dynasty?

Even today God testifies that he a God of grace. Yet we often fail to stake our claim on the gift of grace in Jesus Christ. Like my friend Laura, we face a choice of what we want to participate in. We might call it eternal drudgery or eternal dynasty. So often we choose the drudge—and we end up feeling lost, hopeless, useless, numb, stale, and even obsolete.

God, however, wants us to choose the dynasty and that is why Jesus warns: "The thief comes only to steal and kill and destroy; I have come that [you] may have life, and have it to the full" (John 10:10).

What keeps us from making the obvious choice—the life-giving choice of God's grace? I believe for most of us it is a fundamental misunderstanding of grace. Jerry Bridges wrote, "I suspect most of us would say we declared permanent bankruptcy. Having trusted in Jesus Christ alone for our salvation, we realized we could not add any measure of good works to what He has already done. However, I think most of us, actually declared temporary bankruptcy. Having trusted in Christ alone for our salvation, we have subtly and unconsciously reverted to a works relationship with God in our Christian lives. We recognize that even our best efforts cannot get us to Heaven, but we think they earn God's blessings in our daily lives."[6]

For most of us, just trudging through life day to day blinds us from seeing our need for God's grace. Look at the following areas of life, and think about how each of these can challenge your need for God's grace.

- **Spiritual life:** Do you feel barren or empty? Or do you sense that you're growing and even reproducing life in others?

- **Physical life:** Do you constantly sense a decrease in force or energy? Or are you alive with energy provided by your relationship with the Holy Spirit?

- **Mental life:** Do you feel like you're regressing from a state of stability—maybe feeling lost or even having perverse thoughts? Or do you feel vivid, charged, and stable, with your experiences creating pleasant and fulfilling memories?

- **Emotional life:** Do you go through most days feeling numb, lacking power to respond? Or do you feel passionate about your relationship with the Lord—having a relationship that you could describe as glowing or on fire?

- **Appearance:** When you look in the mirror, would you describe yourself as lacking radiance, cold, or even steely? Or would you say that you're bright, glowing, and animated because of your relationship with Christ?

- **Activities:** As you go through each day, week, month, and year, do you see the things you need to accomplish as decreasing in quality or as too uniform and listlike in nature? Or do you find a variety in your activities that allows you to approach them with a sense of vigor and a satisfaction that you're accomplishing tasks out of your love for God?

- **Relationships**: Do you find yourself easily offended or sense that your relationships with others are stale? Or would you describe your relationships as pure, vital, and functioning because of who you are in Christ?

If the first question in each of these areas describes you more often than the second, you might sum up your feelings by saying that your physical existence is more an experience of death than life.

But is that really what you want? Instead, most of us would rather answer yes to each area's second question. Those questions describe true life when we embrace God's precious treasure of grace.

How conscious are you of God's desire to extend his grace to you each day? Maybe your image of God is one of a detached king in an air-conditioned heaven, feasting on grapes and wine. But that's not who God is at all! Instead, he is working, creating you in Christ to be a work of grace and to do his works of grace. God is a hands-on God, who works efficiently, extending grace with his hand of Light—Christ. God touches us with the Holy Spirit, causing us to grow, have life, and bear fruit for him. Jesus said, "You did not choose me, but I chose you and appointed you to go and bear fruit—fruit that will last. Then the Father will give you whatever you ask in my name" (John 15:16).

"I chose you." Those three words alone illustrate how God actively works in our lives. Pastor and teacher Oswald Chambers commented on those three words: "That is the way the grace of God begins. It is a constraint we cannot get away from; we can disobey it, but we cannot generate it. The drawing is done by the supernatural grace of God, and we can never trace where His work begins. Salvation is not merely deliverance from sin, nor the experience of personal holiness; the salvation of God is deliverance out of self entirely into union with Himself."[7]

The King's Throne: God's Throne of Grace

I will never forget one of the most dramatic examples of God's grace at work that I have ever witnessed. In October 1996 Yankee Stadium was filled with people on their feet. The roar was deafening. The pitch was thrown, and the home crowd went wild as the pop-up was caught, and the New York Yankees won the World Series. John Wetteland, the thirty-year-old closing pitcher, was swept up in the air by his teammates. My husband, Steven, and I sat in front of our television set with tears streaming down our cheeks as we watched John scan the stands, searching for his wife, Michele.

I first met Michele in the spring of 1990, when both of our husbands were in major league spring training camp with the Los Angeles Dodgers. Yet I'd heard of Michele much earlier. Before either of us got married, our future husbands, Steven and John, were roommates during winter ball in Puerto Rico. Apparently, the women pursuing John in his single days were notorious, and the other ballplayers teased John about his pursuers, referring to them as a harem.

Michele was busy pursuing God's will for her life, attending college and working part-time. When John, the renowned "king of the ladies," visited her hometown of Shreveport, Louisiana, for a series of games, Michele was certainly intrigued and fascinated, but not captured. Michele already considered herself part of a harem—she was a bride of the Lord Jesus, and she resided in his court, respecting his kingdom's rule.

This posed a problem for John, who indeed *was* captured by Michele. Instead of being lured by John's gold and the prospect of more gold, Michele turned away. Like the Grinch in the Dr. Seuss book *How the Grinch Stole Christmas*, John was struck with amazement: What's this? No cards? No calls? No boxes? No bows?

Intrigued and fascinated by whatever commodity could compete with his own, John met the lover of Michele's soul—the Lord Jesus Christ. Admitting that he'd been trying for years to fill a void in his life that he never could fill, John surrendered himself to God's kingdom and received an overabundance of grace—the spiritual gold that really satisfies.

Steven and I watched as John stood beside Michele and their twin daughters to receive the trophy for the Most Valuable Player in the World Series. Emotion-filled words choked from his lips: "I would first like to thank Jesus Christ—my point man. Then my wife, Michele, who is my rock." John was correct with this declaration, because the Rock of Jesus Christ is inside Michele Wetteland. Her spiritual grasp was stretched in her courtship with John, and now she's richer in every way for choosing to possess God's grace, instead of merely the world's gold.

Thrones of Gold

All of us must make the same choice that Michele faced. Will we place ourselves or the world or a myriad of other things on the throne of our lives? Or will we become royal children of God, placing him on the throne to rule and make us rich with his grace? As followers of Christ, each believer becomes part of God's royal spiritual kingdom. Since we are his royal children, God doesn't withhold any good thing from our spiritual life. The psalmist wrote, "The LORD God . . . gives us grace and glory. The LORD will withhold no good thing from those who do what is right" (Psalm 84:11 NLT).

Of course, the false thrones of the world certainly look attractive. This was true even in ancient civilizations. The pharaohs and high priests of Egypt sat on gold thrones, and their palaces and temples sparkled and gleamed with gold. They sat on hammered gold-sheathed furniture surrounded by golden statues. Gold thread shimmered in draperies, tapestries, and clothing. The very walls shone with gold. At night royalty slept on gold beds. When Queen Hatshepsut rose from her morning bath, she powdered her body with gold dust. The Egyptians buried their royalty in gold, wrapping their bodies in yards and yards of linen strips with golden jewels placed in the wrappings. The coffins that held the wrapped bodies and the jars that held their vital organs were covered in gold. We could say that a royal Egyptian's journey through life to afterlife was a path of gold.[8]

In contrast, God offers us his true throne of grace. He and Jesus are seated on this throne of grace. Yet God's grace also pervades every part of his kingdom. He purchased his royal children's salvation with grace. We, his heirs, are covered with grace. We display his grace, and we sit with him by grace. Because we are royal children of God, our journey through life to eternity is a path of grace.

The writer of Hebrews described the Lord's throne this way: "We have a great high priest who has gone through the heavens, Jesus the Son of God. . . . Let us then approach the throne of grace with confidence, so that we may receive mercy and find grace to help us in our time of need" (Hebrews 4:14, 16).

God's Grace: Spiritual Wealth

You might recall the Old Testament account of Sarai and Abram. God gave this husband and wife an opportunity to exercise their faith and to increase their capacity to receive spiritual wealth—God's grace. God initiated his grace by calling Sarai, and by faith she received grace when she obeyed God by following her husband.

Sarai was stunningly beautiful. Living in the excitement of a metropolitan city, this woman had looks, wealth, love, and servants. Even her name was a blessing: "my princess." Yet for all the things Sarai had, she lacked one thing—a child. In her day, nothing she possessed compared with what she lacked.

Then God told Sarai, through Abram, to leave her familiar surroundings and travel with Abram to an unknown land that he would show them, promising that it would be worth their while. The land they journeyed to was occupied by another nation, and the people there were experiencing a famine. This meant that

Sarai and Abram faced famine as well when they arrived. What were they to do? Trust in self-rule or God's rule? God had placed them on the road, and they would learn that God would preserve them on the road. They would learn to follow, not lead.

Fearing for his life, due to the famine in the land, Abram decided to take an independent journey, traveling from the land of God's choosing down to Egypt and right out of God's perfect will. Then, fearing that the pharaoh might kill him and seize Sarai for his harem, Abram stepped further out of God's will and hatched his own plan.

Abram said to Sarai, "I know what a beautiful woman you are. When the Egyptians see you, they will say, 'This is his wife.' Then they will kill me but will let you live. Say you are my sister, so that I will be treated well for your sake and my life will be spared because of you" Genesis 12:11–13).

The choice Sarai faced didn't appear to be a grace-laden path at all. Instead, it appeared to be a dead end, where she would lose her chastity, her honor, and her promise for a happy and fulfilled life. She found herself at a crossroads of two kingdoms: not Egypt's or her husband's, but self-rule or God's rule. Certainly, self-rule seemed reasonable, because Sarai thought she would lose everything. Assertiveness, as we will see later, wasn't something she lacked. Yet God promised her what self-rule could never give her: a child.

So Sarai trusted God, yielding to her husband and obeying his wishes. This placed her right in the gold-adorned court of Pharaoh, Egypt's ruler. The Egyptian courts at this time were lavish in golden décor. The Egyptian goldsmiths were experts at combining different colors of gold in their patterns. Adding iron gave gold a purple hue, copper made it red, and silver made the gold pale yellow.

Draped in an array of physical gold as part of the king's harem, Sarai remained obedient to God. Although she was physically trapped in Egypt, she had not ventured spiritually from the court of the King of Kings. God rescued this royal child and, consequently, her husband and their entire entourage, sending "great plagues" on Pharaoh and his household. This all happened before Egypt's king could violate her in any way. Abram, her husband, was shamed for his lack of faith in attempting to sustain his life apart from obedience to God.

With Sarai's spiritual grasp stretched by exercising her faith, she possessed more grace/gold than when she arrived; she left Egypt as a wealthy woman spiritually as well as materially. Pharaoh treated Abram well for Sarai's sake, and Abram acquired sheep, cattle, donkeys, camels, and servants.

The Golden Path of Grace

Sarai chose the path of grace. This golden road leads away from trusting in self-rule toward complete reliance on God. As Christ's followers, we all face this choice. Will we place ourselves or Jesus Christ on the throne of our lives? If we choose to let Jesus reign, God promises that we will experience the richness of his grace in our present life and in eternity. The apostle Paul eloquently described this great gift of grace: "For we are God's [own] handiwork (His workmanship), recreated in Christ Jesus, [born anew] that we may do those good works which God predestined (planned beforehand) for us [taking paths which He prepared ahead of time], that we should walk in them [living the good life which He prearranged and made ready for us to live]" (Ephesians 2:10 AMP).

Did you catch that? God has prepared paths for us, and *we should walk in them*! Yet we so often stumble on the path, failing to live the abundant life God has for us. Paul addressed the reason for our stumbling: "What then shall we say? That the Gentiles, who did not pursue righteousness, have obtained it, a righteousness that is by faith; but Israel, who pursued a law of righteousness, has not attained it. Why not? Because they pursued it not by faith but as if it were by works. They stumbled over the 'stumbling stone.' As it is written: 'See, I lay in Zion a stone that causes men to stumble and a rock that makes them fall, and the one who trusts in him will never be put to shame'" (Romans 9:30–33).

How interesting that Paul described Jesus as a stumbling stone. Think about that. You don't stumble over a mountain or even a huge boulder. You stumble over a nugget that's right under your nose, because you didn't see it. That's the way it is with God's grace. His grace is right under our noses, there to meet our every need throughout each day. But instead of realizing it, and instead of kneeling down and receiving it, we stumble along in unbelief.

Walking the golden path of grace isn't a scurry through the mall or a race measured by speed. It's a deliberate, intentional climb up the jagged face of a mountain with stones mixed in with hard dirt.

When we think about the consequences of stumbling while

climbing a mountain compared to stumbling on a flat terrain, we understand why the psalmist declared, "Your word is a lamp to my feet and a light for my path" (Psalm 119:105). A light on a dark and dangerous mountain, pointing out nuggets that when overlooked would become stumbling stones, would be the difference between a steady assent and a bloody heap of broken bones.

In the same way, as we travel up the golden path of grace, God's written Word is the light that points to who Christ is and the grace we can receive. When we see and receive nuggets of truth of who he is on our individual, prearranged path and trust him completely, we are never put to shame. "I want those already wise to become the wiser and become leaders by exploring the depths of meaning in these nuggets of truth" (Proverbs 1:5–6 LB). Possessing his spiritual richness and abundance sounds better than a bloody heap of broken bones!

─────────────── *Nuggets* ───────────────

G od's
R iches
A t
C hrist's
E xpense

─────────── *A Prayer of Grace* ───────────

Lord God, we acknowledge we exist only because of your grace toward us. You are our Creator, and we praise you for our very existence, our planet, and all that spans beyond our universe. We acknowledge the rarity and beauty of your grace given to us in Jesus Christ, and we know that no one can come to you apart from him.

Father, we acknowledge that you are always working in and around us, pouring out your grace as you re-create us in Christ Jesus to do the very works of grace you have preplanned for us. We acknowledge that two roads exist in life. One we walk by our natural resources that lead to destruction. The other we walk intentionally as a spiritual road of grace that leads to life. Thank you for providing this *golden* road of grace and the gate, Jesus Christ, by which we gain access.

Help us, Lord, to slow our pace, to take our steps cautiously, so as to live the abundant life you have prearranged and made ready. Amen.

—————— *Questions for Reflection* ——————

• Reflect on a time when you or your family was lost. How did it make you feel?

• What were some of the reasons you lost your way?

• If walking the golden path of grace isn't a scurry through the mall or a race measured by speed, how conducive is your lifestyle to carefully walking the golden road of grace? Is your goal to keep pace with grace or pace with the world?

• Consider a time when you have stumbled in unbelief in difficult circumstances. How did God show you he was present and there for you?

2

The Qualities

*I*f you have ever been to the circus, you might share the sentiments of best-selling author and pastor Juan Carlos Ortiz:

> Watching a trapeze show is breathtaking. We
> wonder at the dexterity and timing. We gasp
> at near-misses. In most cases, there is a net
> underneath. When they fall, they jump up and
> bounce back to the trapeze. In Christ, we live on
> the trapeze. The whole world should be able to
> watch and say, "Look how they live, how they love
> one another. Look how well the husbands treat
> their wives. And aren't they the best workers in the
> factories and offices, the best neighbors, the best
> students?" That is to live on the trapeze, being a

show to the world. What happens when we slip? The net is surely there. The blood of our Lord, Jesus Christ, has provided forgiveness for ALL our trespasses. Both the net and the ability to stay on the trapeze are works of God's grace. Of course, we cannot be continually sleeping on the net. If that is the case, I doubt whether that person is a trapezist.[1]

Where do the people around us find us? Do they find us "sleeping on the net" instead of "living on the trapeze"? The apostle Paul wrote of a "secret wisdom" when it comes to living in God's grace in full view of the world (1 Corinthians 2:7). Later Paul described it this way: "We know we are not able in ourselves to do any of this work. God makes us able to do these things. . . . All of us, with no covering on our faces, show the shining-greatness of the Lord as in a mirror. All the time we are being changed to look like Him, with more and more of His shining-greatness. This change is from the Lord Who is the Spirit" (2 Corinthians 3:5, 18 NLV).

Sometimes I think we fear living in full view of the world, simply because we don't understand the wonderful qualities of God's treasure of grace. Let's look together at the qualities of God's gold so we can avoid sleeping in the net and live on the thrill of the trapeze.

Grace Is Workable

At times our life trapeze feels like it has all the chaos of a circus! These times can be brought on by blissful and enjoyable events in our lives. But they often occur during times of catastrophe or crisis.

I still remember the day several years ago when a major crisis hit Sheila,[2] one of my closest and dearest friends. She was diagnosed with thyroid cancer. At the time, she was in her midthirties with two children under four years of age. My heart sank at the news.

For myself, as well as for Sheila, I tried to hold on to faith. Maybe it's more accurate to say that I tried to keep my hand and heart open to faith. I decided that I could not and would not tell her anything that wasn't real to me at the present moment. In other words, I wouldn't give her the *what* of Scripture in place of the *who* (see John 5:39–40).

I immediately felt inadequate to offer anything of substance to Sheila. As helpless and insignificant as it made me feel, all I could do is what I do every day—just receive God's nuggets of grace in the truth of who he is. Between the Thursday when Sheila received the news and the next Monday when she went in for a high dose of radioactive iodine, I, *coincidentally*, had three people from Colorado Springs staying at my house who are part of my ministry's intercessory prayer team. Their arrival had been planned weeks earlier. While our kids played in another room, these three prayer supporters, my husband, and I sat on the floor in our living room, petitioning and praising the God of the universe, our King of Kings, waging warfare prayer on the frontlines for Sheila's life.

Meanwhile, another friend—a busy mother of three children under four years of age—received a nugget of grace in her schedule, enabling her to take dinners to Sheila and her family. Then, a Christian nurse at the hospital received grace polished into encouragement when she assured Sheila of personal attention and care.

The list goes on of people who were faithful to receive God's precious commodity of grace, which is workable into many forms: prayer, service, encouragement, as in this case, each to meet the needs of Sheila and her family. What seemed like a dusty road of death to Sheila and me eventually became to us a righteous road paved with gold—God's grace—that sustains as it leads to life and as we walk it by faith.

Now seven years later, Sheila and her husband are doing well. She later faced another life-threatening ailment but, again, walked the mysterious road of grace. God continues to provide nuggets of grace, and Sheila is still witnessing the good life God has prearranged and made ready for her—a golden road of grace.

An Amazing Resource

During Sheila's time of crisis, God's grace in its many forms had already been prepared, waiting on deposit. As God's royal heirs in Christ, we only need to receive his grace, and then we can share this abundance with those around us, as so many people did with Sheila.

When people face tough times, we often encourage them to have faith—to reach out and receive God's grace. But I've discovered that people find it more meaningful when we communicate through our God-dependent lives the amazing attributes of grace. Imagine a woman living in poverty, and you said, "Reach out and take this gold coin." If she couldn't see the coin, she might be skeptical that it even existed. However, if you held out the coin for her to see, she would probably reach to receive it. Here's the point: Telling people to have faith in God's grace isn't nearly as effective as allowing God to use our dependent lives as canvas for him to display his grace.

Whether a gold coin or this precious metal worked into another form, physical gold can help us understand God's grace to a greater degree. Gold is a highly workable commodity, and yet it's nearly indestructible. Gold can be pressed into molds, stretched into threads, pounded into sheets, and polished smooth as glass. It's not simply workable; it's *extremely* workable into many forms.[3] Just think of all the ways we encounter gold—gold jewelry, gold coins, gold cloth, gold buildings, gold statues, gold powder, and much more.

Grace, God's gold, is the highly workable spiritual commodity that is completely indestructible. Grace can be pressed into prophecy, stretched into service, pounded into teaching, and polished smooth as encouragement. Grace isn't simply workable; it's *extremely* workable into many forms of service for the kingdom of God. Just think of all the ways we encounter grace—including seeing grace in people who are fashioned into leaders, teachers, givers, and extenders of mercy.

The apostle Paul addressed how God demonstrates grace through us as followers of Christ:

> For by the grace given me I say to every one of you: Do not think of yourself more highly than you ought, but rather think of yourself with sober judgment, in accordance with the measure of faith

> God has given you. Just as each of us has one body
> with many members, and these members do not
> all have the same function, so in Christ we who are
> many form one body, and each member belongs to
> all the others. We have different gifts, according to
> the grace given us. If a man's gift is prophesying,
> let him use it in proportion to his faith. If it is
> serving, let him serve; if it is teaching, let him
> teach; if it is encouraging, let him encourage; if
> it is contributing to the needs of others, let him
> give generously; if it is leadership, let him govern
> diligently; if it is showing mercy, let him do it
> cheerfully. (Romans 12:3–8)

The opportunity for using our gifts of grace isn't just a nice thing God provides. It's a significant choice we each face. It's a choice of two roads. We can choose to try to walk in our own strength, which seems natural, but this road ultimately leads to destruction. The other road we can choose to walk is a spiritual road of grace, which immediately leads to life.

God provides this golden road of grace. What's more, he provides the gate—Jesus Christ—so that we can gain access and begin the journey. If you're reading this book and you've never entered God's kingdom, he invites you to start that journey now! God is the King of the universe *and* a loving spiritual Father who has a remedy for the sinful state of your and my soul. Yes, he knows your heart inside and out! He knows how far you have fallen from the person he created you to be. To remedy and restore you, God provided a gift that you must receive—his own Son, Jesus Christ.

This gift is all of *grace*, because he offers you Jesus with no strings attached. And when I say no strings attached, that is exactly what I mean. There can be no strings tying you to self-reliance. To receive God's grace, you must surrender your sinful self—that selfish will inside that has ruled your life. You exchange your will for God's will, and the kingdom of darkness for the kingdom of light. But you must choose to enter through the gate.

Once we take that step, inviting Jesus to be our Lord and Savior, God's grace lives right within us in the nature of Christ by the Holy Spirit. We just need to receive this grace humbly. Jesus is the gate, the "new self," the continual grace resource, and our example: "You have taken off your old self with its practices and have put on the new self, which is being renewed in knowledge in the image of its Creator. Here there is no Greek or Jew, circumcised or uncircumcised, barbarian, Scythian, slave or free, but Christ is all, and is in all" (Colossians 3:9–11).

Life-Giving Commodity

The road of grace is a path we walk continually in a humbled posture before God, the King of the universe. On that road we will have unexpected and incalculable encounters with grace. In John's Gospel is the story of one unlikely woman whose road intersected with grace. She was a Samaritan, a descendent of Israelites who had intermarried with Gentiles, creating a mixed race.

She had traveled far from home during the heat of day, a time when no sensible person traveled. Why? For water. When she approached the well, to her utter shock, Jesus initiated communication, asking her for a drink. She must have thought, *Doesn't he know that I'm a woman, a Samaritan woman at that? Doesn't he know my ancestry? And what did he say—"Would you give me something to drink?"* The woman knew that most Jews of Jesus' stature wouldn't even be seen with her, much less touch something of hers. Certainly, they would never drink from the same cup!

The woman couldn't contain herself: "You are a Jew and I am a Samaritan woman. How can you ask me for a drink?" (John 4:9).

Jesus cut to the heart of the matter: "If you knew the gift of God and who it is that asks you for a drink, you would have asked him and he would have given you living water." With his statement, Jesus exposed her ignorance in two areas: she didn't know whom she had just encountered, and she didn't know what gift was available.

She avoided both points and diverted the conversation to logistics: "You have nothing to draw with and the well is deep." Basically, she responded by arguing, as if saying to Jesus, "Let me expose two points where *you* are ignorant."

Yet instead of getting angry or offended, Jesus cleared up the woman's confusion by plainly stating that two kingdoms exist: physical and spiritual: "Everyone who drinks this water will be thirsty again, but whoever drinks the water I give him will never thirst. Indeed, the water I give him will become in him a spring of water welling up to eternal life."

The woman didn't understand. She was still thinking strictly of physical water when she said, "Sir, give me this water so that I won't get thirsty and have to keep coming here to draw water."

Jesus knew he'd have to singe the woman's heart to get to the bottom of it. He proceeded to reveal that he knew about her—her sin and deceit. She immediately recognized him as a prophet. And again he drew her toward the spiritual dimension: "Believe me, woman, a time is coming when you will worship the Father neither on this mountain nor in Jerusalem." In other words, he wanted her to stop thinking merely of the physical realm. "Yet a time is coming and has now come when the true worshipers will worship the Father in spirit and truth, for they are the kind of worshipers the Father seeks. God is spirit, and his worshipers must worship in spirit and in truth." Jesus meant that God isn't looking for worship from within the interior of our own wills; rather, God desires that we surrender our will to the Holy Spirit, who offers authentic worship. By God's standard, religious worship that comes from our own wills isn't true worship.

Jesus' words registered with the woman, and even if she was ignorant about a lot of things, she did know about the Messiah who would teach God's standard. "'I know that Messiah' (called Christ) 'is coming. When he comes, he will explain everything to us.'"

Then the woman looked intently at Jesus, her breath suspended as Jesus declared unequivocally, "I who speak to you am he" (John 4:26).

A flood immediately rushed into her soul! What she lacked, what she risked her physical life to attain, was spiritual water—*grace*. She was no longer ignorant of the gift available to her—*grace*;[4] and she knew the One who gives it—Jesus Christ.

With this living water now within her, the Samaritan woman left her water jar under the midday sun. She realized that no physical commodity could compare or compete with the spiritual commodity of grace, and she wanted to share with others both this gift and the one who offers it. Immediately, this spiritual commodity of grace was pressed into strength for the journey, stretched into service for the people who saw her as an outcast, pounded into courage to speak openly about her sin and her Savior, and even polished into encouragement to help others go see for themselves (John 4:29).

The prophet Isaiah spoke of this same spiritual commodity, the living water that Jesus provides and that he *is*: "Come, all you who are thirsty, come to the waters; and you who have no money, come, buy and eat! Come, buy wine and milk without money and without cost" (Isaiah 55:1). Jesus himself announced to the crowds gathered for a feast, "'If anyone is thirsty, let him come to me and drink. Whoever believes in me, as the Scripture has said, streams of living water will flow from within him.' By this he meant the Spirit, whom those who believed in him were later to receive" (John 7:37–39).

Using and Caring for the Gift

There is only one spiritual commodity and only One who gives it: grace is given by the Spirit of Christ when we surrender self-rule and receive it. When we receive this gift, we have a responsibility to both use it and care for it.

Imagine that someone gave you a beautiful and powerful high-tech automobile. As a condition of the gift, the giver said that you needed both to use the car and to care for it. So as you drove the car each day, what would you do?

I must admit that I'm not a "car person." Each car I've owned, I've owned for years, usually until it just dies. I also don't spend a lot of time washing my car. It's clean, just not sparkling clean, and it runs even though I just provide the required maintenance. I don't care a lot about the car I'm driving as long as it gets me where I want to go. These aren't the confessions of a slovenly car owner, but a perspective I have on transportation. I see owning a car as a means, not an end. It's a means to transport the people I love to where I want them to go.

How does this correlate to God's gifts of grace? The ways he shows his grace through us shouldn't be an end, but rather a means. Instead of endlessly polishing our gift of teaching or continually tinkering with a gift of administration, we need to get out and put it to use. Start transporting people to the kingdom of God.

What's great is that our gifts of grace come with their own vehicle control system—the Holy Spirit. He's our GPS (Global Positioning System). He points out areas of maintenance and flashes warning lights. So when you feel red hot with anxiety, stop and take notice. When a light within you flashes "low fuel," take a break from your busyness and fill up your soul's tank with Christ's life through Bible study and prayer. If you run on empty, you'll break down.

But once you fill up with this spiritual fuel, you can follow Jesus' commission to his disciples (see Matthew 28:19–20), which for the purpose of this analogy might be paraphrased as, "Go, get the car out of park, and take with you those who want a lift to my kingdom, teaching them to follow my instructions for how to drive their own cars. And don't worry, because I'm always with you; your control system will never fail."

Grace Is Strong

Grace is not only workable; God gives it a strength that won't snap under heat or pressure—or even because of stupidity on our part! I'll never forget how the strength of God's grace surprised me during one of the most foolish episodes of my entire life.

I was nineteen years old, and I had just made a commitment to devote myself to seek the Lord: "You will seek me and find me when you seek me with all your heart" (Jeremiah 29:13). For me, seeking him meant leaving my family, friends, and hometown of Fort Worth, Texas, and traveling to Virginia to attend Bible college.

However, my ignorance quickly emerged. I figured that Christianity was like any other arena in the world—that I could succeed by hard work. Independently, I began trying to work out my salvation instead of yielding to the Holy Spirit, who works it out within. The Scriptures were proved true: "The trouble is with me, for I am all too human, a slave to sin. I don't really understand myself, for I want to do what is right, but I don't do it. Instead, I do what I hate. . . . I want to do what is right, but I can't. I want to do what is good, but I don't. I don't want to do what is wrong, but I do it anyway" (Romans 7:14–15, 18–19 NLT). During this time, I felt a lot like those words. I was like a yo-yo. Fleeting moments of goodness were quickly followed by sin's rampant appearance.

Frustrated in my Christian experience, I spent time with my family in Colorado during Christmas break—it was a welcome diversion. When it came time to return to school, I had two connecting flights. I traveled from Colorado, through Dallas, onto Washington DC, then on a commuter flight into Virginia. On the flight from Colorado to Texas, I decided to escape my impending responsibility of becoming a "good Christian" by drowning my dread with orange juice and champagne. Landing in Dallas with an hour layover, I thought, *What the hey*, and ordered a Bloody Mary to pass the time. Now in the air, with each mile bringing me closer to a sense of failure, I got depressed and ordered a glass of wine to cheer my mood. Keep in mind that I wasn't a drinker at all, so these cocktails were quite out of the ordinary.

Arriving in Washington DC, I had a delay before I could catch my small commuter flight to my final destination. So I passed the time in the airport bar. As night quickly approached, I heard over the public-address system that the airline had oversold my commuter flight. They were offering a free airline ticket to be used later if someone would give up his or her seat, take a later flight to a nearby city, and then make a connection to a final destination. It sounded good to me—anything to delay returning to my self-imposed prison.

So with twelve hours and several drinks behind me, I boarded a plane to a destination completely unknown to my family. At about 10:00 p.m., I arrived at a small airport an hour away from my college, car, and safety. I entered the small, vacant terminal and decided to pass the remaining time until my final connecting flight in the bar, of course! "Sorry, miss, we're closed."

Probably just as well, I thought. "Do you mind if I just sit here and wait?" The bartender nodded his head to say yes as he continued to wash glasses.

After a few minutes, two guys sitting at the bar turned to me and said, "There's a great band playing across the street at the Ramada. Would you like to go over and listen to some music?"

"Sorry, I'm waiting for a flight. Thanks anyway."

"It's right across the street, and we'll bring you right back."

In the dark bar, staring past the men in the shadows, I thought, *I do have fifty minutes to kill.* "Okay."

Now for the climax of this low and utterly unwise time of my life—and an amazing display of God's grace! I crawled into the white van, sitting beside one of the men in one of the two front seats. I knew the Ramada was just across from the airport, and it should take less than five minutes to get there.

We traveled along a dark road, and as time passed, the road got darker. I couldn't see the lights of the city or the airport. "I think you took a wrong turn," I said casually, completely unaware of any impending evil and danger.

"No, it's right up ahead," the driver said as the man in the passenger seat began groping my neck.

This is ridiculous, I thought. *I didn't ask for this.* "Well, I think I'm going to have pass on hearing the band. So why don't you just take me back to the airport." Just then, the driver made a sudden turn down a bumpy, desolate road. "Where are we?" It suddenly didn't seem right.

The man in the driver's seat turned off the engine, reached behind my seat, and pulled out a machete. He placed the long blade to my throat and said, "Take off your clothes."

In that brief moment, my entire day flashed before my eyes. Hugging my mom, dad, and brothers goodbye at the ski resort. Arriving for a brief moment back in my hometown. Then all the drinks, all the attempts to escape failing at Christianity again. And then giving up my flight.

No one knows I'm here, I realized. *They'll never even know where to look for me!* Completely aware of my inadequacy, I cried out internally, *God, help!*

Before I could calculate a move, words started coming out of my mouth, declaring loudly, "I am in the Father and she is in me. All authority in heaven and earth has been given to me and it's in her!" Immediately, I reached up and moved the knife from my neck and continued boldly, "Vengeance is mine; I will repay. It is a dreadful thing to fall into the hands of the living God."

The arm of the man holding the knife flung backward, and the knife hit the doors at the back of the van. The man who had been holding the knife demanded that I shut up, but I couldn't. More words came out: "Lo, I am with her always even until the end of the age." The man beside me pleaded, "Make her shut up."

Up to this point, none of the words I spoke to these men had ever been put to memory, and it was all spoken in first person. I knew it was Christ speaking from within me! And at that instant, I understood what the King James Bible means when it reads "*sore* afraid": "There were . . . shepherds abiding in the field, keeping watch over their flock by night. And, lo, the angel of the Lord came upon them, and the glory of the Lord shone round about them: and they were *sore* afraid" (Luke 2:8–9 KJV, emphasis added). These men, aggressors just a moment earlier, became terrified. And I was at "perfect peace," as I kept my mind "stayed on thee" (Isaiah 26:3 KJV).

Becoming keenly aware of what was happening, I began praising the Lord. This made the men even more submissive. The man in the driver's seat stammered, "We weren't really going to hurt you. We're actually policemen, and we were just trying to frighten you."

"Take me back to the airport!" I demanded, keeping my mind fixed on the Lord and remembering the first line of a psalm: "God is our refuge and strength, a very present help in trouble" (Psalm 46:1 KJV).

They did, but they had driven so far away from the airport that by the time we returned, I had long since missed my connecting flight. "Well, it looks like you're just going to have to drive me an hour to the other airport."

Of course, now I look back and it seems ludicrous that I would stay in the van one more second with these would-be assailants. But I was at perfect peace while they were sore afraid. And I knew it! This wasn't knowledge merely on a rational level, any more than I knew all those Bible verses on a rational level. This was a knowledge that Someone else was in charge—Someone whose authority, when initiated, we must all submit to.

They drove me an additional hour to my original destination and dropped me off at my car at the airport.

Avoiding the Masquerade

Long before this incident, God's spiritual gold, grace, had been deposited in me. Although his grace seemed buried as I pursued Christ with my vain efforts and labor, God's treasure of grace resurfaced. What's more, this grace was authenticated by its strength, and it didn't snap in the heat of the moment.

Unfortunately, we often foolishly choose the spiritual equivalent of copper, which turns spongy or snaps under heat or stress. Gold won't. Although copper and gold resemble each other at first glance or at a distance, with closer scrutiny, their value is easily distinguishable.[5]

Similarly, grace differs from works of the flesh, such as using self-effort to succeed at the Christian life. These vain works turn spongy or snap under heat. Grace won't. Although works of the flesh and grace can resemble each other at first glance or at a distance, with closer scrutiny, their values are easily distinguishable, especially in their abilities to be of spiritual use. Why would we ever be so foolish to choose works of the flesh in place of God's gift of grace?

That's the question the apostle Paul seemed to be asking the Christians in Galatia: "You foolish Galatians! Who has bewitched you? Before your very eyes Jesus Christ was clearly portrayed as crucified. I would like to learn just one thing from you: Did you receive the Spirit by observing the law, or by believing what you heard? Are you so foolish? After beginning with the Spirit, are you now trying to attain your goal by human effort? Have you suffered so much for nothing—if it really was for nothing? Does God give you his Spirit and work miracles among you because you observe the law, or because you believe what you heard?" (Galatians 3:1–5).

Grace in Christ—who is authentic and strong—won't snap under heat or stress. The works of the flesh are merely a vain masquerade of this highly valuable grace!

Works or Grace?

Scripture tells the stories of two sisters who had very different responses to Jesus. One tried hard work, while the other tried grace. Jesus and his disciples arrived at the home of these two sisters and their brother. One of the sisters, Martha, was distracted by all the necessary preparations for these guests, while her sister, Mary, simply sat at the Lord's feet and listened to what he said. Upset, Martha went to Jesus and asked, "Lord, don't you care that my sister has left me to do the work by myself? Tell her to help me!"

"Martha, Martha," the Lord answered, "you are worried and upset about many things, but only one thing is needed. Mary has chosen what is better, and it will not be taken away from her" (see Luke 10:38–42).

Later, when these women faced a difficult and desperate situation, they definitely felt the heat—the fire of testing. Lazarus, their dearly loved brother and only legal representative of the family, became ill and died. Martha and Mary handled this devastating news differently, revealing how bankrupt each perceived the situation to be.

Martha, again worried and upset about many things, abruptly abandoned the mourning ceremony and ran out to meet Jesus as he approached. When she reached him, she scolded him: "If you had been here, my brother would not have died" (John 11:21). This was the response of a woman who saw her situation as hopeless.

Mary's response was quite different. She too grieved the loss of her brother. But she did so appropriately, inside her home as part of the mourning ceremony. When Martha returned, she told Mary that Jesus was asking for *her*. When Mary went to meet Jesus, she didn't criticize him. Instead, she fell to her knees out of worship and respect: "Lord, if you had been here, my brother would not have died" (John 11:32).

Jesus responded very differently to these two women. With Martha, he countered her statements as if in a legal debate. With Mary, he wept. He was deeply moved in spirit and troubled as he spoke with Mary, and he *immediately* took action to raise Lazarus from the dead.

The grace that Mary received from initially choosing Jesus Christ over works sustained her strength, showing the immeasurable value of grace in the heat of desperate circumstances. And when she faced the desperate circumstances surrounding the death of her brother, she continued to receive grace from her faith as she humbly confessed Jesus as Lord. By exercising her faith, her spiritual grasp was stretched. Immediately, she, her sister and brother, and the entire community were richer—by having Lazarus's life returned to them.

Weakness and Strength

We might sum up Mary's attitude as one of surrender. When we think of the word *surrender*, we often define it as giving up. But it also means to submit. That's what Mary did. Instead of working to make something happen, she was willing to humbly submit to the Lord and wait for his strong grace to carry her through the heat of her circumstances.

On our own, we can't do anything more than that. If we try to offer up any other works of our own, they're woefully unacceptable in the Lord's sight. Left to our own strength, we're powerless to maintain and reproduce spiritual life.

The apostle Paul appropriately called this lack of power "weakness." His words to the Christians at Corinth remind us that only when we admit the futility of trying to be spiritual on our own and humbly submit to Jesus Christ will we truly understand the strength of God's treasure of grace: "I will boast all the more gladly about my weaknesses, so that Christ's power may rest on me. That is why, for Christ's sake, I delight in weaknesses, in insults, in hardships, in persecutions, in difficulties. For when I am weak, then I am strong" (2 Corinthians 12:9–10).

My prayer is that we will admit to ourselves how desperately weak and dependent we are on God's grace. Only then can we experience the strength of his grace to survive the heat that life inevitably brings.

Grace Is Durable

In addition to its workability and strength, grace is also durable. Just as physical gold won't corrode in the air—and can even be buried for centuries and returned to light unchanged[6]— spiritual gold won't corrode in the atmosphere of Satan's influence. And even if grace is buried for centuries, it returns to light unchanged.

The apostle Paul emphasized the durability of God's grace, noting that this treasure is the very source of life:

> As for you, you were dead in your transgressions and sins, in which you used to live when you followed the ways of this world and of the ruler

of the kingdom of the air, the spirit who is now at work in those who are disobedient. All of us also lived among them at one time, gratifying the cravings of our sinful nature and following its desires and thoughts. Like the rest, we were by nature objects of wrath. But because of his great love for us, God, who is rich in mercy, made us alive with Christ even when we were dead in transgressions—it is by grace you have been saved. (Ephesians 2:1–5)

When Grace Resurfaces

In the Old Testament, we find an example of the durability of God's grace in the story of Esther, a young Jewish orphan girl who became the queen of Persia.

Esther's story begins with another woman. Vashti, the queen of Persia, refused to obey her husband's request. So Xerxes, the Persian king, decreed that a new queen should be found. Unlike the other young women brought before the king as potential queens, Esther took nothing special with her. Yet she won the grace of the king and the favor of all who saw her (Esther 2:12–15).

Four years passed, and it seemed that Esther's valuable commodity was buried. A plot arose in the kingdom to exterminate the Jewish people. Esther worried if her commodity, grace, would hold value for the Jewish people. Amazingly, the king asked her to tell him her request: "Then Queen Esther answered, 'If I have found favor with you, O king, and if it pleases your majesty, grant me my life—this is my petition. And spare my people—this is my request. For I and my people have been sold for destruction and slaughter and annihilation. If we had merely been sold as male and female slaves, I would have kept quiet, because no such distress would justify disturbing the king" (Esther 7:3–4). Xerxes then extended Esther grace far beyond what she asked. Her buried commodity—grace—remained powerful and destroyed the evil plan of the enemy.

Everyone benefited from Esther's grace, especially those closest to her. To honor this great deliverance from destruction, a Jewish holiday is still observed today, the Feast of Purim. This memorial of grace recalls this "time when the Jews got relief from their enemies, and as the month when their sorrow was turned into joy and their mourning into a day of celebration" (Esther 9:22).

When God Says, "I Can"

I'm no queen, but I do remember a time in my life when grace seemed completely buried. I grew up in a Christian home, and we attended a wonderful church where I was introduced to our Lord and received his grace for salvation. Sad to say, however, that while this grace changed my eternal destiny, my relationship with Christ stagnated out of my ignorance. I wasn't ignorant about the Scriptures; I was ignorant about the *person* of the Scriptures. Jesus' own words describe exactly how ignorant I was: "You diligently study the Scriptures because you think that by them you possess eternal life. These are the Scriptures that testify about me, yet you refuse to come to me to have life" (John 5:39–40).

That's pretty blunt. Yet after years of studying the Scriptures on my own, three years of Bible education at the university level, and a short overseas stint as a missionary, I was experiencing very little life. The chasm between who I was and who I wanted to be was tortuous. This agony in my soul eventually manifested itself as an eating disorder, bulimia.

I vividly remember the time I was staying at my parents' home. I read the apostle Paul's words to Timothy: "Be strong in the grace that is in Christ Jesus. And the things that thou hast heard of me among many witnesses, the same commit thou to faithful men, who shall be able to teach others also. Thou therefore endure hardness, as a good soldier of Jesus Christ" (2 Timothy 2:1–3 KJV). I wept as I read these words, because I wanted so badly to be a good soldier of Jesus Christ. Yet my best efforts always seemed to fall short. I realized that I had been numbing my inadequacy with food. That day I penned this poem:

A Dialogue with My Soldier

So alone, no one to care.
I'm just an unfinished project going nowhere.
Please, I want to be complete
You with the pencil in the drawing seat.
Energy and imagination are in Your hand
Sketch me with feet in which to stand.
Lift me from this dimension and let me go.

I AM. And I will tell you all you need to know.
I will give you a mind like My own

For the wisdom I know you've never known.
I will give you a heart in which to feel
And dreams that are Mine, in you I'll instill.
I AM the person you cannot be.
Within Me lies your being and creativity.
I give you courage without tears
And love with ambition without fears.
You see I AM listening to your every thought
Let Me fight the battles that must be fought.

As soon as I poured these words onto paper, I immediately went into the living room and announced to my parents that I was going to the hospital. Sweetly, they responded, "To visit a friend?"

"Uh . . . no, I have an eating disorder, and I need professional help."

At the eating disorder hospital, among a sea of New Age advisers, I, *coincidentally*, was assigned to Gwen, the only Christian on staff. In the third week of the six-week program, Gwen looked at me and said, "Pam, your problem isn't with food or your family. You simply have a problem with one word in the Bible that you know nothing about."

Wait a minute, I thought, *I know the Bible*. Then Gwen continued, "You know nothing of the word *grace*." My mind raced, mentally searching the glossaries of my theology textbooks. Then Gwen said, "For you, recovery is simply an understanding of God's grace."

I went back to my hospital room and, in a moment, received the One I had been introduced to as a child, as if he had walked out of the shadows of my soul. For me, it was as simple as admitting, *I can't*, and God was saying, "I can." No more torturing and comforting myself with food for being inadequate. I discovered that I can receive God's unearned spiritual blessings only when I cease trying to earn them. Christ himself satisfies the emptiness and hunger of the soul.

At times God extends his grace as complete deliverance, as he did for me with my eating disorder. From that moment until now, I've never seen food as anything other than sustenance to sustain life. In the face of the supernatural power of his grace, God rendered impotent the power that food had over me. At other times, according to God's good prearranged plan, he allows us to experience what seem like prolonged times of suffering and hardship. As the apostle Paul wrote, these times teach us the sufficiency of God's grace: "Three times I pleaded with the Lord to take it away from me. But he said to me, 'My grace is sufficient for you, for my power is made perfect in weakness'" (2 Corinthians 12:8–9).

We are fragile vessels of grace, and God desires to show his strength in our lives precisely at our points of weakness. Unfortunately, we often see this as a negative experience, but only when we're exposed as fragile beings who must completely depend on God can the durability and strength of his grace show through us.

Grace Is Heavy

We've compared several qualities of physical and spiritual gold, including workability, strength, and durability. Now let's look at a quality that speaks of quantity: the weight of gold and grace.

For us to understand how grace is heavy, it is helpful to understand how physical gold is heavy. The atomic number of seventy-nine is attributed to gold because of the collective number of protons found in the nucleus, or core, of its atom.[7]

Likewise at the core of grace are the collective attributes of God, which make it spiritually heavy. The Bible translates the Hebrew word *kabad* as "heavy"; it is often also translated as "glory." However, it "does not mean simply 'heavy' but a heavy or imposing quantity of things."[8] So we see at the core of God's grace the collective quantity of God's attributes. Therefore, when we receive grace, we are receiving the spiritual weight of God, which is glorious.

When speaking of Jesus, the apostle John said he possessed the full measure of grace. "In the beginning was the Word, and the Word was with God, and the Word was God. . . . The Word became flesh and made his dwelling among us. We have seen his glory, the glory of the One and Only, who came from the Father, full of grace and truth" (John 1:1, 14). Jesus was full of grace, weighty in all the attributes of God.

To be "full" denotes a measure. For something to be full, it must also have the potential to be empty. Quite literally, our hearts are vessels, and though immaterial they are still vessels—vessels that can be either full or empty, in this case either full of grace or empty of grace. What gain is there to being spiritually full or heavy with grace? To understand this, let's first examine the implications of being full or heavy in gold.

Solomon was a man in the Bible whose life God used as a

canvas for teaching the weighty implications of gold and grace. Solomon said to God:

> O LORD my God, you have made your servant king in place of my father David. But I am only a little child and do not know how to carry out my duties. Your servant is here among the people you have chosen, a great people, too numerous to count or number. So give your servant a discerning heart to govern your people and to distinguish between right and wrong. For who is able to govern this great people of yours? (1 Kings 3:7–9)

God responded to Solomon's humble request.

> The Lord was pleased that Solomon had asked for this. So God said to him, "Since you have asked for this and not for long life or wealth for yourself, nor have asked for the death of your enemies but for discernment in administering justice, I will do what you have asked. I will give you a wise and discerning heart, so that there will never have been anyone like you, nor will there ever be. Moreover, I will give you what you have not asked for—both riches and *honor*—so that in your lifetime you will have no equal among kings." (1 Kings 3:10–13, emphasis added)

The word *honor* in the above verse is the Hebrew word *kabod*, a derivative of the same Hebrew word *kabad* we looked at earlier, denoting an imposing quantity of things. Indeed, Solomon's possessions were an imposing quantity of things. He was heavy in cattle, servants, and wives; and "the weight of the gold that Solomon received yearly was 666 talents" (2 Chronicles 9:13). Clearly, this man's bank was filled with gold, but what about his heart?

The Bible attributes the number 666 to man: "If anyone has insight, let him calculate the number of the beast, for it is man's number. His number is 666" (Revelation 13:18). "The best interpretation to the number 666 is that it is one less than the perfect number seven, and the threefold repetition of the six would indicate that for all their pretensions to deity."[9] Solomon took for himself the weight of 666 talents of gold. The man who once saw himself as a humble child in need of God's grace, used the weight of heaven's commodity not "to distinguish between right from wrong" but to build an empire whose glory would reflect his own tastes.[10] At the end of his life Solomon proclaimed that even though he had stored up gold in his bank, his heart was empty, without meaning. "'Meaningless! Meaningless!' says the Teacher. 'Everything is meaningless!'" (Ecclesiastes 12:8). The exclamation marks in the text serve as a warning echoed by the rhetorical words of Jesus: "What good will it be for a man if he gains the whole world, yet forfeits his soul? Or what can a man give in exchange for his soul?" (Matthew 16:26).

If being weighty in spiritual gold—grace—is God's utmost desire for us, then at what measure is our heart presently? Each one of our spiritual hearts, apart from God's grace, has no weight, regardless of how weighty our physical bank accounts are. "Trust in him at all times, O people; pour out your hearts to him, for God is our refuge. Lowborn men are but a breath, the highborn are but a lie; if weighed on a balance, they are nothing; together they are only a breath" (Psalm 62:8–9). But this weightless state is not God's plan for us. As a matter of fact, he desires that we succeed: "Commit to the LORD whatever you do, and your plans will succeed" (Proverbs 16:3).

This verse has caused many to stumble because they have taken it out of context. They falsely believe that they can begin any endeavor and claim God's promise of success, because they have committed it to him. The verses preceding it speak to the fact that before God administers grace for success, he first weighs the heart. "To man belong the plans of the heart, but from the LORD comes the reply of the tongue. All a man's ways seem innocent to him, but motives are weighed by the LORD" (Proverbs 16:1–2). God knows exactly why we are doing what we are doing, regardless of what we say. The Scriptures say, "Your attitude should be the same as that of Christ Jesus: Who, being in very nature God, did not consider equality with God something to be grasped, but made himself nothing, taking the very nature of a servant" (Philippians 2:5–7).

There is a weighing going on. In the world, our bank accounts are being weighed, determining our right to survive and thrive materially and possess influence. In heaven God weighs our hearts, determining our right to survive and thrive spiritually and possess spiritual influence. Let us not be ignorant: "God opposes the proud but gives grace to the humble" (1 Peter 5:5).

What can we expect when we humbly reach in faith for God's grace with pure motives to serve? Paul said, "God is able to make all grace abound to you, so that in all things at all times, having all that you need, you will abound in every good work"

(2 Corinthians 9:8). Notice the words "all things . . . all that you need . . . every good work." We will be aptly supplied by God when we are truly about what he defines as a "good" work.

Abraham Booth (1734–1806), an English pastor and author, wrote, "To constitute a work truly good, it must be done from a right principle, performed by a right rule, and intended for a right end. The right principle is our love for God. The right rule is God's revealed will as contained in Scripture. The right end is the glory of God."[11]

So, as we overcome the natural desire to serve self, we reach in faith to receive God's grace to serve others. Jesus said: "To him who overcomes, I will give the right to sit with me on my throne, just as I overcame and sat down with my Father on his throne. He who has an ear, let him hear what the Spirit says to the churches" (Revelation 3:21–22).

Matter That Matters

I am fortunate to have a humble friend who provided a wonderful example of being filled with grace. In the midst of difficult circumstances, she chose what matters.

Kay Daniels, my friend since the seventh grade, taught me how receiving grace can make us heavyweight champions in God's kingdom. Even though Kay[12] has a small frame and is quiet—a much more passive person than I am—she and I have been classmates, cheerleaders, and coconspirators in all sorts of mischief and fun. In other words, we've known each other through many glorious and not-so-glorious times.

When we were in high school, Kay lost her mother to cancer.

Because of Kay's passive nature, I feared that she lacked the personal aggressiveness to cope with her tragic loss. Unbelievably, in the aftermath of the family's first trauma, Kay soon lost her father as he was undergoing heart surgery. Devastated, she latched on—with leechlike tenacity—to the only secure thing in her life: the Rock of Ages, Jesus Christ.

When we were twenty years old, Kay and I began a weekly Bible study together, which has continued throughout the years. Over this time, I've observed a difference between us. Consistently, instead of just hearing God's Word, Kay receives and obeys the Word as a personal promise. She always acts on the truths she receives from God's Word, as if those truths are buoys that keep her from sinking in a sea of hopelessness.

Throughout the years, Kay and I have both studied the Scriptures—me from my lawn chair and umbrella on the beach of life and Kay in the middle of crashing waves of uncertainty. In essence, the difference was that Kay became more glorious, while I became spiritually fat. The difference between her glory and my fat was simply a question of *matter*.

What mattered to Kay was knowing Christ by experience. As a result, the matter of his life—grace—was deposited within. For me, what mattered was knowing Christ by intellect, knowing facts about him without having to rely on him to live those facts. As a result, I was puffed up. The prophet Habakkuk described my condition: "See, he is puffed up; his desires are not upright—but the righteous will live by his faith" (Habakkuk 2:4).

When we know facts about Jesus but don't rely on him to live those facts in us, we quickly become foolish and fat. "Knowledge puffs up, but love builds up. The man who thinks he knows something does not yet know as he ought to know" (1 Corinthians 8:1–2).

I realized that when Kay spoke the Word to someone in need, she had already heard, received, and processed it! She was relying in faith on the living Word, Jesus Christ. In addition to the *what* of facts, Kay was able to offer the *who* of Jesus Christ. She ministered with *glorious grace,* demonstrating what the apostle Paul wrote: "For God, who said, 'Let light shine out of darkness,' made his light shine in our hearts to give us the light of the knowledge of the glory of God in the face of Christ. But we have this treasure in jars of clay to show that this all-surpassing power is from God and not from us. We are hard pressed on every side, but not crushed; perplexed, but not in despair; persecuted, but not abandoned; struck down, but not destroyed" (2 Corinthians 4:6–9).

Instruments of Glory

The Old Testament contains the account of a man who obeyed God's word and then not only saw God's glory, but also became the expression of that glory. He journeyed from a place of authority and weight in the world's kingdom to authority and weight in God's kingdom.

Moses was rescued at birth, groomed with education and social class, and ended up living in the richest golden civilization of the time, Egypt. Believing he had the necessary resources to make a difference in the lives of God's children, he killed an Israelite slave-master. This presumption and murder caused his exile to the far side of the desert, tending sheep.

Yet in this unlikely place, Moses encountered the word of God from within a burning bush. He humbly obeyed God's instructions and began a simple cycle of hearing God, obeying God, seeing the manifestation of God, and becoming an instrument of God's glory.

Years later when Moses ascended Mount Sinai—a physical picture of the spiritual reality of ascending the golden road of grace—he again encountered the Lord and said:

> "Now therefore, I pray, if I have found grace in Your sight, show me now Your way, that I may know You and that I may find grace in Your sight. And consider that this nation *is* Your people." . . .
>
> So the LORD said to Moses, "I will also do this thing that you have spoken; for you have found grace in My sight, and I know you by name." And he said, "Please, show me Your glory." Then He said, "I will make all My goodness pass before you, and I will proclaim the name of the LORD before you. I will be gracious to whom I will be gracious, and I will have compassion on whom I will have compassion." . . .
>
> Now it was so, when Moses came down from Mount Sinai (and the two tablets of the Testimony *were* in Moses' hand when he came down from the mountain), that Moses did not know that the skin of his face shone while he talked with Him. (Exodus 33:13, 17–19; 34:29 NKJV)

Although Moses didn't see God's face, God revealed his

identity to Moses through his word. This wasn't merely an encounter with the *what* of God's identity; it was a personal encounter with *who*: "When Moses came down from Mount Sinai with the two tablets of the Testimony in his hands, he was not aware that his face was radiant because he had *spoken with* the Lord" (Exodus 34:29, emphasis added).

Speaking to God and obeying his voice demonstrate our heart's belief. This is the way that we both receive his grace and reflect his glory. The apostle Paul explained that this heavy glorious grace is not just for a celebrated few, but for all of us: "All of us, as with unveiled face, [because we] continued to behold [in the Word of God] as in a mirror the glory of the Lord, are constantly being transfigured into His very own image in ever increasing splendor and from one degree of glory to another; [for this comes] from the Lord [Who is] the Spirit" (2 Corinthians 3:18 AMP).

Grace Is Reflective

Like a mirror, grace by its very nature is reflective. This quality of grace correlates with gold, because both reflect light and heat.

Refined to Reflect

Gold has an excellent reflective quality. In the ancient world, a goldsmith would work over a pot of gold, removing the impurities from the gold by carefully refining it in a fire. When he saw a reflection of himself in the gold, he knew that it was pure and ready for use.

Engineers in the twentieth century used gold foil's reflective quality to cover parts of the *Apollo* spacecraft to protect the astronauts from solar radiation. We also see the reflective quality of gold film used on windows in large office buildings to reflect heat without reducing light.[13]

Similarly, grace has an excellent reflective spiritual quality. God sees the soul of each spiritual child as a pot of gold. As the "spiritual goldsmith," Jesus Christ works over all his spiritual children's souls, removing our impurities and carefully refining us by the fire of the Holy Spirit. When Christ sees a reflection of himself in our souls, he considers us pure and ready for his chosen use. "He will sit as a refiner and purifier of silver; he will purify the Levites and refine them like gold and silver. Then the LORD will have men who will bring offerings in righteousness" (Malachi 3:3). Preacher and author John Piper wrote, "He created us 'in his image' so that we would image forth his glory into the world. We were made to be prisms refracting the light of God's glory into all of life."[14]

Reflections of Christ

During his ministry on earth, Jesus taught, spoke, and took actions that provide many clues about how God wants us to live. Of course, from our perspective, we can never really ever measure up to Christ, because Jesus was the exact manifestation of God in a human body.

But God sees us differently. When we become God's children, he sees us as reflections of Jesus Christ. The author of Hebrews wrote: "In the past God spoke to our forefathers through the prophets at many times and in various ways, but in these last days he has spoken to us by his Son, whom he appointed heir of all things, and through whom he made the universe. The Son is the radiance of God's glory and the exact representation of his being, sustaining all things by his powerful word" (Hebrews 1:1–3). Miraculously, when we spiritually see Jesus for who he is, transfigured into the very glory of God, we are also transformed into reflections of him.

Because God provides the Holy Spirit to do this work in us from the inside out, we easily overlook it or take it for granted. But three of Jesus' disciples provide an illustration of just how, in Christ, our transformation remarkably makes us reflections of God's glory and grace.

When I think about the story of Jesus and his disciples going to the Mount of Transfiguration, I envision it like this:

> Just a little bit farther . . .higher, Jesus thought as he turned, looking at the sweat pouring off the brows of Peter, James, and John. Each disciple held in his mind that Moses had encountered God high on a mountain, so they pressed on, following Jesus.
>
> As the salty air from the Sea of Galilee filled Peter's nostrils, he looked up and realized that Jesus had changed! No longer were his tunic timeworn and his sandals dirty. He was white—dazzling white—and Peter shielded his eyes.
>
> John stammered, "Jesus, your face is like the sun and your clothes are whiter than light." The three disciples blinked at the sight before them. Now Jesus was standing beside Moses and

Elijah, talking. As Peter tried to make sense of the astonishing sight, his mind raced. "It is good to be here," he blurted. "I'll make three shelters—one for you, Jesus, and Moses and Elijah."

Suddenly, a bright cloud enveloped Jesus, Moses, and Elijah. And God spoke, "This is my descended One, my Son, whom I love; with him I am well pleased. Now listen to him!"

At that, all three disciples fell facedown in awe, worship, and fear. Jesus touched them and said, "Get up now and don't be afraid." (author's summary of Matthew 17:1–8)

Grace in its fullness appeared to Peter, James, and John. When Jesus was transfigured—unveiled from his body of flesh— his reflection of God's glory evoked awe, worship, and fear in the disciples. How could they ever be the same? How could they not be transformed themselves, becoming reflections of God's glory and grace?

Bible teacher and speaker Chuck Swindoll wrote,

> As the face of the moon reflects the sun, so the face of a person reflects grace. Sometimes that grace is eclipsed by the sin in our life. Other times it beams full and radiant. At such shining moments we reflect a glimmer of the Lord Jesus. That's what the poorest of the poor in India's streets see when they look up at the wrinkled face of Mother Teresa. They see the eyes of Jesus, the tears of Jesus, and the smile of Jesus. They see a reflection of grace.

What do people see when they look at your face? Do they see the worries of the world etched in a wrinkled forehead and knitted brow? Do they see the harshness of the dog-eat-dog business world chiseled in a stone jaw? Do they see the frazzle of depression and fatigue scribbled in bloodshot eyes? Grace is really amazing, for it will not only change the way you look at others but the way others look at you.[15]

Bone Weary and Bedraggled

I find it humorous that we often try so hard to exhibit God's grace on our own—unsuccessfully, of course—when all he really wants for us is to set ourselves aside so his grace can reflect off us. Interestingly, all our awareness or preparation doesn't matter, because God chooses when and how he uses us.

That's exactly what happened with my friend Gretchen.[16] By the time we met, she had attended a prestigious boarding school and university and traveled extensively. Her candid personality bluntly let others know where she stood on most of life's issues. Immediately, I liked her.

Since she regarded herself as open-minded and well traveled, we discussed her disbelief in what she called "narrow-minded Christianity." She expressed that she was simply more comfortable with a more tolerant and inclusive religion.

I was open-minded, too, tolerating Gretchen's need to feel comfortable. Yet I was a bit surprised when she accepted my invitation to a weekly Bible study I led for a group of women.

Gretchen loved it—the heart-to-heart girl talks, the love expressed in laughter as well as tears. She found acceptance and love after a life of wandering. Still, even after two years of weekly Bible studies and endless talks and prayers, she refused to accept Christ and his "narrow way."

One spring weekend, our Bible study group joined with other women's small groups for an overnight retreat. It was like a big slumber party! We stayed up all night, talking, laughing, and eating junk food, as well as praising and praying to the Lord.

As we left the overnight retreat, my tired eyes burned when they met the morning rays. Our group piled into the car. Bone weary and bedraggled, we all grew more and more cranky with each passing moment—all except Gretchen. "That was a blast!" she exclaimed exuberantly.

I muttered, slumped in the front seat, "Yeah . . . I suppose heaven will be one endless slumber party." A few faint chuckles followed. Gretchen chirped in, "That'll be great!"

Candidly, I countered, "It's too bad you won't be there."

"What?" A hush cloaked the car. But I couldn't stop my bluntness, and I answered, "You'll be in hell." Immediately, I was shocked at what I had said. No one blinked. But I recalled how Gretchen's own candor made her appreciate when others told her what they thought. So I simply continued, "Gretchen, you know that. We've studied that for two years."

She leaned back and whispered, "I know . . . I know."

When we finally arrived at my apartment, I had pretty much forgotten about Gretchen. Instead, I could only focus on getting some sleep. But Gretchen asked, "Do you mind if I come in?" I nodded, stumbling up the stairs, thinking, *Whatever she wants, she better make it quick.* She looked at me, her eyes fresh and alert. "I want to go to the slumber party. The slumber party in heaven. You women are the most wonderful friends, and I want to be at the endless slumber party in heaven!"

I was shocked. For two years I had rehearsed the steps of salvation. I never went to work or dinner with Gretchen without bringing my Bible. Countless times I had asked her if she wanted to receive Christ, but each time she refused. Now—when I'm exhausted beyond belief and completely unprepared—she wants to accept Christ!

I wasn't prepared.

Still, we knelt right there in the doorway of my apartment. I didn't have any wise or rehearsed words, yet the God of the universe deposited in Gretchen's soul grace for eternal life. What she saw in our bone-weary, bedraggled appearance was a reflection of Christ: his love, his acceptance, his longsuffering, his narrow "slap in the face" truth.

Not needing our awareness or preparation, God, by reflective grace, had fashioned Christ in us as we simply beheld him in his Word.

Surrendering to Grace

During those years with Gretchen, I saw the apostle Paul's words come to life: "When we tell you these things, we do not use words that come from human wisdom. Instead, we speak words given to us by the Spirit, using the Spirit's words to explain spiritual truths. But people who aren't spiritual can't receive these truths from God's Spirit. It all sounds foolish to them and they can't understand it, for only those who are spiritual can understand what the Spirit means" (1 Corinthians 2:13–14 NLT).

God opened Gretchen's ears to hear what before sounded narrow and "foolish" to her. He opened her eyes to see in my tired appearance the reflection of God's glory and grace.

Sadly, we easily forget that God gives us everything we need for life. He grants us everything we need to live godly lives. We can't add a single thing to what he provides! We need to learn to see and confess our utter dependence on him, realizing that we will find a true position of security only when we surrender to his grace. Then, by reflecting who he is, we can deliver the message of his grace to the people around us.

Grace Is Powerful

We have looked at many qualities of God's spiritual gold, examining how grace is workable, strong, durable, heavy, and reflective. Of course, not enough paper and ink exist to fully explain the qualities of God's grace. Even as I've tried to provide just an overview, this chapter became the longest one in this book. Yet I hope you've enjoyed hunting through these treasures of God's grace. Before we move on, let's look at one more important quality.

Another amazing quality of God's spiritual gold is its power. Physical gold is a great conductor of electricity; and because of its malleability and resistance to rust, engineers prefer gold for televisions, calculators, and other fine circuitry.[17] In a mystical and miraculous way, spiritual gold—grace—is the great conductor of the power of God into our lives.

Our souls serve as the receivers of God's grace. Grace is the conductor, the Holy Spirit is the power of God, and our bodies become the output devices. To turn on this power, we need to activate the switch of faith. When God's power is channeled through us, the level of charge can't be controlled!

The Current of Grace

I will never forget one electrifying experience when I was the receiver of God's grace. Like many experiences with the Lord, this happened when I least expected it.

I was asked to speak at a mother-daughter retreat on the subject of the biblical perspective of beauty. I felt prepared to address this topic, but I wanted to make sure I was yielding to what God wanted to say through me. So I decided to fast and pray a few days before the retreat. Little did I know that God was preparing my soul to receive his grace.

When the day of the retreat came, I was ready to go. I had my notes and I looked the part—well dressed, conservative yet fashionable. In a beautiful banquet room in a fine hotel, I awaited my time to speak. At the last minute, the woman scheduled to speak before me canceled, and a young woman in college gave her testimony.

As I listened to her speak about how God bestowed his grace on her after a season of rebellion, it was as if God had fastened gold conductors to my mind, emotions, and will. Immediately, I connected with this young woman's story, because I had also experienced God's grace after a season of rebellion. Somewhere during her talk, I began to cry and tremble, not out of sympathy, but because I was again experiencing the overwhelming goodness and grace of God.

I had gone to this event "so together," and by the time someone said, "Pam, they introduced you," I realized that I was now a tear-stained mess.

I gathered my notes, stood, and shuffled to the podium. But my mind was blank. There was nothing more to say. "God is so good!" I declared, before bursting into tears. A few women rushed to my aid with tissues. The mascara on my painted lashes was now down at my chin. My eyes were completely bloodshot as the church historian snapped a photo of the speaker who came to talk about *beauty*.

I laughed on the inside at God's sense of humor and went to plan B, not having any idea what it was. All I could think to do was to follow up the young woman's testimony with my own. So I spoke: "All I have learned about beauty—whatever beauty I have—is merely what God has reconstructed out of my failed attempts. When all is said and done, true beauty, lasting beauty—that quality that attracts admiring pleasure—is actually grace, God bestowing his favor on us."

Visibly shaken, I left the podium.

Visibly shaken, I drove home.

All I know is that God's power came upon my soul. I couldn't shut off or control this power, which seemed to be channeled through me when I reconnected personally with God's grace. My mouth, voice, eyes, and tears were all the output of this transaction. And no one more than I recognized the presence of this very real yet foreign current: the power of God's grace. I'm happy to say that God used this experience to powerfully touch the girls and women in attendance.

That day I truly understood how the apostle Paul could say, "I became a servant of this gospel by the gift of God's grace given me through the working of his power. Although I am less than the least of all God's people, this grace was given me" (Ephesians 3:7–8).

Charged with Power

A scholar in his own right—part of the Who's Who of Judaism—Paul, the writer of most of the New Testament, asserted in his teachings that Jesus Christ is the spiritual and physical Messiah, the Savior. Paul's perspective reminds us that there's an unseen spiritual world with unseen powers that work for and against us.

Paul's power to work in this unseen spiritual realm didn't come from the power of his persuasive prose or anything he brought physically to the equation. In the end, if Christ didn't manifest his power through Paul when the apostle spoke or wrote, no one would ever see the light of the good news Paul proclaimed. Certainly, Paul daily faced the real possibility that his labor would be in vain unless Christ's power charged it. That's why he clearly and frequently wrote of the power of the Lord working in and through his life.

- "My message and my preaching were not with wise and persuasive words, but with a demonstration of the Spirit's power, so that your faith might not rest on

men's wisdom, but on God's power." (1 Corinthians
2:4–5)

- "For the kingdom of God is not a matter of talk but of
power." (1 Corinthians 4:20)
- "He said to me, 'My grace is sufficient for you, for my
power is made perfect in weakness.' Therefore I will
boast all the more gladly about my weaknesses, so that
Christ's power may rest on me." (2 Corinthians 12:9)

Spiritual Receivers

Amazingly, God offers all his followers the same incredible
power that the apostle Paul tapped into so that others can see the
light of the good news proclaimed through our lives. But, like
Paul, we need to make sure we're connected to the conductor of
God's power: his grace.

Is it possible to possess all the components for receiving and
reproducing God's power and yet not sense God working in
our lives? When we accept Christ, we can think of our souls as
becoming the receivers of God's grace.

Often, we aren't aware of the powerful path and all that God
is desiring and willing to do in and through us. Jesus explained
it to his disciples this way: "The Father . . . will give you another
Counselor to be with you forever—the Spirit of truth. The world
cannot accept him, because it neither sees him nor knows him.
But you know him, for he lives with you and will be in you"
(John 14:16–17).

Just as we cannot see the electric current that empowers
our computers and television sets—but we know it exists—

we cannot see the Spirit of grace empowering us, though his presence is undeniable as we witness him. When we receive God's power, he can work through us in amazing ways. He will use us to speak boldly for him as he confirms the message of his grace by enabling us to do things beyond our natural ability (see Acts 14:3).

A Choice

In this chapter, as we've looked at the qualities of physical gold and God's grace, we can understand the words of the apostle Paul: "For since the creation of the world God's invisible qualities—his eternal power and divine nature—have been clearly seen, being understood from what has been made, so that men are without excuse" (Romans 1:20).

In order for us to understand and value God's kingdom commodity—grace—God wisely gave earthly kingdoms the commodity of gold, because the truth of his grace is like gold. The Russian novelist Leo Tolstoy once said, "Truth, like gold, is to be obtained not by its growth, but by washing away from it all that is not gold."[18]

Let's be sure we don't hold on to the dirt—choosing the lesser for the greater, the temporal for the eternal—and be a fool with grace by choosing something over God's authentic spiritual gold—his grace: "They became fools and exchanged the glory of the immortal God for images" (Romans 1:22–23). Again quoting John Piper, "The way we 'fall short' of the glory of God is we exchange it for something of lesser value. All sin comes from not putting supreme value on the glory of God."[19]

---------- *Nuggets*----------

G ive God the right to be God of your life

O pen your heart to perceive him

L isten to his inaudible voice

D are to believe

---------- *A Prayer of Grace* ----------

Lord God, we are sobered yet exuberant at the invisible gift of grace you've given us—your Son's life within. Forgive us when we haven't been attentive. Thank you that we're forever part of your heavenly family.

Father God, we acknowledge your desire that we each be content with your gifts of grace as thankful children, living interdependently with each other in love. Open our spiritual eyes to see your gifts of grace in our lives, as well as in our brothers' and sisters' lives, so we may praise you and offer them encouragement. Thank you that it is not our responsibility to get others to see our gifts of grace. Let each of us be devoted to you and our family, doing our designated part in your kingdom . . . joyously.

Forgive us when we insult you by offering up to you our works of flesh. Lord God, we acknowledge that you do not lower your standards. You steadfastly remain holy and righteous. Help us to realize deeply that Christ would not have been offered up if we could offer up anything acceptable in your sight. Thank you for providing us with sufficient grace.

Let us not be deceived into thinking that building with grace in our lives and in others is easy for our flesh. Enable us to be merciful, extending to others grace when we and they fall short of your glory. Amen.

──────────── Questions for Reflection ────────────

• Excluding your house and cars, what's the most valuable material possession you own? What makes it so valuable?

• When Jesus lived the abundant life on earth, he possessed all the power of God, yet he worked. He possessed all knowledge, yet he studied and taught from the Scriptures. He had all strength, yet he got tired and grew hungry. Does your image of the abundant life look anything like the life Jesus and the disciples experienced?

• How does the world describe the abundant life?

• Which perspective, the world's view or a biblical view, describes your life desires now? Consider this: "Do not love the world or anything in the world. If anyone loves the world, the love of the Father is not in him. For everything in the world—the cravings of sinful man, the lust of his eyes and the boasting of what he has and does—comes not from the Father but from the world" (1 John 2:15–16).

The Reward

*L*et's be real with each other. Imagine that someone gives you a gold mine worth millions of dollars. What would this new possession allow you to do? Maybe you've been ill, and with your newfound riches, you could see a specialist and receive the best medical care available. Or perhaps you're exhausted, and your new wealth could provide rest and a vacation. Or maybe you'd like a new home, new cars for every member of your family, fully paid college tuition, the finest clothes—the list goes on with possessions and desires that would be available to you if you were rich in gold.

Of course, material possessions aren't the only thing your gold would provide. You'd also receive the close relatives of possessions—influence and power. The vast rewards gold yields are one of the reasons why Jesus chose to use this term when he counseled Christians on grace. He wants us to experience abundant rewards and to live rich lives. But to do so we need to buy from him gold *refined* in the fire so we can become rich (Revelation 3:18).

Pure Gold Is Refined Gold

In the last chapter, we noted how a goldsmith in the ancient world would work over a pot of gold. When he could see a reflection of himself in the gold, he knew it was pure and ready for use. As we noted, this provides an excellent image of how Christ removes impurities of self-reliance from each one of us, so that we see our need to live in total dependence on God. Even Jesus depended completely on the Father. He said, "When you have lifted up the Son of Man, then you will know that I am the one I claim to be and that I do nothing on my own but speak just what the Father has taught me" (John 8:28).

Imagine that! Jesus—who was fully man and also fully God—did nothing based on his own independent desires or initiative. He was pure from selfish motives and a selfish agenda, completely submitting to the Father's will. This is the same Jesus whom Paul described as the One who created all things "visible and invisible, whether thrones or powers or rulers or authorities; all things were created by him and for him. He is before all things, and in him all things hold together" (Colossians 1:16–17).

Even though we are imperfect reflections of him, Jesus' pure state reflects God's work in us. The prophet Daniel had a vision of this: "Some of the wise will stumble, so that they may be refined, purified and made spotless until the time of the end, for it will still come at the appointed time" (Daniel 11:35).

A Rock and a Hard Place

Today, right now, God refines us from our independent ways. He carries out this refining process both for our benefit and for the benefit of the world at large. Look at how he refined Ananias, a Christian man who lived in Damascus in the first century.

"The Lord called to him in a vision, 'Ananias!' 'Yes, Lord,' he answered. The Lord told him, 'Go to the house of Judas on Straight Street and ask for a man from Tarsus named Saul, for he is praying. In a vision he has seen a man named Ananias come and place his hands on him to restore his sight'" (Acts 9:10–12).

Ananias knew about Saul. This man, who saw the fledgling followers of Jesus as a threat to his Jewish faith, was determined to destroy the lives of Christians. Undoubtedly, Ananias knew many of these early martyrs personally. But instead of warning Ananias to flee Saul's Hitler-like rampage, God instructed Ananias to help Saul.

What would you have done? How many of us would have believed that the dream wasn't really God speaking but was a nightmare cause by something spicy we ate? Most of us simply wouldn't want to do what God was asking. Ananias was made out of the same independent flesh we all are, so he asked the Lord to clarify his instructions.

"Lord," Ananias answered, "I have heard many reports about this man and all the harm he has done to your saints in Jerusalem. And he has come here with authority from the chief priests to arrest all who call on your name."

But the Lord said to Ananias, "Go! This man is my chosen instrument to carry my name before the Gentiles and their kings and before the people of Israel. I will show him how much he must suffer for my name."

Then Ananias went to the house and entered it. Placing his hands on Saul, he said, "Brother Saul, the Lord—Jesus, who appeared to you on the road as you were coming here—has sent me so that you may see again and be filled with the Holy Spirit." (Acts 9:13–17)

If this decision had been left to Ananias's independent will, I'm guessing he would have either denied the dream or at least stalled before he finally obeyed. But he yielded his will and allowed the Rock to crush his independence. Why? The Scriptures say that Ananias was more than just a follower of Jesus Christ. He was a *disciple* of Jesus Christ (Acts 9:10). He submitted his own will to the will of God, his commanding officer. Again and again, he would deny himself and follow Jesus.

Ananias's obedience made him a trophy of God's grace, a victor in the grace race. Here's how the apostle Paul later expressed this concept to his protégé Timothy: "No one serving as a soldier gets involved in civilian affairs—he wants to please his commanding officer. Similarly, if anyone competes as an athlete, he does not receive the victor's crown unless he competes according to the rules" (2 Timothy 2:4–5).

Gold-Medal Living

Just as Ananias went through a refining process, God calls on all of his followers to submit to his refinement. This process is God's rule for gold-medal living.

We can see the depth of commitment this process requires when we look at how dedicated athletes must live. Read the biography of almost any Olympic gold-medal athlete, and you will find long, grueling workouts, time tests, weigh-ins, practice, practice, practice, and hard work after hard work. It doesn't matter when they won or what country they represented; each of these athletes will speak of the hard work, dedication, and grueling cost of being a champion and taking home the gold prize.

Swimmer Michael Phelps was a six-time gold medalist in the 2004 Summer Olympics. His mother, Deborah Phelps, said that once Michael competed in the 2000 Summer Olympics and held his own, he believed he could win the swimming events in the 2004 Summer Olympics. He not only believed he could win, but he saw himself shattering world records. He visualized standing on the center stand with the gold medal around his neck. He visualized what winning those gold medals would look like and how they would feel.[1]

The apostle Paul also visualized winning. He was both a spiritual athlete and a spiritual coach. And he trained for just one vital race: "I consider my life worth nothing to me, if only I may finish the race and complete the task the Lord Jesus has given me—the task of testifying to the gospel of God's grace" (Acts 20:24).

Paul realized that many Christians start this race. But he

knew that finishing the race is another matter: "Do you not know that in a race all the runners run, but only one gets the prize? Run in such a way as to get the prize. Everyone who competes in the games goes into strict training. They do it to get a crown that will not last; but we do it to get a crown that will last forever. Therefore I do not run like a man running aimlessly; I do not fight like a man beating the air. No, I beat my body and make it my slave so that after I have preached to others, I myself will not be disqualified for the prize" (1 Corinthians 9:24–27).

Paul had the kind of passionate dedication it takes to visualize the prize and pursue it wholeheartedly. Yet his prize was completely selfless: spreading the thrilling message of God's grace—undeserved favor—so that anyone who believes in Christ receives forgiveness of sins and an abundant eternal life!

Pure-Gold Trophy

While Paul could only visualize his prize, the apostle John later wrote the book of Revelation and described this trophy for us. Remember Jesus' counsel in Revelation 3:18? He said, "Buy from me gold refined in the fire." The Greek word for *refined* in this verse means "ignited" or "glowing." It speaks of proven quality. Just a couple of chapters earlier, John used the exact same Greek word to describe the risen Jesus: "His head and hair were white like wool, as white as snow, and his eyes were like blazing fire. His feet were like bronze *glowing* in a furnace, and his voice was like the sound of rushing waters" (Revelation 1:14–15, emphasis added).

I'm always struck by the words, "His feet were like bronze

glowing in a furnace." I spent seven years working in the outward image business—as a fashion model, an image consultant, and doing makeup on post-cosmetic-surgery patients. During that time, I learned that people's hands and feet reveal more about them than any other part of their bodies Hands and feet are the most difficult body parts to camouflage. Our hands and feet reveal our age, our nationality, our health, and even our attention to detail.

So, look closely at how John described Jesus' feet: "like bronze glowing in a furnace." The phrase "like bronze" is translated from the Greek word *chalkolibanon*. It means "a metal like gold, if not more precious."[2] Unfortunately, the English language sometimes has limitations when translating from Greek. In English we don't have "a metal like gold, if not more precious," so translators chose the word *bronze*.

I don't think of bronze as more precious than gold. In fact, I think just the opposite. We give the winner at the Olympics a gold medal while the person or team finishing in third receives a bronze medal. So, a more accurate translation of what John saw would be: "Jesus' feet were 'like gold, if not more precious,' glowing in a furnace."

Did you catch that? "Like gold, if not more precious." Indeed, grace is like gold, as we have seen, but it is more precious. Jesus Christ is the gold trophy and the crowned reward of God's kingdom: "'You made him a little lower than the angels; you crowned him with glory and honor and put everything under his feet.' In putting everything under him, God left nothing that is not subject to him. Yet at present we do not see everything subject to him. But we see Jesus, who was made a little lower than the angels, now crowned with glory and honor because he suffered death, so that by the grace of God he might taste death for everyone" (Hebrews 2:7–9). Jesus' sacrificial love made him God's ultimate trophy of grace, crowned with glory and honor.

In the same way, as we yield our plans to God and sacrificially love and serve, God refines us and makes us trophies of his grace. The people we serve become our crown. Paul expressed it this way: "For what is our hope, our joy, or the crown in which we will glory in the presence of our Lord Jesus when he comes? Is it not you?" (1 Thessalonians 2:19).

Trophy-Making Process

To understand how God makes us trophies of his grace, we can look at the process of making a physical golden trophy. This process is called "lost-wax casting." The artisan starts by making a figure out of wax and then setting the wax figure in soft molding clay. The clay must be fitted with a pouring vent. After the clay hardens, molten gold is poured into the vent. The heat of the gold vaporizes the wax, leaving the void filled with the precious metal. When the casting cools, the artist breaks away the clay, leaving a golden replica of the original lost-wax figure.[3]

Now consider how this process works spiritually. Genesis describes how God created Adam: "So God created man in his own image, in the image of God he created him; male and female he created them. . . . The LORD God formed the man from the dust of the ground and breathed into his nostrils the breath of life, and the man became a living being" (Genesis 1:27;

2:7). In other words, you could say that our bodies are the clay, the original figure is the image of God, and our hearts are the pouring vent. When we ask Christ to be our Savior, God pours in golden grace, and when our clay bodies break, what's left is an image of God.

The apostle Paul recognized this process of being made into God's image when he wrote: "In all things God works for the good of those who love him, who have been called according to his purpose. For those God foreknew he also predestined to be conformed to the likeness of his Son" (Romans 8:28–29).

Amazing and Unexpected Trophy!

Think of the amazing process God accomplished through the life of Jesus, by sending Jesus to earth as a human baby. Even though he was fully man, Jesus was born with a unique soul that existed before the foundations of the world. Further, it will exist wholly (as well as holy) throughout the ages. This unique individual the Holy Spirit placed in Mary's womb was encased in soft molding clay (a body), fully equipped with a pouring vent (a spiritual heart).

During the first thirty years of Jesus' life, his body and his faculties were formed. This included the forming of his mind, emotions, and will for the unique purposes of God. The Bible records that "Jesus grew in wisdom and stature, and in favor with God and men" (Luke 2:52). When Jesus' clay was fully formed, the Spirit of Grace descended on him. Luke described this amazing scene: "As he was praying, heaven was opened and the Holy Spirit descended on him in bodily form like a dove.

And a voice came from heaven: 'You are my Son, whom I love; with you I am well pleased'" (Luke 3:21–22).

Just as God planned and prearranged Jesus' life, he has planned and prearranged ours. We are his workmanship, trophies of grace displayed in heaven! The apostle Paul described why God proudly displays us as his trophies:

> Because of his great love for us, God, who is rich in mercy, made us alive with Christ even when we were dead in transgressions—it is by grace you have been saved. And God raised us up with Christ and seated us with him in the heavenly realms in Christ Jesus, in order that in the coming ages he might show the incomparable riches of his grace, expressed in his kindness to us in Christ Jesus. For it is by grace you have been saved, through faith—and this not from yourselves, it is the gift of God—not by works, so that no one can boast. For we are God's workmanship, created in Christ Jesus to do good works, which God prepared in advance for us to do. (Ephesians 2:4–10)

Today's Trophies

Trophies of grace stand all around us today. These men and women have made a lifetime of choices to surrender their wills to Jesus Christ. Ruth Opiyo, a friend of mine, is a missionary *from* Africa *to* the United States. Ruth serves in children's ministries in a local church, and her husband is the chaplain of the Children's Medical Center in Dallas, Texas.

I asked Ruth what compelled her to leave her home and family and travel halfway around the world to share God's grace with people in the United States. She replied with the story of her grandmother—a woman Ruth clearly sees as a trophy of God's grace.

Although birth records weren't kept, Ruth's grandmother, Bathsheba Mugure Ngugi, was probably born in 1920 in Gatundu, Kenya. As a child, Bathsheba worked on the farm, helped her mother prepare and cook meals, and cared for her siblings. When she was fourteen years old, Salvation Army cadets came to her village to share the love of Jesus Christ. When she heard the gospel story, she felt God tug on her heart. She responded by kneeling in prayer and deciding to become a follower of Jesus Christ. She immediately liked the Bible name Bathsheba and took it as her Christian name.

She met in homes of Christians who taught her the Bible. But her mother and brothers weren't happy with her new faith. They believed that girls didn't need to learn how to read and write and that girls certainly didn't need to go to church. When Bathsheba bought a dress for church, her brothers were so displeased that they beat her and burned her dress. But this didn't stop Bathsheba from following Christ. Soon, she would be able to read the Bible for herself. With her only church dress burned, Bathsheba gathered managu leaves, a green vegetable that flourished in maize fields after the harvest, and sold them to buy another dress. Her family members saw her dedication and devotion to Christ, realizing that even if they beat her, she would follow the Savior she had grown to love.

At sixteen Bathsheba met Joshua Ngugi, another African Christian, at a church fellowship. Bathsheba and Joshua eventually got married, started a family, and then joined the Salvation Army training to share the good news of God's grace. While they attended the training, their family consisted of two boys and two girls. Sadly, however, two of the children died—one from measles and one from an unknown cause. For Bathsheba and Joshua, the loss of these children was very painful as they trained to be ambassadors of Christ. Yet God blessed their devotion to him with more children. In all, Bathsheba gave birth to fourteen children—ten more than when she and Joshua joined the Salvation Army.

Christian work for the Ngugi family was a family call to serve Christ. Bathsheba shared all the pastoral responsibilities with Joshua. She would preach on Sunday mornings, lead worship, help the sick, and perform funerals. But Bathsheba's first priority was always to minister to her children, because she wanted to see them come to the saving knowledge of Jesus Christ. Bathsheba's children, her grandchildren, and her great-grandchildren became living lights to the good news of God's grace in Christ Jesus, largely because of Bathsheba's choice as a young girl to embrace the God who tugged at her heart.

"My grandmother's love for people and life was contagious," Ruth says. "We all wanted what she had. We saw by her life— her enduring strength, matchless joy, and honeylike love toward the people she served—that surrendering our plans to Christ was worth the price."

Nuggets

R ight under your nose

O n your path by sovereign design

C hrist Jesus, God's pure gold, is in you

K neel to your Maker, the craftsman of your soul, to
recover it

A Prayer of Grace

Lord God, we acknowledge that we can't realize our identity
and purpose on this planet apart from your grace, because you
are the initiator of the new life within. We acknowledge that it's
impossible for us to transform ourselves; we can't control the
metamorphosis of our old nature to yours.

Help us to humble ourselves as soft moldable clay in your
hands. Lord, teach us to continually receive your grace by keeping
the secret environments of our hearts pure and by allowing your
Holy Spirit to replicate in us your original Christlike design.

Enable us, Lord, to see the people we serve as crowns that
honor our participation in your kingdom. Remind us, Lord, as a
son matures and grows strong enough to be able to carry his mother
someday, Christ maturing in us will carry us in our weakness. Lord,
make us vessels of spiritual gold to bless your world. Amen.

Questions for Reflection

- Think of a time when you felt caught between a rock and
  a hard place. What part do you believe God played in that
  situation?

- What's your favorite Olympic event and why?

- Imagine the dedication it takes—in hours and days and years—to be an Olympic athlete. Do you think the reward is worth the cost?

Peter says that as believers we have waiting for us in heaven "an inheritance that can never perish, spoil or fade . . . ready to be revealed in the last time" (1 Peter 1:4–5). As you think about heaven, ponder Jesus' description of heaven's gold-medal ceremony:

> When the Son of Man comes in his glory, and all the angels with him, he will sit on his throne in heavenly glory. All the nations will be gathered before him, and he will separate the people one from another as a shepherd separates the sheep from the goats. He will put the sheep on his right and the goats on his left.
>
> Then the King will say to those on his right, "Come, you who are blessed by my Father; take your inheritance, the kingdom prepared for you since the creation of the world. For I was hungry and you gave me something to eat, I was thirsty and you gave me something to drink, I was a stranger and you invited me in, I needed clothes and you clothed me, I was sick and you looked after me, I was in prison and you came to visit me."

Then the righteous will answer him, "Lord, when did we see you hungry and feed you, or thirsty and give you something to drink? When did we see you a stranger and invite you in, or needing clothes and clothe you? When did we see you sick or in prison and go to visit you?"

The King will reply, "I tell you the truth, whatever you did for one of the least of these brothers of mine, you did for me."

Then he will say to those on his left, "Depart from me, you who are cursed, into the eternal fire prepared for the devil and his angels. For I was hungry and you gave me nothing to eat, I was thirsty and you gave me nothing to drink, I was a stranger and you did not invite me in, I needed clothes and you did not clothe me, I was sick and in prison and you did not look after me."

They also will answer, "Lord, when did we see you hungry or thirsty or a stranger or needing clothes or sick or in prison, and did not help you?"

He will reply, "I tell you the truth, whatever you did not do for one of the least of these, you did not do for me."

Then they will go away to eternal punishment, but the righteous to eternal life. (Matthew 25:31–46)

4

Prospecting

One of the things I love to do is dig deeply into the gold-rich dirt of the Bible. I remember a time, not long after our first child had been born, when I had most of an afternoon to myself while she napped. So I got my concordances, a few Bible translations, and my journal. I wanted to dig into a verse in Ephesians, a prayer of Paul's, that had captured my interest: "I pray also that the eyes of your heart may be enlightened in order that you may know the hope to which he has called you, the riches of his glorious inheritance in the saints" (Ephesians 1:18).

I had read this verse many times, but the phrase that caught my attention was "eyes of your heart." I wondered, *If we have eyes in our hearts to see, do we also have the senses of hearing, smell, taste, and touch?* I decided to look up every verse in the Bible that has anything to do with our physical senses and record my thoughts in my journal.

Fortunately, the baby took a nice long nap! After I wrote about the last verse I'd looked up, I closed my Bible and thought about what I'd been studying. *God seems to personify himself. He smells, hears, sees, can be touched, and even spits from his mouth.*

Suddenly, it was as if the Spirit of God stepped out from the shadows of my soul. At that very moment, I realized that God is a personal being! Up until that day, when I thought of God, I thought of him sitting somewhere encircled on a throne beyond the last known planet. Or maybe I thought of him two thousand years in the past, a historical figure dressed in a tunic and sandals.

Yet there in my living room, I realized that God isn't just a transcendent, out-there being. He is also an immanent, in-here, in-my-heart being—as real as I am and as real as our sleeping newborn daughter.

Wow! The God of the universe is real, alive, and in me!

That day, my entire relationship with God changed, and I understood the Bible in a new light. "The kingdom of God does not come with your careful observation, nor will people say, 'Here it is,' or 'There it is,' because the kingdom of God is within you" (Luke 17:20–21). What an amazing truth to grasp: Our search for God's grace in Christ—mining for spiritual gold—must be done on the inside, within our individual souls.

Where to Look

Even though grace is close at hand, mining the spiritual gold hidden in our lives isn't easy. In fact, it's very similar to the difficulty of mining physical gold. Interestingly, gold actually exists almost everywhere: in your own backyard, in the creek at the edge of your town, in the natural rock under your city. Yet even though this valuable commodity is spread throughout the earth, the cost to recover it makes it too expensive to seek and own.[1]

Even when gold is found in concentrated quantities—usually in quartz, the most common gold-bearing rock—mining these gold deposits is so difficult that it's often called hard-rock mining. Usually the layers of quartz gold are so thin that they can't be seen with the naked eye. This means that the rock must be crushed and processed to recover the gold before it can be used.[2]

Spiritual gold is everywhere also—in everything in life. It's exclusively bestowed by Christ and for Christ: "[Jesus Christ] is the image of the invisible God, the firstborn over all creation. For by him all things were created: things in heaven and on earth, visible and invisible, whether thrones or powers or rulers or authorities; all things were created by him and for him" (Colossians 1:15–16). However, even though this invaluable spiritual commodity bestows every blessing, if we want to receive its benefit, the cost is our very selves. Jesus expressed this cost when he said, "If anyone would come after me, he must deny himself and take up his cross and follow me" (Matthew 16:24).

Just as quartz bears physical gold, Jesus Christ is the Rock who bears grace. Retrieving this grace is hard labor on our flesh. We usually can't see the layers of grace in Christ with the naked eye. Jesus Christ must crush the independent spirits of our souls for grace to be processed and recovered: "I have been crucified with Christ and I no longer live, but Christ lives in me. The life I live in the body, I live by faith in the Son of God, who loved me and gave himself for me. I do not set aside the grace of God, for if righteousness could be gained through the law, Christ died for nothing!" (Galatians 2:20–21). As we identify with Christ's sacrifice, we also share in his grace. So, receiving grace is simple, but it's not easy on our flesh.

Hard-Rock Mining

Seeking God's grace is so tough on our flesh that we can compare it to hard-rock mining for gold. This process can involve deep tunneling into the heart of a mountain, drilling, blasting, and pick-and-shovel work. Why do we have to dig and pick and shovel—and even drill and blast—to find God's grace? Think again about Jesus' words in Revelation. After he described the pitiful state of the Laodicean Christians, he said, "I counsel you to buy from me gold refined in the fire, so you can become rich" (Revelation 3:18). When Jesus said, "Buy from me," he was saying, "Dig into the soil of my soul. I am gold Rock." As we pick and shovel, drill and blast, and tunnel deeply into the Rock of Jesus Christ, we discover the adventure that other spiritual prospectors discovered before us.

Digging for grace, like looking for gold, can take us on a long trek across a wasteland of years. That's how Edward Hammond Hargraves felt when he left his Australian ranch to seek California gold in the 1850s. However, he found nothing but loneliness and exhaustion in California. And to make things worse, he was homesick; the Sierra foothills reminded him of the hills around his ranch in New South Wales. One day while writing home, he was struck by simple logic. If gold lay buried in this land that looked so much like home, could gold lay buried *at home*. He returned to Australia as quickly as he could. On February 12, 1851, Hargraves panned the sand in the mountain streams near his home. He found gold dust—great quantities of it. Again and again, each pan yielded the gleaming stuff, initiating Australia's gold rush.[3]

Like Hargraves, we can search everywhere trying to find God's grace. We can travel halfway around the world, but as we've discussed, God's grace dwells right within us, waiting to be mined. I like what Joyce Meyer, one of the world's leading practical Bible teachers, said:

> The problem is a lack of abiding—lack of believing. The church is filled with "unbelieving believers"—people who are trying to believe God, or those who believe in certain situations, but in many others, they are filled with doubt and unbelief. This was my testimony for many years. I admit those were frustrating miserable years. I was saved and on my way to heaven, but I was not enjoying the trip! I depended on myself most of the time. My life was filled with dead works—my plans, my ideas, my efforts being expended trying to make things happen in my life. We are partners with God, and as such we do have a part for which we are responsible. There is a gold mine hidden in every life—but you have to dig to find it.[4]

So, if we know we're going to have to dig deep within ourselves to find God's gold, how will we know when we've discovered the rich veins of grace?

Risky Business

Gold miners come in all shapes, sizes, genders, and ages. The one unifying aspect is they all want to get rich. They may have a myriad of reasons why they want to get rich, but the fact is they want to find gold and they are willing to engage in the risky business of finding it.

Like gold mining, grace mining is risky business. When I set out on the business of sharing God's grace, I excitedly told my uncle, who had just retired from a long ministerial career as a pastor, "I'm so happy that God has given me a message of grace to share, rather than a message of destruction like that of Jeremiah." I continued with zeal, "Every Christian will *certainly* embrace the message of grace." My uncle's silence spoke volumes. He lowered his chin and looked at me from pools of wisdom. "Pam, the divisive message *is* grace. Be prepared."

At the time my zeal ignored his statement, but soon my naiveté couldn't keep his words from proving true. Another seasoned pastor for thirty years, Martyn Lloyd-Jones of England's Westminster Chapel, noted the risky business of teaching grace: "First of all let me make a comment, to me a very important and vital comment. The true preaching of the gospel of salvation by grace alone always leads to the possibility of this charge being brought against it. There is no better test to whether a man is really preaching the New Testament gospel or salvation than this, that some people might misunderstand it and misinterpret it."[5]

The reason that mining for grace is risky business is that most Christians, as Charles Swindoll wrote, "want a moral report card that objectively measures their progress. Works, good works, provide that. But if works are not the basis of our relationship with God, then there is no *external* proof of salvation or spirituality. If, on the other hand, grace is the basis of our relationship with God, then the reality of our faith is *internal*. It can be seen—and judged—only by God."[6]

Indeed, mining for God's grace is risky business because possessing it means you may

- lose the desire to do the things that once made you look spiritual
- be free to do and be what your religious code once disapproved
- lose the ability to feel self-righteous
- be reduced to broken humility
- perceive with heightened senses the stench of your own character
- become wild-eyed and compelled to exclaim, with heels clicking, "Good news! I've struck gold!"

Once you're willing to embark on the risky business of mining for God's grace, like gold mining, you better know what you are looking for. Unless an experienced prospector shows you what raw gold looks like, you will set out on your quest without an idea of what to look for.

The Art of Prospecting

John and Dick were two soldiers on a three-day pass in the Sierra Nevada, and they were curious about some nearby old-time gold camps. A gas station attendant advised them to go up the Feather River to Quincy, where he said gold could still be found. After they checked into a hotel, the counterman suggested they hike down the valley a few miles and walk along the Feather River toward Spanish Ranch and Gold Bar, which had produced gold during the placer mining days a hundred years earlier.

The following day the soldiers headed down the valley. They found a riverbed and worked their way up several of the streams. They reported back to the counterman at the hotel that they didn't find anything, because they didn't know what they were looking for. And even if they had, they didn't have any tools to recover it.

The hotel counterman suggested they talk to the sheriff about renting some tools. The next day the sheriff loaned them a gold pan, a shovel, and a map. John and Dick hitchhiked down the highway with the borrowed tools, heading for another stream.

Almost as soon as they arrived at the intersection of the main road and town road, an old pickup truck stopped, and the driver offered them a ride. He was an older man in coveralls with a large-brimmed hat that hid his face, and he wasn't overly talkative. Dick explained to him that they were on an army pass and wanted to try their luck at prospecting for gold. As they neared a small side creek leading off the Feather River, the old-timer slowed the truck and told the soldiers that this was the most likely spot to look for specks of gold.

John explained that they had never seen gold, much less used a pan or read a geological map. The old-timer reached down and turned off the engine. He got out of his truck, walked around to where the young men were standing, reached into his pocket, and pulled out a vial. "This is gold."

John and Dick stared at the nuggets of shiny, worn-smooth gold. The old-timer explained that those nuggets had come out of the same creek they were standing beside. He led them to the stream and showed them how to take the gold pan, kneel beside the stream, scoop up a pan full of sand and gravel, and put the pan in motion. Then he walked away without so much as a wave.

When John asked to see the vial of gold again, the experienced prospector refused, leaving the two amateurs' interest forever captured. In fact, they were so enamored that John Dwyer went on to become an expert in the field of gold prospecting. The primary lesson John and Dick learned that day was that in addition to a map and tools, they needed the help of an experienced prospector who was acquainted with gold.[7]

Spiritual Prospecting

Just as these two men tried to determine what to look for when they prospected for gold, we might take time out of our regular lives to prospect for grace in Christ. We might ask other Christians where to look. We might collect some tools and head in the correct general direction.

Yet if we want to recover grace, the presence of the Holy Spirit in our lives is essential. The Spirit serves as the Eternal

Prospector who leads us to a place in our thinking, our feelings, and our will where grace can be recovered as we grow in our understanding of Christ. However, the Holy Spirit never intends to make us independently rich in God's grace. Instead, he allows us to work with him so that Christ can prosper. When that occurs, we benefit from the increase.

We can find spiritual gold—grace—only with the help of the Holy Spirit. He is the Spirit of Grace, and he alone has possession of it. Jesus explained it this way: "When he, the Spirit of truth, comes, he will guide you into all truth. He will not speak on his own; he will speak only what he hears, and he will tell you what is yet to come. He will bring glory to me by taking from what is mine and making it known to you. All that belongs to the Father is mine. That is why I said the Spirit will take from what is mine and make it known to you" (John 16:13–15).

Such was the case for Philip, one of the seven servants chosen to serve the widows of the early church (see Acts 6:1–6). An angel of the Lord came to Philip and said, "Go south to the road—the desert road—that goes down from Jerusalem to Gaza." Even though he had been spiritually prospecting north in the Samaritan villages, Philip went where the angel instructed (Acts 8:5, 26).

As Philip started south, he spotted a "lump of clay" in the form of an Ethiopian eunuch. The Spirit essentially told Philip to go near this lump of clay, because he would find God's pure gold—grace. Philip didn't walk. He ran at the prospect of uncovering God's grace.

Philip listened to the Ethiopian read from the prophet Isaiah and then asked the important official—who was in charge of all the treasury of Ethiopia—if he knew what he had found. Philip asked a man who had spent his life acquainted with physical gold if he recognized the spiritual gold before him.

The Ethiopian didn't. But as Philip shared the good news of God's grace available in Christ Jesus, the eyes of the Ethiopian eunuch were opened, and he perceived true wealth. The Ethiopian repented and received God's spiritual wealth, and the new life of Christ was deposited within him. The Holy Spirit—the Spiritual Prospector—in Philip had guided, counseled, and helped him to share God's grace. This became the transforming agent in the Ethiopian's life. The Holy Spirit made both men richer in Christ. "This is the good news: we are no longer waiting for the Holy Spirit—He is waiting for us. We are no longer living in a time of promise, but in the days of fulfillment."[8]

Which Tools to Use?

Even if we know what to look for, God's gold—grace—won't do us much good if we spot it but leave it untouched. If you saw a gold coin on the ground, wouldn't you stop to pick it up? If you went wading in a mountain stream and saw a glimmering nugget on the bottom of the riverbed, wouldn't you reach down and grab it? Of course! You'd make the effort in order to have a chance at gaining wealth.

What kind of effort would you make if you realized a whole chest of coins was buried under the coin you picked up? Or if you believed that the nugget of gold in the stream was just one of many? Chances are that you'd make a significant effort to keep looking for the richness the gold could provide.

Let's say you wanted to prospect for gold in the stream. Which tools would you need? You'd start with a pan, a map, and a shovel. The pan doesn't need to be fancy; in fact, a worn one works better. When you got your pan, you might even want to practice the elliptical racetrack motion of shifting the dirt and debris. Without a good map, you'd end up wandering around randomly in a nonproductive manner. Likewise, a shovel—essential for recovering loads of gold-rich gravel—would make your efforts much more productive.

Grace-Prospecting Tools

If you want to prospect for God's treasure of grace, you would start with a grace pan, map, and shovel. Let's look at what each of these items represents:

> **Pan.** Each of us is equipped with a reservoir for God's grace. Sometimes we call this pan our soul—a word that represents our mind, will, and emotions. For most of us, our souls aren't fancy or without blemishes. In fact, when we've lived a little, the process of recovering grace is easier. We need to spend time practicing the elliptical motion of shifting the dirt and debris of the fallen nature in order for our souls to recover grace. For example, a fallen thought starts in the mind, swirls through the will, and then swishes through the emotions. We must keep swirling until it shifts out of the soul. If we don't, we're left with a pan full of the dirt and debris of the fallen nature.

Map. The Bible, God's written word, is the map that guides us toward spiritual wealth. Without a Bible to guide the way, we can end up wandering spiritually in a nonproductive manner (see Psalm 119:105). God's map, the Bible, serves not only as a guide to your desired location—spiritual wealth— it also points out, "You Are Here." Paul said that we have been released from the law (Romans 7:6). But being released in no way negates or abolishes God's moral law. Paul continued, "I would not have known what sin was except through the law" (Romans 7:7). In other words, I wouldn't have known where I was—which is sinful in nature— unless the law pointed out, "You Are Here." Jerry Bridges wrote, "The good news of the gospel is that God has removed the guilt we incur by breaking His law and has bestowed on us the righteousness of Christ, who perfectly kept the law."[9]

Shovel. Bible dictionaries and other study tools are essential for recovering loads of spiritual gravel, making our efforts more productive in the recovery of grace. Remember the shovel and the map aren't gold; they're tools that aid in the recovery of gold. Likewise, the Bible and biblical teachings aren't grace; they're tools that aid us in recovering grace (see John 5:39–40).

Of course, we also need the right place to find grace. The only true source of grace is the stream of Christ living within us.

Jesus said, "'Whoever believes in me, as the Scripture has said, streams of living water will flow from within him.' By this he meant the Spirit, whom those who believed in him were later to receive. Up to that time the Spirit had not been given, since Jesus had not yet been glorified" (John 7:38–39). A pan full of any other water will not yield the spiritual gold of God's grace.

Israel's king David was a man after God's wealth and heart (1 Samuel 13:14). David revealed himself as a skilled spiritual prospector and acknowledged his need for the true Spiritual Prospector as his ever-present guide: "Where can I go from your Spirit? Where can I flee from your presence? If I go up to the heavens, you are there; if I make my bed in the depths, you are there. If I rise on the wings of the dawn, if I settle on the far side of the sea, even there your hand will guide me, your right hand will hold me fast" (Psalm 139:7–10).

David cooperated with the removal of his fallen nature from the pan of his soul: "Search me, O God, and know my heart; test me and know my anxious thoughts. See if there is any offensive way in me, and lead me in the way everlasting" (Psalm 139:23–24).

He acknowledged his need for a map: "The law of his God is in his heart; his feet do not slip" (Psalm 37:31).

David also acknowledged the connection between shoveling his heart full of God's Word and the recovery of spiritual wealth: "I desire to do your will, O my God; your law is within my heart" (Psalm 40:8).

David's spiritual mining clearly proved prosperous, yielding the spiritual gold of God's grace. This is how he eagerly expressed his experience of mining for grace: "Praise the LORD, O my soul;

all my inmost being, praise his holy name. Praise the LORD, O my soul, and forget not all his benefits—who forgives all your sins and heals all your diseases, who redeems your life from the pit and crowns you with love and compassion, who satisfies your desires with good things so that your youth is renewed like the eagle's" (Psalm 103:1–5).

Panning for God's Gold

Remember what we said about panning for gold? You need a pan that serves as a reservoir for the gold. The pan doesn't need to be fancy—a worn pan can actually work better. In the same way, the soul functions as a pan, a reservoir for grace. Our souls don't need to be fancy either—and a worn soul actually works a little better.

Isn't that interesting? An experienced prospector would never exchange an old pan for a new one. It wouldn't recover gold as well. In the same way, when we've lived long enough to put our soul to use recovering God's grace and can see within us the propensity for sin, then our worn pan—soul—is in an invaluable condition.

Paul spoke of the pan of his soul: "I see another law at work in the members of my body, waging war against the law of my mind and making me a prisoner of the law of sin at work within my members. What a wretched man I am! Who will rescue me from this body of death? Thanks be to God—through Jesus Christ our Lord!" (Romans 7:23–25). A soul aware of its fallen nature, a worn pan, makes the recovery of grace easier.

Why?

Remember that you use your grace pan—your soul—to recover God's grace. The skill is similar to using a pan for recovering gold. With physical gold, first you scoop up some dirt where you think gold might be present. Then you put the pan in an elliptical racetrack motion to start the shifting process. In a similar way, you scoop up the grace-rich words of the Bible, place them in your soul, and put your soul in motion. You take in a biblical truth from God's Word, your mind processes it, it shifts through your will, then it goes to your emotions, then back to your will, and it continues in this motion—until no more shifting can take place. Oswald Chambers wrote, "The profound thing in man is his will, not sin. Will is the essential element in God's creation of man: sin is a perverse disposition that entered man. In a regenerated man the source of the will is almighty. You have to work out with concentration and care what God works in: not *work* your salvation, but *work it out,* while you base resolutely in unshaken faith on the complete and perfect Redemption of the Lord."[10]

Let's walk through a practical demonstration. Let's use Psalm 139:14: "I am fearfully and wonderfully made."

I start by scooping these words into my soul. Then I put my soul in motion. I start in my mind, thinking, *I am fearfully and wonderfully made.* I argue with the words. Let's say I struggled in school, I can't sing on tune, and I don't look like the way people in magazines look.

My own mind tells me, *You're not fearfully and wonderfully made! Look at this list I've been compiling on you.* But I don't stop there! I keep my soul in motion.

Next I come to my will, praying, *I yield to you, Holy Spirit. I want to believe you, God. The living water of Christ rushes in.* I keep sifting.

Then I move on to my emotions: *I certainly don't feel like I'm fearfully and wonderfully made. In fact, I feel totally inadequate and inferior.*

Then back to my will: *I want to believe you, God.*

Back to my mind: *If I'm fearfully and wonderfully made, then you must have a purpose for me. Maybe you made me specifically for this purpose!*

Back to my will: *I want to believe you, God.*

Then to my emotions: *I don't feel like doing anything mundane, lowly, and insignificant, God—I admit it!*

Back to my will: *I want to believe you, Lord. But I really don't want to follow you just anywhere.* No water. I'm stuck, I live like that for a week, a year, or a decade, pursuing my own dreams that I think are significant. Yet all this time, I feel inadequate and inferior.

Finally, I pick up my pan again. *Where was I? I am fearfully and wonderfully made.* Again, my mind says, *Oh, yeah? Now I have an even longer list of why you're not fearfully and wonderfully made at all!*

But I keep sifting. My will says: *I'll believe you, God, in spite of my mind's list, and this time I'll follow you.*

To my emotions: *I'm afraid. It's too late. I've messed things up too much. Too much time has passed.*

Back to my will: *I believe you and I'll follow you.* Cleansing water washes in once more.

To my mind: *I am fearfully and wonderfully made. God says*

that. He is God and smarter than I am, so I guess he supersedes my list of doubts.

Back to my will: *I will believe you and follow you.* Water washes in.

To my emotions: *I'm feeling more loved and accepted, in spite of it all.*

To my will: *I'll believe and follow you, Lord.* Water washes in.

To my mind: *I am fearfully and wonderfully made. Lord, what do you want to do with me?*

To my will: *I believe and will follow you regardless of where you lead.*

My emotions: *I'm afraid, but I won't let the fear stop me or control me.*

Back to my will: *I believe and will follow you.* Water washes in.

To my mind: *I am* . . . But before I say, *fearfully and wonderfully made,* I pause . . . and I say it again: *I AM.*

My mind says: *I get it! I AM is in me. That's why I AM fearfully and wonderfully made. I am a vessel of God!*

To my will: *I believe! I follow you!* Water washes in.

To my emotions: *I feel excited. This isn't about me. This is about me letting you work in and through me.*

In my mind, I clearly see the nugget of truth: I am fearfully and wonderfully made because I'm a unique creation that almighty God has chosen to live in.

My will responds: *That is utterly amazing.* Water now makes that nugget of truth sparkle!

To my emotions: *God is living in me! I feel aflame, so on fire that it's hard for me to sit here. I feel passionate. I must praise God. I need to tell someone about him. Anything—but I can't sit here!*

My emotions, with the help of my mind, have prodded my will into action. My will says, *I will believe. I will follow you.* And finally, the washing water enables the nugget to be reflective.

What started as a nugget of truth in my soul, I worked through my mind, will, and emotions. In the end, the truth revealed itself to be a nugget of grace—Christ Jesus in me, unveiled by the Spirit of Grace.

I suggest you try this process of panning for God's gold—grace. There's no trick to it—it just takes some discipline and practice. The psalmist expressed it this way: "Search me, O God, and know my heart; test me and know my anxious thoughts. See if there is any offensive way in me, and lead me in the way everlasting" (Psalm 139:23–24).

—————————— Nuggets——————————

M ake time to seek God

I nteract with Jesus Christ

N otice the Spirit's prompting and leading

I nvolve Jesus in all your thoughts, feelings, and decisions

N ow respond to Jesus

G o for the gold

—————— A Prayer of Grace ——————

Lord God, we acknowledge that you give us everything for life and godliness. Forgive us when we neglect the precious gift of your Son's life in us. Help us to be good stewards of the gift, realizing that by this very means you desire to communicate with us.

Remind us, Lord, of the truth that when we hear your silent voice communicating the same truths to our spiritual brothers and sisters, you are bearing witness to the power of your grace.

Help us to be your true and faithful disciples, listening to your voice by your Holy Spirit and allowing you to lead and direct our lives. Help us not to be lazy or passive in following your Helper, but enable us to cooperate, recovering the full treasure in Christ.

Amen.

Questions for Reflection

- Share a "spiritual treasure" you've found. What made it so?

- What was the most pleasant aspect of that time? What was the most unpleasant aspect?

- What's the favored tool in your house? What is its use?

- What sources do you rely on to guide your decision making?

5

Barriers to Receiving Riches

Once upon a time, there was a kingdom whose ruler was enormously rich. Each morning after breakfast, the king's servants covered his body with gold dust, and he strutted about all day, shining gloriously golden. In the evenings after supper, his servants placed him on a flower-decked barge that floated on the royal lake, and the king jumped into the water to wash off the gold dust. Then, to show their devotion to the king, his subjects tossed offerings of golden objects into the lake. The king's legendary country was called El Dorado. In Spanish, it means "the gilded one."

This legend probably grew out of a religious custom of the Chibcha Indians. They lived in the highlands of South America in the region known today as Colombia. The Chibcha anointed each new chief with resinous gums and coated his body with gold dust. The chief then plunged into the sacred Lake Guatavita and washed off the gold as an offering to the gods.

This Chibchan ritual died out before the Spanish conquistadores came to the New World in the early 1500s. But when they arrived, the legend of El Dorado—a whole country filled with golden treasure—was still alive. The conquistadores launched a long series of expeditions to find the fabled riches of El Dorado. Their quest for "the gilded one" unearthed no trace of him or his golden land.[1]

As Christians, we don't have to settle for a legend of riches or fables of wealth. God promises us a true treasure of pure gold—grace in Christ Jesus!

Seeking True Gold

Unfortunately, we easily chase after false treasures instead of true grace. When we look at our actions objectively, we can see just how foolish it is to settle for legends or fables. Perhaps our foolish actions make us fools!

Most of us don't use the word *fool* much anymore. Maybe it's politically incorrect. But from early childhood, we have enjoyed the gags we can play on each other for one day a year—April Fools' Day. The history of this day—sometimes called All Fools' Day—isn't totally clear. The beginning of this tradition may have occurred in 1582 in France. Prior to that year, the new year would begin on March 25 and was celebrated for eight days, culminating on April 1.

However, in 1582 King Charles IX reformed the calendar, moving New Year's Day to January 1. Communication in those days was slow; news traveled by foot, and many people didn't receive the news of the calendar change for several years. Others, a more obstinate crowd, refused to accept the king's authority and his new calendar, and they continued to celebrate the new year on April 1. The general populace labeled these backward folk as "fools." They were subject to ridicule and were sent on "fool's errands." Sometimes, they were the butt of other practical jokes. This harassment evolved over time into a tradition of prank playing on the first day of April.[2]

The Folly of Fools

Several times in this book, we have referred to Jesus' letter to the church in Laodicea (see Revelation 3). Before he counseled the Laodicean Christians to buy from him gold, he said, "You say, 'I am rich; I have acquired wealth and do not need a thing.' But you do not realize that you are wretched, pitiful, poor, blind and naked. I counsel you to buy from me gold refined in the fire, so you can become rich" (Revelation 3:17–18). In other words, Jesus was describing these Christians as fools.

In the Bible a fool is someone who lacks moral sense, who is spiritually blind, and who chooses trash over treasure. Solomon, the wisest and richest of Israel's kings, made eighty statements about fools in the Proverbs: he spoke of their conceit, their self-confidence, and their pride.

Jesus also used the word *fool* to refer to the Bible scholars of his day, the Pharisees. That's especially interesting, because it shows us that just having knowledge of Scripture doesn't keep us from becoming fools. We become fools when we fail to choose what is the most valuable commodity of all—God's grace.

Psalm 14:1 states that this choice begins in our hearts: "The fool says in his heart, 'There is no God.'" We say that God doesn't exist, and then our actions convey what we think and feel. And like the Laodicean Christians, we acquire a kind of wealth that doesn't satisfy. You might recall that the wealth these lukewarm Christians possessed did give them a sense of fullness, because they told Jesus that they didn't need a thing. Although the wealth they had can fill, it can't satisfy.

The word *satisfy* means to be filled to the degree that you no longer want. For example, you go out to restaurant for dinner, and you eat until you're full—satisfied. Then the waiter asks if he can bring a dessert. You might indulge and have one. But your hunger is satisfied long before you ever take a bite of that apple pie à la mode.

In 1965 the Rolling Stones released one of their many hit songs. The lyrics cried, "I can't get no satisfaction!" That complaint could very well be the mantra of the ages, because Christians and non-Christians alike struggle with satisfaction. Yet the psalmist wrote, "Better the little that the righteous have than the wealth of many wicked" (Psalm 37:16).

I recently read an article about how middle-class Americans live better than most of the world's population, both now and throughout the ages. So why aren't we happy? The article quoted Gregg Easterbrook, the writer of the book titled *The Progress Paradox: How Life Gets Better While People Feel Worse.* Easterbrook noted that for the last half century, North Americans and Western Europeans have participated in a grand social engineering experiment to answer the question, Does prosperity bring happiness? Middle-class North Americans and Western Europeans live better than 99.4 percent of all people who have ever existed on earth. So why do we walk around scowling rather than smiling at our good fortune? Interestingly, research shows that more people felt happier in the 1940s when a third of the population still used outhouses. Easterbrook concluded that the reason for our unhappiness is obvious: We have excelled at making a living, but we have failed at making a life. He added, "Everybody needs a certain amount of money, but if money is the priority in your life, woe to you as a person and as a soul."[3]

If most people have failed at making a life, what's the alternative? Do we have any options? How can we make *a life?* Jesus answered these questions long ago: "My purpose is to give them a rich and satisfying life" (John 10:10 NLT). That's why Jesus told these lukewarm Christians in Laodicea to buy from him gold.

The Shine of Gold

Have you ever heard of fool's gold? This type of rock is actually pyrite, and it's called fool's gold because it has a shine that imitates the quality of real gold. Yet the quality of true gold is determined by its inherent features—qualities that are absent in fool's gold.

James Marshall discovered this on a January morning in 1848. Marshall—a newcomer to the West—was inspecting the trail that led away from the water wheel that powered the small sawmill he had just built for his employer, John Sutter. As his eyes grew accustomed to the early morning light, Marshall said that he "caught a glimpse of something shining in the bottom of the ditch. It was about half the size of a pea, worth perhaps fifty cents, if it really was gold, not iron pyrite, known as fool's gold." When Marshall placed the small yellow particle on a river stone and hammered it with a rock, it didn't shatter as brittle fool's gold would. It flattened out and remained in one piece. Eureka! It was true gold! And so began California's gold rush.[4]

Like physical gold, true grace isn't brittle either. When hammered against life's circumstances, it remains intact. However, "fool's grace"—the world's substitution—often seems to shine like grace but is virtually worthless except as an imitation of God's grace.

Think of some of the things we try to substitute for God's true grace: money, medicine, education, job, career, clothes, and people. I call these fool's grace because, *in and of themselves,* each of these lacks the inherent quality of God's grace. They are not Jesus Christ.

Of course, God can use any and all of these as vessels of his grace. Remember, he uses something as common as dirt as a vessel of gold! However, if we use these as substitutes for his grace—even though they might briefly characterize life—sooner or later we'll be poorer for the transaction. Jesus warned: "Do not store up for yourselves treasures on earth, where moth and rust destroy, and where thieves break in and steal. But store up for yourselves treasures in heaven, where moth and rust do not destroy, and where thieves do not break in and steal. For where your treasure is, there your heart will be also. . . . No one can serve two masters. Either he will hate the one and love the other, or he will be devoted to the one and despise the other. You cannot serve both God and Money" (Matthew 6:19–21, 24).

Jesus told a parable about a rich man who stored up the world's treasures. Sadly, this man set his heart on fool's grace instead of seeking true grace. When he died, he found himself in hell, full of reverential fear and regretting that he had been deceived by the world's imitations (see Luke 16:19–31).

Money can buy medicine, but not health. Money can buy a house, but not a home. Money can buy companions, but not friends. Money can buy clothes, but not beauty. Money can buy power, but not love. C. S. Lewis wrote, "Money is not the natural reward of love: that is why we call a man mercenary if he marries a woman for the sake of her money. But marriage is the proper reward for a real lover, and he is not mercenary for desiring it. A general who fights well in order to get a peerage is mercenary; a general who fights for victory is not, victory being the proper reward of battle as marriage is the proper reward for love. The proper rewards are not simply tacked on the activity for which they are given, but are the activity itself in consummation."[5]

If our desire is to be the lover of Christ, willing to be used in his spiritual battle, then God's reward will be the intrinsic reward of seeing his grace flow through us to bless others. "Submit to God and be at peace with him; in this way prosperity will come to you. Accept instruction from his mouth and lay up his words in your heart. If you return to the Almighty, you will be restored: . . . then the Almighty will be your gold, the choicest silver for you" (Job 22:21–23, 25).

Making the Choice

To paraphrase Jesus' words, he says to us, "You must choose one. Either you'll choose allegiance to gold and hate me. Or you'll devote yourself to me and despise gold. You can't choose both. You can't choose to love both God and money. So which do you choose?" (see Matthew 6:24).

Before you answer, think about a typical day in most of our lives. When we wake up, either we start panning for grace or we don't.

When we don't, it's because we say, "I'm rich, I've acquired wealth, and I do not need a thing." Those words should sound familiar by now. Right there in our hearts, whether we voice it or not, we take the first step toward being fools. Then it's just a matter of time before we start experiencing the symptoms of our spiritual poverty. Such as:

In our minds, we think we're inadequate: *I don't know what to do; this problem is too confusing for me. I don't know which direction to go.*

Or we experience bankruptcy in our emotions: *I feel unloved, underappreciated, hopeless.*

Or our wills becomes deficient: *I feel weak, passive, overwhelmed.*

Of course, this is where we should realize that we need to put our souls to use. But something glittery, something that seems easier and quicker, captures our attention. So midmorning in that typical day in our lives—when our poverty starts to settle in—we must resist the temptation to grab for tools in place of the Carpenter, or pyrite in place of God's pure gold.

We also need to resist the temptation to do this in others'

lives as well. When friends come to us with problems, we don't want them to be impoverished, so we point them to a tool instead of the Carpenter. Or we hand them some glittery dirt, because we hope it holds some value. Instead, simply praying with them helps them put their own pans in motion, so they can discover Christ and see what's truly valuable. The apostle Peter told a crippled man who begged for money that what he really needed was Jesus: "Peter said, 'Silver or gold I do not have, but what I have I give you. In the name of Jesus Christ of Nazareth, walk.' . . . He said to them: 'Men of Israel, why does this surprise you? Why do you stare at us as if by our own power or godliness we had made this man walk?'" (Acts 3:6, 12).

This kind of faith-filled, grace-giving life is exactly what Satan tries to stop.

Banishing Squatters

Choosing fool's grace isn't the only thing that can get in the way of choosing to live a rich and satisfying grace-filled life in Christ. We also must contend with spiritual squatters who try to squelch Christ's authority and power in our lives.

Immediately after John Sutter discovered gold on his property, he was forced to deal with a myriad of rugged, violent men who rushed to his property.[6] Known as "forty-niners," they set up camps that they named Hell's Half Acre and Rough and Ready. One was even named Hangtown, because lynch law took the place of any orderly system in these camps. Instead of kicking these squatters off his property, Sutter allowed them to remain. He even built settlements for them in an effort to civilize them.

However, the squatters didn't want to be contained or ruled. In fact, these squatters disputed Sutter's right to his own property. The case went to the Supreme Court. In 1852 most of Sutter's land was taken from him, and he was forced into bankruptcy. The squatters had successfully usurped his property, taking possession of the land by force and without true legal claim.

Satan desires to do the same thing in a spiritual sense when we receive God's grace, Jesus Christ. God promises to replace our old fallen nature with a new nature. Yet Satan works to try to keep that old nature in our lives as a squatter. Satan wants to usurp Christ's authority and power in our lives.

In the earthly world, we fight wars for two basic reasons: to take power over territory or to take the wealth of a land. In the spiritual world, Satan and his forces battle to take both the power and the wealth of each believer's soul. They do this by tempting the fallen nature to remain powerful so that Christ's life within is not controlling us.

Peter was a disciple of the Lord Jesus. He left everything he ever had to follow Christ. Yet when Jesus explained that it was time for him to suffer and die—but also to be raised to life—Peter strongly objected: "'Never, Lord!' he said. 'This shall never happen to you!'" (Matthew 16:22). Jesus' response was equally strong: "Get behind Me, Satan! You are in My way [an offense and a hindrance and a snare to Me]; for you are minding what partakes not of the nature and quality of God, but of men" (Matthew 16:23 AMP).

Jesus then went on to describe what banishing the fallen nature—the spiritual squatter—looks like: "If anyone desires to be My disciple, let him deny himself [disregard, lose sight of, and forget himself and his own interests] and take up his cross and follow Me [cleave steadfastly to Me, conform wholly to My example in living and if need be, in dying, also]. For whoever is bent on saving his [temporal] life [his comfort and security here] shall lose it [eternal life]; and whoever loses his life [his comfort and security here] for My sake shall find it [life everlasting]" (Matthew 16:24–25 AMP).

Satan was tempting Peter to consider and guard his old nature—the squatter that desires comfort and security—in the territory of his soul. Jesus, however, explicitly countered that two natures can't both control the same territory. As we cling to Jesus Christ in faith and obedience to his Word, he banishes Satan's influence over our lives. Apart from that simple faith we place in Christ, even our best efforts are futile.

No Trespassing, Satan!

Carolyn Risher discovered just how futile our own efforts can be. Carolyn was the sixty-two-year-old mayor of Inglis, Florida. She got sick of the sinful nature ruining her town, so she placed four posts at the north, south, east, and west entrances to her town with words of banishment: "Be it known from this day forward," she began, "that Satan, ruler of darkness, giver of evil, destroyer of what is good and just, is not now, nor ever again will be, a part of this town of Inglis."

Risher didn't stop there. She printed these words of banishment on her official stationery. She stamped the declaration containing these words with a gold seal. She signed it and had the town clerk sign it. As a result, Mayor Risher got the attention of the world! Dan Rather called. *Saturday Night Live* and the *New York Times*, as well as the American Civil Liberties Union (ACLU), contacted her.

Gradually, the flood of reporters, lawyers, and comedians left Inglis, but—sad to say—the sinful nature didn't. One of the citizens, who opened a rehabilitation center, said the citizens of Inglis were still hungry for something that can never fill or satisfy them: "Use of cocaine, pot, crack, and methamphetamine is on the rise. Nothing seems to satisfy. Our drunks are still drunk, our hookers still hook." A Korean vet, Floyd Craig, said, "I figure if you start thinking the devil is outside of you, you'll stop taking a good hard look at evil inside you."[7]

This war veteran was exactly right. Just as God's grace is on the inside of our individual souls, so is the sinful, squatting nature. Although this squatter has no rights, it remains because Satan continues to convince us to be passive about banishing it.

Manage Your Soul

Only God possesses the power and authority to banish the demons that try to influence our sinful natures. When we accept Christ's sacrifice, we are accepting his ransom—the price paid to redeem a slave—and we are no longer obligated to live under the rule of Satan and his demons. "You were bought at a price. Therefore honor God with your body" (1 Corinthians 6:20). When we're born again, the deed to the territory of our body and soul belongs to God. He takes his possession seriously; it cost him the life of his Son. Of course, he doesn't kick us off this territory, because he loves us and wants what's best for us. Instead, we become his managers. As managers we will have to give an account for every idle word, thought, and deed. So, let us choose *not* to welcome or entertain the sinful nature; instead, we must banish this squatter through the power of God's grace.

Billy Graham once said, "*Becoming* a Christian can be the act of a moment; *being* a Christian is the act of a lifetime"[8] (emphasis author's). The same is true of grace. For Christians, receiving grace is an act of a moment; continuing in grace is the act of a lifetime. The apostle Paul described exactly what we can expect when we fail to continue to live in God's grace:

> It is obvious what kind of life develops out of trying to get your own way all the time: repetitive, loveless, cheap sex; a stinking accumulation of mental and emotional garbage; frenzied and joyless grabs for happiness; trinket gods; magic-show religion; paranoid loneliness; cutthroat competition; all-consuming-yet-never-satisfied wants; a brutal temper; an impotence to love or be loved; divided homes and divided lives; small-minded and lopsided pursuits; the vicious habit of depersonalizing everyone into a rival; uncontrolled and uncontrollable addictions; ugly parodies of community. I could go on. (Galatians 5:19–21 MSG)

God Is No Fool

"Don't be misled: No one makes a fool of God," Paul wrote to the Christians in Galatia. "What a person plants, he will harvest. The person who plants selfishness, ignoring the needs of others—ignoring God!—harvests a crop of weeds. All he'll have to show for his life is weeds! But the one who plants in response to God, letting God's Spirit do the growth work in him, harvests a crop of real life, eternal life" (Galatians 6:7–8 MSG).

The NIV translates the first part of Paul's words this way: "Do not be deceived: God cannot be mocked. A man reaps what he sows." I used to think this verse said that God *will* not be mocked, as if he willed the consequence of my sinful nature. Perhaps, subconsciously, I thought since God is merciful and forgiving, he *will* not punish the sins that are just in my mind, because I'm not hurting anyone with those sins. So I can just let these aspects of my squatting nature remain.

But that's terribly incorrect! This verse doesn't say that God *will* not be mocked. It says, "God *cannot* be mocked" (emphasis author's). This means that choosing my sinful nature will always lead to my destruction. Only by the mercy of God's discipline does he at times step in to spare us from the devastating results of our sinful natures.

After Adam and Eve ate from the tree that God had told them not to eat from, God drove them out of the garden and posted angelic guards so they wouldn't eat from the Tree of Life and live forever. They missed out on the pleasures of living without sin in his beautiful garden. But the merciful discipline of banishing them for the garden kept them from living *forever* in their fallen state.

"The LORD is gracious and compassionate, slow to anger and rich in love" (Psalm 145:8). Compassionate love and merciful discipline are demonstrated by a shepherd with his sheep.

At times, if a sheep continues to wander from its shepherd, the animal becomes easy prey for wolves or falling off cliffs. So acting in love to protect the sheep, the shepherd has to break the animal's legs. The shepherd then carries the sheep with him on his shoulders until its legs are healed. By that time, the sheep has come to love and know its master's voice above all other voices. This sheep is now so loyal and committed to the master that it can become the bell sheep, the one on which the master hangs the bell and the other sheep follow the shepherd.[9]

Jesus the Good Shepherd extends us merciful discipline, which at the present time is painful, but in the end it is for our benefit. "No discipline seems pleasant at the time, but painful. Later on, however, it produces a harvest of righteousness and peace for those who have been trained by it" (Hebrews 12:11).

A Modern-Day King Wanders

Wandering from the Shepherd in Las Vegas in the 1970s, Elvis Presley struggled with womanizing, pill popping, reclusiveness, and uncontrollable weight gain. He turned to uppers, downers, and pain killers to dull the ache of depression and loneliness. Fame was a harsh taskmaster, and Elvis and his entire entourage knew it.

In December 1976 Elvis requested that television evangelist Rex Humbard and his wife, Maude Aimee, meet with him in Las Vegas. "Jesus is coming back really soon, isn't he, Rex?" Elvis asked, as he began quoting all kinds of Scriptures about the second coming. But what really shook Elvis up during their time together was when Maude Aimee told Elvis about her prayer that he would become a "bell sheep" for God. Elvis asked her about what that meant, and she explained: "In the Holy Land, they put a bell on one sheep, and when he moves, all the rest of the flock move with him. I have been praying for years for you, Elvis, that you would become a bell sheep. If you fully dedicated your life to God you could lead millions of people into the kingdom of the Lord."

According to Humbard, "Elvis went all to pieces. He started crying. She shook him up by that statement." As they held hands and prayed, "he rededicated his heart to the Lord," recalled Humbard. "I asked God to bless him and to send His spirit into his heart and meet his every need."

Right after their prayer time, Maude Aimee went to the hotel gift shop and purchased a symbolic bell with a little diamond in it. During the evening's second show, Elvis held up the small bell and smiled to Maude Aimee and then dedicated "How Great Thou Art" to the Humbards.

"Elvis recommitted his life to Jesus Christ on that night," says Rick Stanley, Elvis's stepbrother. On the day before Presley died at forty-two years old, Elvis Presley said, "People who talk to you about Jesus really care." Within hours Elvis was dead.[10]

Satan knows the result of the sin nature is always destruction. So he says in a faint whisper, "Go ahead. What will it hurt?" And we passively allow the sinful nature to linger on the soil of our mind, the soil of our emotions, and soil of our will. There gluttony, greed, sexual impurity, deceit, envy, and selfish ambition remain (see Galatians 5:19–21). And they won't be contained and ruled—just like John Sutter's squatters whom he allowed to remain on his soil during the gold rush. Instead, these sinful behaviors remain rough and wild, bent on control of the entire territory of our souls, not content until they force us into moral and spiritual bankruptcy. Then Satan throws his head back, cackling a heinous laugh, mocking God, and spewing the words, "Trophies of your grace, huh?"

God is so grieved for us as his children and the pain we reap for ourselves. Before Jesus tells us that he has good and satisfying lives planned for us, he says: "The thief comes only to steal and kill and destroy" (John 10:10).

Strength in Numbers

I often hear a particular verse at wedding ceremonies: "Though one may be overpowered, two can defend themselves. A cord of three strands is not quickly broken" (Ecclesiastes 4:12). Think about the core truth of this verse. If it's true that we enjoy strength in numbers to defend ourselves, it's also true that the sinful nature has strength in numbers. In other words, sexual immorality can steal love from our lives; sexual immorality *and* a gluttonous appetite can kill us; and sexual immorality *and* a gluttonous appetite *and* drunkenness can destroy not only our lives, but also the lives of those around us.

The news is littered with stories of incest, rape, and promiscuity. Generation after generation, people are painfully affected by these sins. In the same way, greed alone will steal the blessing of God; greed *and* lying will kill our efforts and productivity; greed *and* lying *and* stealing will destroy our financial future and the inheritance of our children.

God has an intimate knowledge of our thought lives and has authority and power to enable us to banish the squatting sinful nature. But he calls on us to manage the territory of our souls and not be passive.

Secure in a Gold Standard

In recent years many big companies deceived their employees and left their investors broke. Because of war, terrorism, and natural disasters, we've lost much of our financial security. However, another group of people suffered an even greater reduction of their assets.

The year was 1865. A long, bitter, and blood-stained battle between the States had ended. Fighting for authority to rule had led to dead bodies laid out across the land. More soldiers died during the Civil War than during all other US wars from the Revolution through the end of the Vietnam War.

The hopes of the people in 1865 were further crushed by the failed banking system. Some sixteen hundred banks across the United States had circulated around seven thousand bank notes. Many of these were worthless, while others were only as valuable as the bank that issued them. By the end of the war, all of this wildcat currency had the appearance of value, yet it was worthless because the new government issued a new currency based on gold.

Gold has been the standard of wealth throughout history, and it remains so today. The *gold standard* means a monetary system where the value of currency is defined by a fixed quantity of gold. The value of a US dollar or a British pound is tied to the worth of a specific amount of gold. If a country is on the gold standard, it has to hold stock of gold in some safe place in order to back up its paper currency and meet its obligations.[11] Alan Greenspan, retired chairman of the United States Federal Reserve, said, "In the absence of the gold standard, there is no way to protect savings from confiscation through inflation. There is no safe store of value, except gold."[12]

In a similar way, if you've been born again, you've left Satan's government. You are a citizen of a new government: the kingdom of God. At Calvary God issued a new means for living based on grace. We can call it the *grace standard*. To borrow Alan Greenspan's words, in the absence of the grace standard, there is no way to protect our lives from confiscation through the sin of inflated self. There is no safe store of value, except God's grace.

——————— *Nuggets* ———————

F orgetting our identity

O bjecting to God's authority

O bliging our self-interest

L usting after temporal satisfaction

——————— *A Prayer of Grace* ———————

Father God, help us not to be deceived by the shine of fool's grace that would leave us regretful and impoverished spiritually.

Instead, help us to be mindful that everything good and perfect comes from you.

Lord God, it's so simple. You've made it so simple, and yet we confess how difficult it is not to act as gods over our own lives. Remind us that we are merely the creation and that you are the Creator. You are the only One who has the right to dictate the way to life.

Father God, we acknowledge your mercy in your willingness to live within sinful people and your holiness that requires grace. Thank you for Jesus, who alone makes our souls fit places for the King.

Father, you've warned us of the enemies of our souls. Help us not to be fearful, but to submit to you and resist our enemies, knowing that you are preparing within us your kingly dwelling. Amen.

———————— *Questions for Reflection* ————————

- Consider a person in history or presently in the sports or entertainment industry whose life you would spiritually characterize as full of fool's gold.

- What spiritual fool's gold—an imitation of grace—has the most tempting glitter for you?

- The Bible says, "The fear of the Lord is the beginning of wisdom" (Psalm 111:10). What does "fear of the Lord" mean to you?

- What strategies has Satan used to keep you from seeing the spiritual gold right under your nose?

6

Staking a Claim

*H*ave you ever noticed—and maybe even marveled at the fact—that the bodies and skills of musicians, athletes, models, scientists, and accountants are all so obviously different. I've always been fascinated at how God *prearranges our lives,* beginning with the very body and skills and gifts that we each come equipped with.

The person I've most clearly seen God's handiwork in is my husband, Steven. His mother liked to tell me that even when Steven was an infant, his strong left-handedness was apparent. He was the only son born into a family that loved sports—especially baseball. So it was no shock that he grew to be a left-handed baseball player—a major league pitcher at that.

As Steven grew up, he stepped from Little League to Pony League to Colt League. And he really had few other internal pressures except baseball. He easily formed both inside and outside into a career player.

However, God didn't just prearrange Steven's steps to be a baseball player. Although Steven was unaware of it, God also prearranged each of Steven's steps to lead him to Christ. Steven was taken aback when at college in the athletic dorm he was introduced to Christ and received him as his Lord and Savior.

All of Steven's heroes, interest, and desires lay in the arena of baseball. By God's will, he remained there. But it was like a riverbed containing animals, debris, and gravel—as well as gold. During his years in baseball, he became more aware of his need for Christ, as the number of his heroes dwindled because of their weaknesses. His interest and desire for baseball waned as he accomplished his goals but found the satisfaction fleeting. This river he had spent twenty-five years in was drying up. He held in his hand what remained: memories of a few heroes along the way, debris of some pitching records broken, and gravel—time spent in the "big leagues."

Yet, as he left the game at age thirty-one, the treasure he valued most was that he had staked a claim to God's grace: Jesus Christ. Today, we have a plaque in our son's room below one of my husband's jerseys that reads, "A boy is the only thing that God can use to make a man." For my husband, Steven, who had boylike dreams of being a big leaguer, the bravado has been chipped away, and what is left is a sincere man who asserts that his identity is in Christ.

Gold Claims and Grace Claims

Sincerity is a word that has lost its strength in our commercial world. Advertising "can sell a buffalo off a nickel," as my grandmother used to say. But God still examines hearts. He looks for sincere claims to his grace. The word *sincere* comes from the Latin word for "without wax." In ancient Rome, when statues were sold in the marketplaces, an artist would fill in any cracks or flaws with wax that matched the original wood or stone. This gave an impression of perfection until the piece of artwork was taken out into bright light or when heat melted the wax, revealing the hidden flaws. Shrewd buyers learned to ask, "Is this artwork without wax—is it sincere?"[1]

We are the artwork, the workmanship of God. And he won't allow us to fill our cracks. Instead, he searches us and grants grace to our sincere hearts. "O righteous God, who searches minds and hearts, bring to an end the violence of the wicked and make the righteous secure. My shield is God Most High, who saves the upright in heart" (Psalm 7:9–10).

In the same way, the United States government requires that anyone who stakes a claim to property must assert rightful ownership of the property. They must have sincere motives about the use of the property. In other words, the law prohibits people from falsely staking claim to a property, such as saying they plan to use the land for a cabin site or a cheap source of commercial sand, gravel, or clay supplies when they really intend to mine for gold. Therefore, staking a claim to prospect for gold is shown by actions. Evidence for this is that the property is occupied and utilized—put to use in the search for gold.[2]

Staking a claim to recover God's grace also takes sincere action. It involves asserting the rightful ownership of being in Christ, claiming the right to the privilege and title of being God's heir in Christ. This establishes the fact that whatever belongs to Christ is also available to the believer (see Romans 8:17). In God's kingdom, under his governmental rule, he prohibits anyone from falsely staking claim to grace. This means that we must be interested in mining the precious commodity of *grace in Christ*, rather than just staking a claim to gain a reputation, accumulate money, or to further personal endeavors. The apostle Paul wrote, "If anyone teaches false doctrines and does not agree to the sound instruction of our Lord Jesus Christ and to godly teaching, he is conceited and understands nothing. He has an unhealthy interest . . . [and has] been robbed of the truth and . . . think[s] that godliness is a means to financial gain" (1 Timothy 6:3–5).

In the Old Testament, we read the story of a powerful man who found himself in need of grace. King David had died, and his son Solomon realized the depth of his own inadequacy to rule Israel's kingdom. Assertively and dependently, he said to God, "You have shown great kindness to your servant, my father David, because he was faithful to you and righteous and upright in heart. You have continued this great kindness to him and have given him a son to sit on his throne this very day" (1 Kings 3:6).

Solomon then detailed his reason for needing God's grace: "Now, O LORD my God, you have made your servant king in place of my father David. But I am only a little child and do not know how to carry out my duties. Your servant is here among the people you have chosen, a great people, too numerous to count or number. So give your servant a discerning heart to govern your people and to distinguish between right and wrong. For who is able to govern this great people of yours?" (1 Kings 3:7–9).

After examining Solomon's motive and finding his claim true, God responded to Solomon's plea:

> Since you have asked for this and not for long life or wealth for yourself, nor have asked for the death of your enemies but for discernment in administering justice, I will do what you have asked. I will give you a wise and discerning heart, so that there will never have been anyone like you, nor will there ever be. Moreover, I will give you what you have not asked for—both riches and honor—so that in your lifetime you will have no equal among kings. And if you walk in my ways and obey my statutes and commands as David your father did, I will give you a long life. (1 Kings 3:11–14)

As Solomon governed God's people, he experienced peace from his enemies and prosperity, a kingdom rule that exhibited God's grace.

Governmental Grace

While we may not think of God's kingdom as a real kingdom, it is just as real as the kingdom Solomon governed and just as real as kingdoms today. God's kingdom has a governmental structure, and it operates on real rules. For example, God transacted eternal business when he purchased our sinful souls with the life of his Son, Jesus Christ. As the apostle Paul explained, "Do you not know that your body is a temple of the Holy Spirit, who is in you, whom you have received from God? You are not your own; you were bought at a price" (1 Corinthians 6:19–20).

According to God's kingdom rules, we incurred a debt. And as citizens of his kingdom, we must pay for the sinful state of our souls. Of course, we possess nothing of value to equal the debt. Only God has a resource of adequate value to pay for our individual sinful state, as well as all sin at all time. This resource is his gold—his grace—in his Son, Jesus Christ. God's mercy and love extend this payment: "Because of his great love for us, God, who is rich in mercy, made us alive with Christ even when we were dead in transgressions—it is by grace you have been saved" (Ephesians 2:4–5; see also Colossians 2:13–14 NASB).

While this all seems almost mystical, the truth is that a real debt occurred, God provided a real payment, and this transaction happened in real time and space. From the cross, Jesus' last words were, "It is finished" (John 19:30), or literally "Paid in full." That Greek word *teleo* means "to perform," "to execute," "to complete," "to fulfill," "to pay," so that the thing done corresponds to what has been said.[3]

Christ Jesus satisfied God's justice in real time and space when he died to pay for our sins. In fact, the punishment for our sins can never occur again because that would violate God's justice.[4]

Abraham understood God's governmental rule. "What does the Scripture say? 'Abraham believed God, and it was credited to him as righteousness.' Now when a man works, his wages are not credited to him as a gift, but as an obligation. However, to the man who does not work but trusts God who justifies the wicked, his faith is credited as righteousness" (Romans 4:3–5).

The good news of God's grace is that we are freely pardoned and in good standing with God, so that we can freely and boldly come to his throne of grace and receive mercy and grace to help us in our times of need (see Hebrews 4:16).

God's Gold on Account

If you have received God's gift of grace in Jesus Christ, then you have heaven's gold on account. It's yours! What's more, God expects you to use it. Jesus described God's expectation in the parable of talents:

> Again, it will be like a man going on a journey, who called his servants and entrusted his property to them. To one he gave five talents of money, to another two talents, and to another one talent, each according to his ability. Then he went on his journey. The man who had received the five talents went at once and put his money to work and gained five more. So also, the one with the two talents gained two more. But the man who had received the one talent went off, dug a hole in the ground and hid his master's money.
>
> After a long time the master of those servants returned and settled accounts with them. The man who had received the five talents brought the other

five. "Master," he said, "you entrusted me with five talents. See, I have gained five more."

His master replied, "Well done, good and faithful servant! You have been faithful with a few things; I will put you in charge of many things. Come and share your master's happiness!"

The man with the two talents also came. "Master," he said, "you entrusted me with two talents; see, I have gained two more."

His master replied, "Well done, good and faithful servant! You have been faithful with a few things; I will put you in charge of many things. Come and share your master's happiness!"

Then the man who had received the one talent came. "Master," he said, "I knew that you are a hard man, harvesting where you have not sown and gathering where you have not scattered seed. So I was afraid and went out and hid your talent in the ground. See, here is what belongs to you."

His master replied, "You wicked, lazy servant! So you knew that I harvest where I have not sown and gather where I have not scattered seed? Well then, you should have put my money on deposit with the bankers, so that when I returned I would have received it back with interest.

"Take the talent from him and give it to the one who has the ten talents. For everyone who has will be given more, and he will have an abundance. Whoever does not have, even what he has will be taken from him. And throw that worthless servant outside, into the darkness, where there will be weeping and gnashing of teeth." (Matthew 25:14–30)

Sometimes we get confused when we hear this story, because we don't even know what a talent is. A talent was a measurement equal to a sum of money. A talent of gold in Israel weighed about two hundred pounds.[5] Jesus used this parable of talents to teach that God doesn't want us to shrink from needs—even extreme needs—that surface in our lives and in those around us. Instead, he wants us to put his gold—grace—to work.

The Bible records the story of Moses, a man who was acquainted with great physical gold. He went from a shack in Goshen to the stately, rich court of Egypt. As the adopted heir of Pharaoh, he would have sat on a golden throne. His bedroom walls would have shone with gold. He would have worn gold-threaded garments. He would have walked hallways laced with golden idols, and even his bed would have been made of gold.

Yet, unexpectedly, when a great need surfaced, Moses quickly discovered that he was broke: "When Moses was forty years old, he decided to visit his fellow Israelites. He saw one of them being mistreated by an Egyptian, so he went to his defense and avenged him by killing the Egyptian" (Acts 7:23–24). The next day when Moses tried to settle a dispute between two Israelites, "the man who was mistreating the other pushed Moses aside and said, 'Who made you ruler and judge over us? Do you want to kill me as you killed the Egyptian yesterday?' When Moses heard this, he fled to Midian" (Acts 7:27–29).

This man of exceptional wealth spent the next forty years

getting acquainted with his poverty. In fact, when God arrived with grace, Moses exclaimed his threefold poverty: "I don't know your name, God. . . . They won't believe me. . . . I don't speak so well" (author's paraphrase of Exodus 3:13; 4:1, 10). Moses' plea of poverty culminated with his words, "O Lord, please send someone else to do it" (Exodus 4:13).

Haven't we all felt like this at times? Yet the Bible is clear. Once God interrupts our circumstances and points out a need in another person's life, he expects us to meet that need: "Do not withhold good from those who deserve it, when it is in your power to act. Do not say to your neighbor, 'Come back later; I'll give it tomorrow'—when you now have it with you" (Proverbs 3:27–28). The problem lies in the fact that most of us don't believe we have the resources to meet people's needs.

The great missionary to China Hudson Taylor faced this feeling of lack—not just in his financial resources but in his emotional resources as well. In the 1800s God laid the spiritual needs of the people of China on Hudson Taylor. Although his father had died, leaving Hudson's mother a widow, Hudson Taylor reached out in faith, believing that God would give him grace to strengthen his resolve to go to China.

He wrote of his faith struggle to receive God's grace:

> My beloved, now sainted, mother had come to see me off from Liverpool. Never shall I forget that day, nor how she went with me into the little cabin that was to be my home for nearly six long months. With a mother's loving hand she smoothed the little bed. She sat by my side, and

joined me in the last hymn that we should sing together before the long parting. We knelt down, and she prayed—the last mother's prayer I was to hear before starting for China. Then notice was given that we must separate, and we had to say good-bye, never expecting to meet on earth again. For my sake she restrained her feelings as much possible. We parted; and she went onshore, leaving me her blessing! I stood alone on deck, and she followed the ship as we moved towards the dock gates. As we passed through the gates, and the separation really commenced, I shall never forget the cry of anguish wrung from that mother's heart. It went through me like a knife. I never knew so fully, until then, what 'God so loved the world' meant. And I am quite sure that my precious mother learned more of the love of God to the perishing in that hour than in all her life before. "Praise God, the number is increasing who are finding out the exceeding joys, the wondrous revelations of His mercies; vouchsafed to those who 'follow Him,' and emptying themselves, leave all in obedience to His great commission."[6]

By the end of Hudson Taylor's life in 1905, God birthed by his grace an estimated 125,000 Chinese Christians through a man who was willing to bank on God.

A Claim Exchanged for Wealth

Once you've staked an authentic claim to mine for gold, you go through the process of recovering it. The ruling government will determine the value of the gold you mine. And once you exchange your gold for currency, the ruling government will establish your usable wealth. The steps look like this:

- Staking a claim
- Mining
- Value assessment
    Determination of authenticity
    Determination of weight
- Exchange for usable wealth

We can also apply these steps to God's grace. We begin by surrendering our old nature's identity and asserting our identity in Christ. Then as we walk with God in faith along his grace path, he points out needs in other people's lives. There, we stake a claim to Christ's life and begin to pan for nuggets of grace. We do this by putting our soul in motion: our mind, will, and emotions, scooping up the gold-rich dirt found in the Bible or in clay: other Christians.

When this gold—grace—runs low, we pursue the labor of hard-rock mining. We allow the Rock to come against the reality of our circumstances, humbling us before God. With dim understanding, we empty our dependence on everything but God and stretch our faith and receive his grace. We then allow God's governmental rule to evaluate the weight of grace: God weighs the thoughts, motives, and intents of the heart (see Proverbs 16:1–3).

Further, God is the perfect grace exchanger. For example, he exchanges the value of grace into encouragement in the very portion needed. Another time he may exchange grace into teaching. For another Christian, God may exchange grace into leadership, and so on. This makes the entire family of God mutually wealthy, as we respond to each other's needs and as we pursue the labor of recovering his grace and sharing this wealth with others.

Miners

All potential miners begin with dreaming about the value of their find. Gold catches their imaginations, and they envision the wealth they'll possess. Suddenly, what they previously valued—the comfort of home and the security of the familiar—is replaced with this new gold-rich vision.

The same is true spiritually. For example, the things valued by Moses changed. The writer of Hebrews expressed Moses' value change this way: "He regarded disgrace for the sake of Christ as of greater value than the treasures of Egypt, because he was looking ahead to his reward" (Hebrews 11:26). Even though Moses once owned gold, he grew to value grace. He valued grace to the extent that he used the "gold-medal strategy" of keeping his eye on the prize. Then Moses pursued spiritual mining: "By faith he left Egypt, not fearing the king's anger; he persevered because he saw him who is invisible. By faith he kept the Passover and the sprinkling of blood, so that the destroyer of the firstborn would not touch the firstborn of Israel. By faith the people passed through the Red Sea as on dry land; but when the Egyptians tried to do so, they were drowned" (Hebrews 11:27–29). Moses was a miner—a spiritual miner—who recovered, gave, and shared in the riches of God's grace.

To stake a claim, mine, and possess heaven's gold comes at a great expense. Oswald Chambers described this incalculable cost: "To be born from above of the Spirit of God means that we must let go before we lay hold. There will have to be a relinquishing of my claim to my right to myself in every phase. Am I willing to relinquish my hold on all I possess, my hold on my affections, and on everything, and to be identified with the death of Jesus Christ?"[7]

Nuggets

C all out to God

L et it be known by thought and deed that he is what you seek

A sk specifically for mercy and grace

I dentify with his death

M ake a conscious choice to let go of your affections and embrace grace

A Prayer of Grace

Thank you, Father, that you have revealed our position in relationship to you as your children, coheirs with Christ, and inheritors of your infinite wealth. Father God, help us to examine the origin of our pursuits and to be mindful of the reverential fear we should have toward you. Help us not to get distracted or be naive under your kingdom rule. Even though our legal right in Christ entitles us to reign with you, we will not experience royal living unless Christ's Spirit occupies the territory of our souls.

Help us to see the crushing experience of our lives as opportunities to receive your grace, honestly agreeing with Scripture that we consider it pure joy when we face all kinds of trials, knowing they are working for our benefit. We love you and do praise you and your glorious grace! Amen.

─────────── *Questions for Reflection* ───────────

• What would you like to leave to your loved ones as an inheritance?

• Who do you admire and why?

• What stirs and grips your affections?

• What are some of the most difficult aspects of submission to God and to others?

Enjoying Wealth

We can't deny the rich life God wants each of us to enjoy in Christ Jesus. The apostle Paul wrote, "The same Lord is Lord of all and richly blesses all who call on him" (Romans 10:12). As we reach in faith for God's riches, let's look at the order that God provides them in.

Wealth in Order

A family trip to SeaWorld in San Antonio, Texas, illustrates the importance of this order. Our children were ages one, six, and nine; and it must have been one hundred degrees on this July day. After we purchased tickets, we had fifty dollars left to spend in the park. Since water bottles were five dollars each, we knew our stash of cash wouldn't last long. Of course, we'd barely walked through the entrance gate when our two older children exclaimed in unison, "Can we have those stuffed dolphins?" The one-year-old flung his hands and pointed as well.

"That's not what you need right now," I explained. "Besides, we'll need lunch later, and we need to buy some water." The children countered, "I'm not hungry. I'm not thirsty."

Of course they weren't. We had just arrived. But I knew they would be hungry and thirsty, and stuffed animals wouldn't meet their needs. Was I cruel and harsh, trying to rob them of all the good things SeaWorld offered? Of course not. I decided that because I love them so much I wouldn't rob them of vital resources to meet their real needs, not just their emotional whims.

In the same way, God knows precisely what will meet our soul's hunger and thirst. And he won't rob us of the vital resource we need to meet our real needs, not just our emotional whims. This is exactly what Jesus referred to when he said, "Do not worry, saying, 'What shall we eat?' or 'What shall we drink?' or 'What shall we wear?' For the pagans run after all these things, and your heavenly Father knows that you need them. But seek *first* his kingdom and his righteousness, and all these things will be given to you as well" (Matthew 6:31–33, emphasis added).

Notice that Jesus didn't say, "Seek exclusively" or "Seek mutually" the kingdom of God. He said, "Seek first." He said this to teach order. Order teaches priorities, and priorities teach value.

That day at SeaWorld we took one step in a long process of teaching our children to value their bodies by providing for their physical needs *first* before their emotional whims. Still, hot and exhausted, we left SeaWorld that day with enough money to purchase those stuffed animals!

As much as we love our children, our love doesn't compare with the Father's love for us. Jesus made this bluntly clear: "If you, then, though you are evil, know how to give good gifts to your children, how much more will your Father in heaven give good gifts to those who ask him!" (Matthew 7:11). God provides his riches for us so that we learn to value the eternal spiritual life over temporal physical life. Jesus knew what he was talking about. Later, when meeting with the disciples to talk about his impending death, Jesus said, "What good will it be for a man if he gains the whole world, yet forfeits his soul? Or what can a man give in exchange for his soul?" (Matthew 16:26).

Highest Value

When we have a proper perspective about wealth, realizing that spiritual wealth is a higher priority than material wealth, we'll begin to value wisdom: "Blessed is the man who finds wisdom, the man who gains understanding, for she is more profitable than silver and yields better returns than gold" (Proverbs 3:13–14). What does it mean to find wisdom? Does it refer to attaining facts like a walking encyclopedia? No. In the Bible, having wisdom or being wise means mastering the art of living according to God's expectations. The words *mastery* and *art* indicate that wisdom involves a process of attaining, rather than accomplishing.[1]

The apostle James wrote about two kinds of wisdom—one from self and one from God: "If you harbor bitter envy and selfish ambition in your hearts, do not boast about it or deny the truth. Such 'wisdom' does not come down from heaven but is earthly, unspiritual, of the devil. For where you have envy and selfish ambition, there you find disorder and every evil practice. But the wisdom that comes from heaven is first of all pure; then peace-loving, considerate, submissive, full of mercy and good fruit, impartial and sincere" (James 3:14–17).

I remember reading the story of a man who, later in his life, chose God's wisdom over the world's wisdom and his own. Andrew Carnegie's family had faced sudden poverty in Scotland and immigrated to the United States to find wealth. Determined to escape poverty, Carnegie went on to become the richest man in the world. After amassing a fortune by crushing competitors and exploiting workers, Carnegie—in a move that underscored his inner conflicts—systematically gave away millions. A great change transpired in his life, and he wrote of investing in others: "Let us cast aside business forever, except for others. Man must have an idol and the amassing of wealth is one of the worst species of idolatry! No idol is more debasing than the worship of money! Whatever I engage in I must push inordinately; therefore should I be careful to choose that life which will be the most elevating in its character. To continue much longer overwhelmed by business cares and with most of my thoughts wholly upon the way to make more money in the shortest time, must degrade me beyond hope of permanent recovery."[2]

The world would call Andrew Carnegie a fool for refusing to worship money. But giving to others accurately represents God's kind of wisdom.

Wisdom Values People over Possessions

Martin Luther King Jr. said, "Everybody can be great . . . because anybody can serve. You don't have to have a college degree to serve. You don't have to make your subject and verb agree to serve. You only need a heart full of grace. A soul generated by love."[3]

As we have looked at the Laodicean church in Revelation, where Jesus counseled the church to buy from him gold, we also see the reason he wants us to be rich. If we experience his richness, we can acquire white clothes to wear to cover our shameful nakedness. The Bible explains the meaning for us: "'Fine linen, bright and clean, was given her to wear.' (Fine linen stands for the righteous acts of the saints)" (Revelation 19:8). Jesus Christ prepares his spiritual bride—those of us who are his followers. He clothes his bride with righteous acts, which she is afforded as she values people and buys from him pure gold—grace.

Dressed in White

A certain doctor in the early twentieth century, physically dressed in white as a surgeon, provides an illustration of the spiritual truth that God wants us to live sacrificially in order to bless others. The surgeon, Dr. Evan O'Neill Kane, performed the surgery in the operating room in Summit Hospital in New York City.

In many ways, the events leading to the surgery were uneventful. The patient complained of severe abdominal pain. The diagnosis was clear: an inflamed appendix. In his distinguished thirty-seven-year medical career, Dr. Kane had performed nearly four thousand appendectomies. So this surgery would be uneventful—except for two unique facts.

The first novelty was the use of local anesthesia in major surgery. Dr. Kane had crusaded against the hazards of general anesthesia. He contended that a local anesthesia was far safer. Many of his colleagues agreed with him in principle, but in order for them to agree in practice, they wanted to see Kane's theory applied.

Dr. Kane searched for a volunteer, a patient willing to undergo surgery while under local anesthesia. Of course, it wasn't easy to find a volunteer. Many were squeamish at the thought of being awake during their own surgery. Others were fearful that the anesthesia might wear off too soon.

Eventually, however, Dr. Kane found a candidate. On Tuesday morning, February 15, 1921, the historic operation occurred. The patient was prepped and wheeled into the operating room. A local anesthetic was applied. As he had done thousands of times, Dr. Kane dissected the superficial tissues and located the appendix. He skillfully excised it and concluded the surgery. During the procedure, the patient complained of only minor discomfort. The volunteer was taken into a recovery room and then placed in a hospital ward. He recovered quickly and was dismissed two days later.

Dr. Kane had proved his theory. Thanks to the willingness of a brave volunteer, Kane demonstrated that local anesthesia was a viable, and even preferable, alternative.

But I mentioned that two facts made this surgery unique. I told you the first: the use of local anesthesia. The second is the patient. The courageous candidate for surgery by Dr. Kane was

Dr. Kane. To prove his point, Dr. Kane operated on himself! This sacrificial act demonstrated Kane's complete devotion and care for patients.

God wants us to be clothed in white spiritually by cooperating with him in righteous acts that he has prearranged for us to do. He also wants us to *see* spiritually, which is why he says, "I counsel you to buy from me gold . . . and salve to put on your eyes, so you can see" (Revelation 3:18, emphasis added).

Grace—the Cure for Spiritual Blindness

Contrary to what our culture sometimes likes to say, God doesn't want us to live in the dark regarding what he wants for our lives. In fact, he said, "I no longer call you servants, because a servant does not know his master's business. Instead, I have called you friends, for everything that I learned from my Father I have made known to you" (John 15:15).

However, our experience often seems to be the opposite. The apostle James called this tossing in doubt about God's will (see James 1:6). When we struggle with this symptom, we need to buy from Jesus gold—or as we've discussed, we need to receive his grace by faith at a cost to our self. When we abandon our ability to trace out God's will—trying to connect the dots about what he's doing in our lives—and instead simply choose to embrace him, we'll receive what Revelation describes as an anointing on the eyes of our hearts. This will enable us to perceive what God is doing in our lives.

The apostle Paul prayed continually for this kind of anointing on those he ministered to: "I keep asking that the God of our

Lord Jesus Christ, the glorious Father, may give you the Spirit of wisdom and revelation, so that you may know him better. I pray also that the eyes of your heart may be enlightened in order that you may know the hope to which he has called you, the riches of his glorious inheritance in the saints" (Ephesians 1:17–18).

So how do we do this? How can we stop trying to figure out God and predict our futures like bad meteorologists and, instead, simply embrace God and trust where he leads us? The story of the movie *Bruce Almighty* provides a surprisingly good example.

In this movie Bruce Nolan, a television news reporter in Buffalo, New York, fails to get his dream job as an anchorman. After a series of other bad-luck incidents, he complains to God about how unfairly God treats him. Surprisingly, God contacts Bruce and grants Bruce all of his supreme power. Bruce quickly uses his newfound powers for personal gain—sabotaging a colleague to get a better job, transforming his car, and enhancing his girlfriend's figure. Then he realizes that he also has to take care of other people's problems. Ultimately, Bruce's self-centered actions endanger his relationship with his girlfriend, Grace. And in the end, Bruce realizes that God's powers are best left for God to handle. And Bruce asks for God to take control of his life.[4]

Of course, Bruce Nolan was just a character in a somewhat silly movie. But Jesus told stories in parables, so we can certainly learn from stories too! In this instance, we can learn that rather than trying to guess at God's will or trying to wrest control away from God for ourselves, we're far better off embracing him and trusting him to take us along for the ride. He guides us one step at time, giving us direction in bite-sized pieces.

The Master's Feast

When I was a missionary in the southern part of the Soviet Union, I had an opportunity to share a supper with some devout Arabs who still practiced the dining customs that would have been practiced in Laodicea when Jesus' words in Revelation 3:20 were written.

The people ate two meals a day: one light meal early in the morning before they went out to work and another meal after work when the sun went down. Their home was a yurt, which is a portable, felt-covered, framed dwelling structure used by nomads throughout central Asia and the Middle East. On the floor of their tentlike home were many colorful woven mats, so the floor was soft and comfortable. Into the center of a ten-square foot space, the owner of the home and master of the feast brought a table. Its surface was two-feet square and set inches off the floor. With pillows to rest on, we followed his example and lounged beside the table. As the night approached, candles were lit inside the dark dwelling.

The master of feast placed a loaf of bread and a small cup of broth on the small table. With no plates or utensils, the master of the feast broke off a piece of bread, dipped it into the broth, and then handed a piece to each one of us. In turn, we opened our mouths and allowed him to feed us. This unhurried meal continued with the master moving from bread to meat.

This kind of relaxed, intimate, and unhurried meal is what Jesus spoke of when he said, "Here I am! I stand at the door and knock. . . . I will come in and eat with him, and he with me" (Revelation 3:20). Notice that Jesus doesn't demand a love relationship. He requests it. And his request is personal and individual, not corporate and impersonal. *I, him, he,* and *me* are singular personal pronouns. Jesus Christ makes an intimate, personal plea within each Christian's heart to receive him.

Jesus describes this setting as he counsels us to buy from him gold. Even though he uses the marketplace language of "buy" and "gold" to identify with our pursuits, he sets the transaction within an intimate relationship, because he loves us: "Those whom I love I rebuke and discipline. So be earnest, and repent" (Revelation 3:19). Jesus Christ develops his tender love relationship with each Christian through rebuke and discipline. This kind of love is the Greek word *phileo*, which speaks of a tender affection that cherishes and always expects a response.[5] This is not the unconditional *agape* love, like a parent for a child. *Phileo* is love in a relationship. It speaks of comradeship, sharing, communication, and friendship. It involves sharing each other's thoughts, feelings, attitudes, plans, and dreams, as well as time and interests. Jesus Christ came so that we might have life to the full as we continually receive his grace in an intimate love relationship with him. He knocks to make us rich.

The Ultimate Purpose

The praise of God's glorious grace is the ultimate purpose of all creation and *the reason why we must go through the spiritual mining process to receive God's grace.*

God is at work within you, stretching your capacity to receive grace. God desires to give you more wisdom and revelation. He wants to enlighten your mind to his riches and power. As a result, you can authentically praise God for his grace more and more.

As I've said throughout this book, the spiritual mining process isn't easy on our flesh. So, what's the point? The answer to that question lies in understanding the three steps of this spiritual mining process:

- God is sovereign, and he allows difficult circumstances to occur in your life.
- This happens so that the Rock of Christ—the truth of his nature—can prove strong, crushing the lies of the enemy. As a result, you will be humbled before God.
- Then, while still under the trying circumstances and with only the dimmest understanding, by faith you must empty your grasp of any other supports you're holding on to and praise God's goodness.

This stretches your grasp and your capacity and enables you to receive more grace. It's imperative that you see the significance of getting rid of anything else that you're relying on and humbly praising God. Only then can you really understand and receive the benefits of your difficult circumstances. If you continue to hang on to other supporting structures, you run the risk of receiving only limited grace—that which you first understood.

But remember, God wants "to do immeasurably more than all we ask or imagine, according to his power that is at work within us." Then we will witness "glory in the church and in Christ Jesus throughout all generations, for ever and ever!" (Ephesians 3:20–21).

Here's another way to look at the spiritual mining process:

DIFFICULT CIRCUMSTANCE

↓

BY FAITH, EMPTYING GRASP OF ALL OTHER RELIANCE

↓

STRETCHING, BY PRAISING GOD'S GOODNESS

↓

RECEIVING GOD'S PURE GOLD—GRACE IN CHRIST

Throughout this book, I have been trying to demonstrate our utter poverty, while at the same time revealing that Christ offers his abundant riches. The goal is to motivate us all to keep on transferring our confidence from our own measly provisions to relying on the richness and wealth of God's grace. As we've discussed, our spirits know this truth, but our minds argue against it: spiritual growth, we mistakenly think, is somehow linked to our strength of character, knowledge, and experience.

And yet, following Christ isn't the work we do, but the relationship we maintain.

Maintaining a relationship with Christ is a simple embrace involving our faith and his grace. Grace is always *in* Christ Jesus, not alongside him as if his way is one option among many. And faith is always in an object *outside* of ourselves. We simply are not reaching in faith if we are still *in* self-reliance.

This exchange doesn't happen in static circumstances as if our spiritual lives exist in a bubble. This embrace is waiting to happen on the battleground of our souls, where a real enemy with legions of warriors constantly fires at us the reasons we should hold on to self-reliance.

Jesus Christ, as commander in chief of God's kingdom, isn't absent from this scene. Not at all! He is ever-present, calling us from Satan's grip of lies. Once we choose to let go of self-reliance and instead embrace grace, we find the amazing power that the apostle Paul described: "Though we live in the world, we do not wage war as the world does. The weapons we fight with are not the weapons of the world. On the contrary, they have divine power to demolish strongholds. We demolish arguments and every pretension that sets itself up against the knowledge of God, and we take captive every thought to make it obedient to Christ" (2 Corinthians 10:3–5).

The love relationship between a soul and Christ is the expert battle strategy of the wise King of Kings: "This is love for God: to obey his commands. And his commands are not burdensome, for everyone born of God overcomes the world. This is the victory that has overcome the world, even our faith. Who is it that overcomes the world? Only he who believes that Jesus is the Son of God" (1 John 5:3–5).

You have a choice, no matter what lies attack you today: "I'll never find a fulfilling relationship"; "I won't have enough money"; "I can't quit this addiction." You have a choice: to surrender, to get out of self-reliance and into an embrace of grace.

What happens next is intimately between you and Christ. If you want to control the outcome, you're still in self-reliance. So abandon the need to know, and instead choose to know the One you need!

Intimacy is simply oneness, which is God's ultimate plan for each of us—that we be one with God through Christ Jesus. Jesus himself said, "I pray also for those who will believe in me through their message, that all of them may be one, Father, just as you are in me and I am in you. May they also be in us so that the world may believe that you have sent me. I have given them the glory that you gave me, that they may be one as we are one" (John 17:20–22).

This oneness isn't just a vertical, spiritual relationship between God and us, but its fulfillment is the expression of oneness we have with our fellow believers in Jesus Christ. Jesus said, "I will remain in the world no longer, but they are still in the world, and I am coming to you. Holy Father, protect them by the power of your name—the name you gave me—so that they may be one as we are one" (John 17:11).

As you are one with God through Christ and one with fellow believers, you'll no longer be wretched, pitiful, poor, blind, and naked (see Revelation 3:17). Instead, you'll be able to endure troubles, be supplied with power to perform whatever God requires, and feel full of satisfaction with a wealth of significance. Instead of being blind, you'll perceive eternal reality and the hope to which he has called you. Instead of being naked—impoverished morally and dishonoring your purpose for existing—you'll be able to offer righteous acts that will revive and comfort our disoriented world.

All this is yours as you buy from Jesus pure gold!

Nuggets

R ight standing with God

I nterceding righteous acts

C hrist at home in you

H eaven-bound perspective

Prayer of Grace

Thank you, Father, that you have predestined us to be conformed to the likeness of your Son, Christ Jesus, and that you are continually working on our behalf through the Holy Spirit.

It is so against our nature to receive your grace. Truly, we are fallen creatures. Help us to go forward, to press on with steady faith. If our faith has been shipwrecked in any area, rescue us and put us back on course. Remind us that the Scriptures tell us we are a different nationality of people—a people of faith with a different country as our homeland, a heavenly one. Therefore, remind us not to be surprised when we feel like aliens in the world as we seek your grace.

Help us to persevere, to feel comfortable in the dark, naked with our spiritual arms open to receive you. Enable us to be the spiritual brides you desire. We do praise you, God, that you are supreme and that everything about you—your goodness, your wisdom, your power, your patience, your love, and your grace—reigns over this world! Amen.

———————— *Questions for Reflection* ————————

- Share a time when you've had a special meal. Who was present? What made it special?

- If you could significantly help one charity, which would it be? Why?

- Who is your best friend? Why?

- The quality of any relationship is measured by the quality of communication. Which factors contribute to quality communication? Is your communication with God of a high quality?

"We make prayer the preparation for work; it is never that in the Bible. Prayer is the exercise of drawing on the grace of God." (Oswald Chambers)[6]

Bible Studies

In addition to reading and discussing passages in the chapters themselves and the questions for reflection at the end of each chapter, you may also enjoy these Bible studies, alone or in a group, to further mine for the God's pure gold: grace in Christ Jesus. Happy treasure hunting!

Chapter 1: Gold and Grace

Read Job 28.

> Commodities of the earth are for the body and for time. The commodity of God is for the soul and for eternity.

- According to Job's poem, what picture is God showing when he hides material riches in the earth?

- Answer Job's question in verse 20 by considering John 14:6–7 and Job 28:23.

- Read carefully Job 28:11. What treasure is worth the hunt?

- How does your view of Christ influence your desire to seek his grace?

- What does "fear of the LORD" mean to you?

Chapter 2: The Qualities

Read 1 Samuel 1:1–2:10.

> Hannah out of her great need sought God, the Trustworthy Rock, and found him to be a Treasure.

- Do you think that at times the Lord allows you to experience great needs in your life? Give an example.

- Does God always shield us from the consequences of painful circumstances?

- How does Hannah handle painful circumstances?

- Eli was the high priest, the intercessor between God and his people. What does Hannah ask of Eli?

- How is Hannah's life a picture of how God wants us to handle painful circumstances and his blessings?

Chapter 3: The Reward

Read Luke 15:11–32.

- According to Luke 15:12 and Romans 2:11, does God show favoritism among Christians?

- What are some of the reasons you think the younger son might have left his father's household?

- How do think Christians play a part in keeping other Christians from staking a claim to God's gold?

- Where was the confusion in the older son's thinking?

- Why do you think the father describes his wayward son as "dead"?

Chapter 4: Prospecting

Read Jeremiah 23:16–32.

Words from self-help books and speakers call to our generation. As the Lord directs his attention and wisdom toward his children, he also directs it against those who spread false hope.

- What do you perceive as the Lord's feelings, based on the tone of his message in this passage?

- Does anyone's counsel go unnoticed by the Lord? How should we approach the advice we give to others?

- What is the test of whether a person speaks the words of God? Has your heart ever burned as you've read a book or listened to a speaker? How can you know if this burning is from the Lord?

- God's words are for our benefit. Can you think of a time when his words benefited you? Explain.

Chapter 5: Barriers to Receiving Riches

Read Acts 4:32–5:1.

> Like Adam and Eve Ananias and Sapphira got their Treasure and Trash mixed up. Believing a lie yields sin. Believing God prevents sin.

- How can spiritual peer pressure be deadly? What do you think motivated Ananias and Sapphira to donate the land? How do we see that same motivation in the church today?

- Read 2 Corinthians 8:1–7. What was lacking in the hearts of Ananias and Sapphira?

- Who was Satan's real target when he tempted Ananias and Sapphira to act on their evil plans? Explain.

- Read Galatians 6:7. When we desire fool's gold in place of grace, does God take it personally? Explain.

Chapter 6: Staking a Claim

Read 1 Corinthians 3:10–15.

> Paul lists varying materials people use to build, which fall into two categories: one set of materials will disintegrate in fire and the other will withstand fire. Wood, hay, and straw speak of those building with "works of the flesh" rather than grace. Gold, silver, and precious stones speak of building with grace, which will survive the fire of God's testing.

- Do you think some Christians invest their lives in "works of the flesh" rather than grace? What does that mean to you?

- The word "careful" means to be slow and consider your approach, your steps. Write your thoughts on how you can be cautious as Christ's disciple each day.

- If someone approached you seeking shelter, would it be easier to provide a shelter of hay or of gold? Likewise, is it easier to build God's kingdom with "works of the flesh" or with grace?

- What value and rank are attached to people who live in shelters of gold? What value and rank does God attach to those you serve?

Chapter 7: Enjoying Wealth

Read Matthew 20:1–16.

- Who is the landowner, and who are the hired men in this parable?

- What was a day's wage called?

- Was the landowner's payment based on the amount of work done by the hired men or based on his generous nature? Was the landowner's payment based on the worker's *need* or his *work*?

- Does God have the right to bestow his gracious gifts on those who in your eyes are less deserving?

- Is it *what we do* or is it *Christ Jesus* that qualifies us for the God's blessings? How does that make you feel?

- Do you respond to people based on what they deserve or the grace you possess?

Notes

Introduction

1. "The California Gold Rush," Wikipedia, http://en.wikipedia. org/wiki/ California_Gold_Rush (accessed January 20, 2008).

Chapter 1: Gold and Grace

1. Arthur W. Pink, *The Doctrine of Sanctification* (Swengel, PA: Bible Truth Depot, 1955), 200.

2. Not her real name.

3. Richard B. Lyttle, *The Golden Path* (New York: Atheneum Books, 1983), 15.

4. Philo Judaeus, *The Works of Philo* (Oak Harbor, WA: Logos Research Systems, Inc., 1995), CD-ROM.

5. Lyttle, *Path*, p. 21.

6. Jerry Bridges, *Transforming Grace* (Colorado Springs, CO: NavPress, 1991), 17.

7. Oswald Chambers, *My Utmost for His Highest* (New York: Dodd, Mead & Co., 1935), 73.

8. Lyttle, *Path*, p. 10.

Chapter 2: The Qualities

1. Juan Carlos Ortiz, http://www.sermonillustrations.com/a-z/g/grace.htm (accessed January 20, 2008).

2. Not her real name.

3. Richard B. Lyttle, *The Golden Path* (New York: Atheneum Books, 1983), 24.

4. The Greek for the word *gift* is used only here in the Gospel of John, emphasizing God's grace through Christ. A different Greek word is used for *gift* in other places in the New Testament. *The NIV Study Bible* (Grand Rapids, MI: Zondervan, 1985), 1600.

5. Milton Meltzer, *Gold: The True Story of Why People Search for It, Mine It, Trade It, Steal It, Mint It, Hoard It, Shape It, Wear It, Fight and Kill for It* (New York: HarperCollins, 1993), 27.

6. Lyttle, *Path*, p. 33.

7. Meltzer, *Gold*, p. 7.

8. W. E. Vine, Merrill F. Unger, and William White, *Vine's Complete Expository Dictionary of Old and New Testament Words* (Nashville, TN: Thomas Nelson, Logos Library System, 1997), s.v. "glory," CD-ROM.

9. John F. Walwoord and Roy B. Zuck, *The Bible Knowledge Commentary* (Wheaton, IL: Victor Books, a division of Scripture Press Publications, Inc., 1985), 963.

10. Ronald F. Youngblood, gen. ed., F. F. Bruce and R. K. Harrison, cons. eds., *Nelson's New Illustrated Bible Dictionary: An Authoritative One-Volume Reference Work on the Bible with Full-Color Illustrations* (Nashville, TN: Thomas Nelson, Logos Library System, 1997), s.v. "Solomon," CD-ROM.

11. Abraham Booth, *The Reign of Grace* (Swengel, PA: Reiner Publications, 1976), 201.

12. Not her real name.

13. http://www.gold.org/discover/sci_indu/indust_app/otherinteresting_apps.html htm (accessed January 20, 2008).

14. John Piper, *Desiring God: Meditations of a Christian Hedonist* (Sisters, OR: Multnomah Books, 1986), 55.

15. Charles R. Swindoll, *The Grace Awakening* (Dallas, TX: Word Publishing, 1988), 1.

16. Not her real name.

17. Lyttle, *Path*, p. 18.

18. http://www.quotationspage.com/quote/4147.html (accessed January 20, 2008).

19. Piper, *Desiring God*, p. 56.

Chapter 3: The Reward

1. http://www.thesykesgrp.com/GoalMedalLifeArt0201.htm (accessed January 20, 2008).

2. *Enhanced Strong's Hebrew Lexicon* (Oak Harbor, WA: Logos Research Systems, 1995), s.v. *chalkolibanon*, CD-ROM.

3. Richard B. Lyttle, *The Golden Path* (New York: Atheneum Books, 1983), 18.

Chapter 4: Prospecting

1. John N. Dwyer, *Summer Gold* (New York: Charles Scribner's Sons, 1971), 2.

2. Richard B. Lyttle, *The Golden Path* (New York: Atheneum Books, 1983), 15.

3. Lyttle, *Path*, p. 2.

4. Joyce Meyer, *Life in the Word*, vol. 13, no. 1 (Fenton, MO: Joyce Meyer Ministries, 1999), 2.

5. D. M. Lloyd-Jones, *Romans: An Exposition of Chapter 6, The New Man* (Grand Rapids, MI: Zondervan, 1972), 8.

6. Charles R. Swindoll, *The Grace Awakening* (Dallas, TX: Word Publishing, 1988), 21 (italics in original).

7. Dwyer, *Summer*, p. 6.

8. Charles Stanley, *The Wonderful Spirit-Filled Life* (Nashville, TN: Thomas Nelson, 1992), 39.

9. Jerry Bridges, *Transforming Grace* (Colorado Springs, CO: NavPress, 1991), 91.

10. Oswald Chambers, *My Utmost for His Highest* (New York: Dodd, Mead & Co., 1935), 158 (italics in original).

Chapter 5: Barriers to Receiving Riches

1. Milton Meltzer, *Gold: The True Story of Why People Search for It, Mine It, Trade It, Steal It, Mint It, Hoard It, Shape It, Wear It, Fight and Kill for It* (New York: HarperCollins, 1993), 3.

2. http://www.april-fools.us/history-april-fools.htm htm (accessed January 20, 2008).

3. Tim Madigan, "The Burden of Materialism," *Fort Worth Star Telegram*, March 17, 2004.

4. Charles Coombs, *Gold and Other Precious Metals* (New York: William Morrow & Co., 1981), 24.

5. C. S. Lewis, *The Weight of Glory and Other Addresses* (Grand Rapids, MI: Eerdmans, 1965), 2.

6. http://en.wikipedia.org/wiki/John_Sutter (accessed January 20, 2008).

7. Todd Lewan, "For Lucifer, a Tough Crowd," *Fort Worth Star Telegram*, March 21, 2004.

8. http://homepages.nyu.edu/~jl867/Thoughts.html (accessed January 20, 2008).

9. http://momorley.blogspot.com/2006/10/wee-like-sheep_15.html (accessed January 20, 2008).

10. http://www.thunderstruck.org/elvis-risen (accessed January 20, 2008).

11. Meltzer, *Gold*, p. 125.

12. http://www.brainyquote.com/quotes/authors/a/alan_greenspan.html (accessed January 20, 2008).

Chapter 6: Staking a Claim

1. Wess Stafford, *From the Desk of the President* (Colorado Springs, CO: Compassion International, 1997), 1.

2. John Dwyer, *Summer Gold* (New York: Charles Scribner's Sons, 1971), 57.

3. *Enhanced Strong's Greek Lexicon* (Oak Harbor, WA: Logos Research Systems, Inc., 1995), s.v. *teleo*, CD-ROM.

4. *Matthew Henry's Commentary on the Bible* (Peabody, MA: Hendrickson Publishers, 1997), s.v. "Romans 5:6–8," CD-ROM.

5. *Enhanced Strong's Greek Lexicon*, s.v. *talaton*, CD-ROM.

6. J. Hudson Taylor, *A Retrospect* (Philadelphia, PA: The China Inland Mission, n.d.), 39–40.

7. Oswald Chambers, *My Utmost for His Highest* (New York: Dodd, Mead & Co., 1935), 68.

Chapter 7: Enjoying Wealth

1. W. E. Vine, Merrill F. Unger, and William White, *Vine's Complete Expository Dictionary of Old and New Testament Words* (Nashville, TN: Thomas Nelson, Logos Library System, 1997), s.v. "wisdom," CD-ROM.

2. http://en.wikipedia.org/wiki/Andrew_Carnegie (accessed January 20, 2008).

3. http://www.1-love-quotes.com/43855.htm (accessed January 20, 2008).

4. http://en.wikipedia.org/wiki/Bruce_Almighty (accessed January 20, 2008).

5. Ed Wheat, *Love Life for Every Married Couple* (Grand Rapids, MI: Zondervan, 1980), 60.

6. Oswald Chambers, *My Utmost for His Highest* (New York: Dodd, Mead & Co., 1935), 178.

Appendix A

Scripture Versions

All Scripture quotations, unless otherwise indicated, are taken from the *Holy Bible, New International Version*®. *NIV*®. Copyright © 1973, 1978, 1984 by International Bible Society. Used by permission of Zondervan. All rights reserved.

Scripture quotations marked NLT are taken from the *Holy Bible*, New Living Translation, copyright © 1966, 2004. Used by permission of Tyndale House Publishers, Inc., Wheaton, Illinois 60189. All rights reserved.

Scripture quotations marked AMP are taken from the *Amplified Bible*, Copyright © 1954, 1958, 1962, 1964, 1965, 1987 by The Lockman Foundation. Used by permission.

Scripture quotations marked MSG are taken from *The Message*. Copyright © 1993, 1994, 1995, 1996, 2000, 2001, 2002. Used by permission of NavPress Publishing Group.

Scripture quotations marked KJV are taken from the *Authorized King James Version*.

The
UNINVITED
GUESTS

The
UNINVITED
GUESTS

Sadie Jones

Alfred A. Knopf Canada

PUBLISHED BY ALFRED A. KNOPF CANADA

Copyright © 2012 Sadie Jones

www.randomhouse.ca

This book is a work of fiction. Names, characters, places and incidents either are the product of the author's imagination or are used fictitiously. Any resemblance to actual persons, living or dead, events or locales is entirely coincidental.

Library and Archives Canada Cataloguing in Publication

Jones, Sadie
The uninvited guests / Sadie Jones.

Issued also in an electronic format.

ISBN 978-0-307-40253-0

I. Title.

PR6110.O54U65 2012   823'.92   C2011-904082-4

Typeset in Perpetua by Palimpsest Book Production Limited, Falkirk, Stirlingshire

Image credits: Christophe Dessaigne / Trevillion Images

Printed and bound in the United States of America

2 4 6 8 9 7 5 3 1

For
Fred, Tabitha, Daisy
with love

Their table was a board to tempt even ghosts
To pass the Styx for more substantial feasts.

Don Juan, Lord Byron *

CONTENTS

1

EDWARD SWIFT DEPARTS

Since her marriage to Edward Swift, three years after the sudden death of her first husband Horace Torrington, Charlotte had changed her position at the breakfast table in order to accommodate her new husband's needs: specifically, aiding him in the spreading of toast and cutting of meat, owing to his having suffered the loss of his left arm at the age of twenty-three in an unfortunate encounter with the narrow wheels of a speeding gig, out of which he had fallen on the driveway of his then home in County Wicklow. Having always faced the window and wide view, now Charlotte sat on Edward's left, and faced him.

Her eldest children, Emerald and Clovis, aged nineteen and twenty respectively, but for whom the word 'children' is not inaccurate at the point at which we discover them, did not like this new arrangement. Nor did they like or approve of Edward Swift; single arm notwithstanding, they found he did not fit.

Clovis Torrington balanced the pearl-handled butter knife on his middle finger and narrowed his eyes at his mother. His eyes were dramatic, and he very often narrowed them at people to great effect.

'We can't leave Sterne,' he stated.

'It would be a great shame,' acknowledged his stepfather.

Clovis curled his lip, loathingly.

'Clovis . . .' his mother growled.

Edward wiped his mouth with a napkin thoroughly and stood up.

'It's all right, Charlotte,' he said, kissing her forehead as he rose. 'I'll know more when I return, Clovis. And neither you nor your sisters – nor your mother – need worry about it until then, but enjoy Emerald's birthday and try not to fret. I'm sorry I can't be here for your guests.'

Charlotte stood, too, and linked her arm through his.

'You're both very naughty,' she said over her shoulder as they left the room.

Emerald had not spoken, but sat throughout breakfast rigid with self-restraint. Now she glanced at Clovis, tears blurring both the scowling sight of him and the vast tapestry that hung behind his head. It was a hunting scene of stags and hounds, a faded, many-layered narrative she knew by heart in all its leaping chases across the flowered forest floor.

'*Fret!*' said her brother with contempt at the word, stable-mates as it was with *sulk* and *pet*.

Emerald shook her head. In his present mood he was the very personification of all three. 'Oh, Clovis,' she said.

From the hall, Edward's voice carried easily to them: 'Clovis! Ferryman needs to be taken out. If you've time today I'd be very much obliged to you.'

His good-tempered authority would have been impressive – lovable – had the very fact of the man not been intolerable to them. Clovis was mutinous. 'He ought to take his damned horse out himself.'

Emerald pushed her plate away.

'He can't very well if he's in Manchester trying to save the house, can he?' she said, and she got up and left the room by the other door so as not to encounter her mother or stepfather again.

He did not go after her. Clovis wasn't somebody who went after people, rather people tended to go after him.

Unable to escape her misery, Emerald wandered up and down in the kitchen for a few moments, aggravating Florence Trieves and Myrtle, and then went out into the garden by the side door.

It was the last day of April. She felt the extraordinary softness of the season on her face and braced herself for a strict talking-to; if it must be audible, she ought at least to get some distance from the house.

The air was complicated with the smells of sharp new things emerging from damp soil. Small tatters of clouds dotted the watery sky. To her left was the door to the kitchen garden and stables. Ahead of her, reaching far and further, in the broadest geometrical sweep, was the country over which Sterne presided. It spread out beneath and beyond, reaching into straining, dazzling blue distance, where the fields became indistinct and hills dissolved to nothing.

The house stood on a piece of land so cleanly semicircular, so strictly rounded, that it might have been a cake-stand left behind in the landscape by some refined society of giants. It was covered with deep, soft turf as one might lay a thick rug over a table, and all the busy pattern of fields, hedges, cows and villages scattered beyond, toy miniatures a child's imagination would produce.

From the front of the house, the edge of the gardens formed a ha-ha between order and free nature. It was bordered by a knee-high sharp-trimmed box hedge, lest dogs should rush at it and fall off. Small children had been known to topple, although happily the slope, on falling, was much gentler than it first appeared. Clovis and Emerald, when much younger, had used to take running jumps off the apparent precipice,

terrifying visitors unfamiliar with the topography, only to emerge laughing hilariously, covered with dandelion fluff or mud or clinging claws of long couch grass.

Emerald walked along the curve of the low box hedge with her head bowed, like a lonely merry-go-round horse.

'This helpless grief over what amounts to a few rooms and a rather poor roof is irrational,' she began, 'and frankly –' she stopped walking, ' – ludicrous.'

She turned her face to the house, the windows of which glowed variously. 'There's no use looking at me like that,' she said to it.

She crossed the gravel, and went towards the other part of the garden, where were the borders and sundial. 'And there's not even the excuse of ancestry!' she said out loud again, and indignant.

And it was true; no generations of Torringtons had lived at Sterne. No generations of Torringtons had lived anywhere particularly, as far as they knew. They were a wandering, needs-must sort of family, who made their livings disparately, in clerking, mills or shipping; travelled to France for work in tailoring, or stopped at home in Somerset, Shropshire or Suffolk, to play some minor role in greater projects: designing a lowly component of a reaching cathedral or a girdered bridge. Some had been in business, one or two in service; there was an artist, some soldiers, all dead. All dead.

Her father's life had been distinguished only by his having the daring to buy Sterne. The house and land had been purchased rashly at the peak of what transpired to be transient – too harsh to call it flukish – financial success when, first married to Charlotte and bathed in her adoration, he had thought Torrington might be the name of the sort of man whose family would live in such a house. Horace had loved Sterne as he loved Charlotte and later, his children: loyally, generously and

gratefully. The children, too, feeling that they were at the end of a line, as children always do (for indeed, they are), loved Sterne as exhausted travellers with lifetimes of migration behind them might love their first and last home. Sterne was the mythology of their parents' marriage, their father's legacy, and it had given them the very best of childhoods. Beyond that, it was beautiful, and the effect of it on their souls was inestimable; once found, they were all of them loath to give it up. Unfortunately, Horace Torrington left business for agriculture, about which he was utterly ignorant, at precisely the worst moment he could have chosen. At his untimely death he was very deeply in debt. Emerald often thought it odd that such dire financial straits should be cheerfully nicknamed 'in the red'; black was a far likelier colour. Her father's increasing debt was a dark hole into which they all might yet fall.

In reality, Sterne was two houses. One was a strange, shallow red-brick manor house of two floors and great charm, built around 1760, where the family now lived; the other – predecessor and companion – was attached behind, as the long side of the L, a great barn-like building of stone, where once one of the first lords of that manor would have laid his fires and roasted his meat, but which now stood almost empty in graceless neglect.

In the busy scullery of the New House there was a brief rise of shallow steps to a door of thick wood, mostly kept barred and bolted, which gave onto the cavern of the Old House. The two were joined utterly in the wide raftered and beamed spaces of their roofs, like Siamese twins. If one were in the attic (as the children often had been, galloping about in the dust or lying reading in the dancing window-light), only close inspection could discover the join, for the ribs of the roofs and the planks of the floors were of similar scale, and in the roof spaces the air was always dim and faded. There had been over the years

much talk of demolishing the older building, but it had so very many convenient and entertaining uses, especially for storage and on rainy days, and they had not been able to do it.

A magnolia tree grew in the courtyard at the crook of the L. As a child, Emerald used to try to touch the thick flowers by leaning out of a landing casement. She would reach as far as she could, until the tight stitches of her dress strained under the arms and her fingers shook. Clovis when young, not yet having acquired a romantic view of himself, had leaned from the same window to spit. His idea was to perfect his aim and range to reach the insides of the flowers. He had to propel his saliva with vigorous conviction in order to span the gap between the tree and the house and by the time he was eight years old he had succeeded, and was triumphant. Emerald, despite her nature, aspired to practicality and surrendered her campaign to touch the petals by the age of twelve, settling instead for drawing the tree, later painting it and, still later, snipping small parts from it for closer observation under her microscope, but still never felt she had *truly* touched it. Perhaps a prosaic ambition – accurate spitting, for instance – is one more easily realised.

Emerald had reached the driveway, a long avenue bordered by giant black yews. The yews had been meant for a hedge and cultivated as one for perhaps two hundred years but had run sluggishly away with themselves and, neglected, they formed a misshapen lumbering procession. They were wrinkles of dense growth. They were resinous twisted towers with pockets like witches' huts hidden within their vastness for playing or hiding. There were gaps between them that ought not to have been there.

Emerald, who was by day a determinedly practical young woman, often dreamed of recklessly galloping down the dark avenue to the house with the noise of hooves in her ears.

Sometimes the dream sent her flying high around Sterne like a bird, with the roofs spinning away beneath her; the chimneys, stables, gardens and country filling her eyes. Then plunged back to earth by waking, she inhabited her bed alone, and wept for her lost infinity.

Now, earthbound, dispirited, she turned from the creeping yews, not caring to gaze into their dreary depths, and having reached the part of the garden laid out to flowers, she knelt by the turned soil of the border and began to cry. She had no smart words now, only childish ones. *If only the Step would find some way to save us*, she thought, bitterly aware that the resented step-parent was now her devoutly wished-for rescuer.

The crying, far from doing its job and clearing up, was threatening to consume her. At any moment she might fling herself face down on the flower-bed. It was her birthday; she must be happy, and soon. She sniffed, blotted her face, hard, against her forearm and stared stonily ahead. 'Good,' she said.

After a moment of listless gazing at the ragged bed she began to pluck at the weeds, inching her fingertips down the weak stems to lift them from the soil. Her hands were soon chilled and muddy and she had made a limp pile beside her on the grass, reflecting that a useful task is a great comforter.

Charlotte's private farewell to Edward was made in their bedroom, which sat squarely in the middle of the house above the front door. The room had a deep bay window, framed by an ancient and extravagant rose whose candy-striped buds – as well as all the county – could be seen from the bed across which Charlotte now draped herself, affecting languor in the hope it would calm Edward, who was pacing the softly bowed boards in his tightly laced shoes and causing the dressing-table mirror to rattle on its stand.

He was of medium height: a stocky, sandy sort of man with

square, broad shoulders (his left arm had been severed cleanly and high up, in such a way as not to interfere with the set of these, although one was necessarily more developed than the other) and piercing, pale-blue eyes. At last, he stopped and sat by her. He had warmth and vigour; he said, 'Charlotte, I'll do my best for you.'

It was the sort of thing Edward often said and, unlike very many people Charlotte had known, he meant it.

Edward Swift was the youngest son of an Anglo-Irish architect. With no expectation of an inheritance, he had made his way in the world with characteristic rigour. He had read law at Trinity College Dublin and moved to London to practise. The intervening years of his life bear no relevance to this story, but suffice to say, on meeting Charlotte Torrington – a woman possessed of a high and trembling beauty, in mourning for Horace Torrington, recently struck down – he fell in love. Edward fell in love as deeply as Charlotte grieved, and there in the far-down places of sorrow and sex they met.

When they married, the older children, Emerald and Clovis, were shocked not only at the speed of their mother's apparent return to cheerfulness, but also – profoundly – at Edward's colouring, which seemed to them a betrayal in itself. Their father had been tall and very dark, with pale, black-fringed eyes so dazzling they deserve the category Torrington Eyes. Both Emerald and Clovis were dark with these same, arresting, grey-blue eyes. Their mother was fair, but had been absorbed and become a Torrington and was, after all, their mother (also, her eyes were not to be sneezed at), but Edward Swift was, well, *blond*.

And then there was the arm. The violent accident; the neatly pinned sleeve – what might have been romantic in another man was abhorrent in a fair-haired step-parent.

What Clovis and Emerald could not know was anything of

the nights that Edward held Charlotte against his body as she cried for Horace, the wet trails of her tears on his neck, chest and shoulder. He had gone with her through the agony of missing a man he had never known, went with her through it still, when called upon, and now would give his all for Sterne; he did not want Charlotte to cry for that, too. Another man might have engineered the incorporating of his new wife into his own milieu, sought to erase her past in the building of his future, but Edward Swift accepted all that she was, including the burden that was Sterne and her opaque and recalcitrant offspring.

Edward reluctantly spent a great portion of his time in Manchester, where he had joined a thriving chambers; reluctant not because he was work-shy – he practised the law with thoroughness and pride – but because he hated leaving Charlotte, upon whom he doted. His imminent journey to the city was not for the benefit of his career but for the attempted rescuing of his wife's house from the auctioneer. There had been a much-needed influx of capital the year before when they had sold the largest of their farms to its tenant, a forthright, handsome young man named John Buchanan. The money had gone a fair way to pay off debts and mend various walls and roofs around the property, but it had dwindled alarmingly. It had dwindled almost to nothing. Edward, seeing Sterne slip through his fingers, turned away from the prospect of a sensible, smaller house nearer the city and a broken-hearted wife and resolved to save it. He was not a gambler, he had nothing to sell; he must borrow the money. It was a distasteful prospect, and it was with this distaste that he now looked down upon Charlotte's fine, pale face.

'Love,' he said, 'don't ask me to *enjoy* asking to borrow money from a man whose employment practices I loathe and whose politics sicken me.'

(This was in reference to the prospective lender; an industrialist of low morals.)

'You needn't do it, you know that,' said Charlotte, looking away from him. A tear rolled from her eye. She brushed it away impatiently – but not so impatiently that he would not see it.

'Of course I must do it!' he said, kissing her damp and salty fingers.

Ten minutes later Edward was in the passenger seat of the car, with his case strapped behind him and an expression of grim resolve as he waited for Robert to crank the starting handle.

Emerald, straightening from her weeding, watched, as with a roar and flying gravel they set off. Their departure had drawn the lurcher Forthright from his doze beneath the yews and he loped after them, barking wolfishly. Edward, catching sight of Emerald, raised his arm and waved.

'Happy Birthday, Emerald!' he shouted above the noise, and very soon the car, the lurcher, her stepfather, Robert and the suitcase were lost to sight in the gloom of the avenue that was dark in any weather, but particularly so this morning, it seemed.

The noise faded, the world was hushed.

Here, then, on the morning of her twentieth birthday, having grown out of her many efforts to capture the magnolia tree or, it must be owned, much else that life might have to offer, having put away her microscope, drawing pad, girlish dreams of Greatness and all, kneeling by the stunted flower-bed, Emerald noticed that water had seeped through the thick linen of her skirt and knitted stockings and onto her knees.

'Happy birthday indeed,' she said. 'I must stop talking to myself.'

There was a drooping bow below her bust. She adjusted it.

Her eye was caught by something and she strained to interpret the shape.

Near the yews, paused in the shadow of them, was a small, white figure. Emerald stood, tucking the pile of weeds into the deep pocket of her dress and wiping her dirty fingers, heedlessly.

'Is that you, Smudge?' she called, and the third young Torrington, the child, replied weakly, 'Yes.'

Emerald crossed the grass towards the figure standing in the overhang, her puff of dark hair merging like a sooty halo with the shadows.

'Good heavens, I thought you hadn't come down. Didn't you say you don't feel well?'

'I don't feel well,' the child responded.

Emerald went to her sister and took her hand. 'Your fingers are like ice,' she said. 'Come inside at once.'

They went in by the back door nearest them to a square, stone-flagged back hall. Pausing by a stand with walking sticks and umbrellas leaning gleamingly at angles, Emerald put her hands on the child's face and tilted it up to look at her, searchingly. 'Why did you come out?'

'I was bored.'

'Is there a fire in your room?'

'I don't want one.'

'Well, let's go up and see about you.'

They started up the echoing back stair, whose treads were naked wood.

'Where's Clovis?'

'I don't know – still at breakfast when I last saw him, sulking.'

'He does sulk. I don't. You wouldn't notice.'

It was true; Smudge was very often forgotten. Like Clovis and Emerald before her, she was left to herself to get on with

the business of her upbringing, but unlike them, she was alone in the endeavour. Clovis and Emerald had had one another as company when marooned by the various tides of their parents' commitments. Smudge's loneliness suited her; she was celebrated by her mother, as well as neglected, and she found much to be cheerful about.

They had reached a landing and went through the baize door onto a corridor, travelled the length of the house and at last reached Smudge's room, the only bedroom to abut the Old House, whose gloomy depths were directly through the wall against which her little iron bed stood. She should have liked to tunnel through the wall with a spoon and dance on the minstrels' gallery.

If Smudge was often forgotten it stood to reason that her room would be too and, taking advantage of the freedom, she did with it exactly as she pleased. She had stuck shells gathered at Southport beach onto the wall above her fireplace to spell her name: _IMOGEN_, and then for sure identification added in charcoal afterwards, (SMUDGE). She had attempted to measure herself against the wall, and then the cat Lloyd, the two King Charles spaniels Nell and Lucy, and the stable dog, the lurcher Forthright, called Forth. In truth, none of these measuring experiments had satisfied. She had never solved the vexing question of whether the dogs and cat ought to be measured to the tops of their heads, which they would keep moving about, or their shoulders, which were easy to confuse with spines and necks. More than this, she had begun in inches and then changed her mind and fixed on hands as a suitable unit, as she knew that was the proper way of measuring horses, and ought therefore to do for all four-legged creatures. The brindled cat Lloyd, incidentally, was usually two-and-a-half hands (or ten inches), and the spaniels somewhat more.

Unfulfilled by her annotated charcoal marks, she had spent many hours drawing the outlines of the animals whilst squashing them against the walls with her legs and body. (Unaccustomed to house manners, the lurcher Forth's sitting had been less than easy. He was, in his dogs' way, no respecter of carpets. He had dragged Smudge the length of the corridor, emitting booming cries of distress at being imprisoned for so long in the small upper bedroom between Smudge's ruthless, childish arms and the damp and dirty wallpaper.)

She intended to paint the fur in later, but hair and fur are uncommonly difficult to paint well and she hadn't yet got around to it. Suffice it to say, her walls were less than immaculate.

Emerald led Smudge to the bed and tucked the quilt around her. 'Have you been on the roof again?' she asked.

'Not recently.'

'Well, you're not to. You'll fall and break your neck and then what will Ma say?'

'You and Clovis do it.'

'Yes, and look at all the problems with leaks.'

Smudge burrowed downwards until only her black eyes, set in purplish pools, and her insubstantially dark hair poked above the faded garlands of the quilt.

'Em?' she said, and her voice was muffled.

Emerald was at the door.

'Will I be well enough for your birthday party?'

'I should hope so, otherwise who will help me blow out the candles? I'm much too old to manage them all by myself.'

'Are you having a cake, then?'

'Oh Lord! Not unless I see to it,' said Emerald and went out, closing the door.

Immediately she had gone, Smudge poked her pale face from the bed. She seemed to listen, sharply, for something.

She sat up and laid her ear against the wall behind her, that joined to the Old House.

'Hmm,' she said, and frowned, 'nobody there.' Then she looked around the room and its apparent emptiness, before lying back down and pulling up the covers to her chin once more, while outside the cold spring wind began to blow.

Emerald, passing the morning room on her way to find Mrs Trieves, came upon Clovis, lying crumpled before the fire and listlessly plucking at the edges of a newspaper. The spaniels Nell and Lucy reclined on the battered velvet chaise near to him, lifting snuffy noses in her direction as she stopped in the door.

'Not taking Ferryman out?'

Clovis glanced at the window with hooded, gloomy eyes.

'My word, Emerald, have you ever thought of joining the police force?' he said. 'I hear they need bullies to suppress the disgruntled.'

'I shall be taking Levi out at ten, if you've a mind to accompany me. I think the weather's on the turn, so the sooner the better, I'd say. At what hour is the train that will bear your beloved to my revels?'

Clovis uttered a groan and rolled onto his back. He stared up at the plaster curls of the ceiling.

'Patience Sutton,' he said. '*At what hour will the train bearing Patience Sutton and her mother arrive?* Is that what you meant to ask? She's *not* my beloved – and won't be.'

'She's a very fine girl. And anyway, we're grown up, she won't baby you now . . .'

Clovis ran his fingers through his hair as a poet might, one who is in the agony of creation, but Clovis was not in the agony of creation, he was in the throes of a worse pain, hubris.

'As if I care what she does. *Insignificance* Sutton,' he said roughly.

14

'I can't think why you've taken against them! I've missed them awfully since—' She broke off, then, 'Don't you remember the fun we all used to have? If you're unkind to *Patience*, or her mother—'

'Her *mother* is the death of hope.'

'*Or her mother*, then I shan't have you at my birthday party, do I make myself clear?'

'Yes, Officer.'

'And it isn't much of a birthday as it stands, I have to admit . . . But I'm counting on you to be a gentleman.'

'Yes, Officer.'

'You know that I love you beyond reason – and for no good reason. I'm going to talk to Mrs Trieves about my cake.'

'Make it chocolate, would you?'

'I don't believe we have any.'

Clovis groaned again and returned to plucking at the newspaper. The dogs laid their chins on their silky paws and gazed at him with love.

At the threshold Emerald changed her mind and returned, like a whirlwind.

'That fire is obscenely hot!' she exclaimed, crossing the room and waving the air in front of her with violent movements.

'I'm freezing to death.'

She slammed the guard down in the grate. 'Have you any idea of the price of coal?'

Clovis rolled onto his back. 'No – and nor have you.'

'Sterne cost us more than twelve guineas in fuel just this last winter, *actually*.'

'Aren't you going to add "so there"?' he said.

Emerald plumped down on the chaise next to the dogs, looking about the room. She pinned a stray lock of hair back to the majority. 'So there', she said.

Clovis had covered his face with his arms in self-defence, but Emerald, surprising him, withdrew her attack.

'The horses' summer coats are coming through,' she remarked, conversationally. 'Levi is beginning to look quite glossy, and Ferryman would be, if he hadn't been clipped out so late in the year. You know, outside feels rather grand once you're in it – and I saw a swallow this morning whilst I was gardening . . .' She was pulling the spaniels' speckled paws absently as she talked. 'I thought I might go down past the tithe barn and around the edge of Hurtle . . . Won't you come, too?'

'Not to oblige *him*.'

'No, Clovis, for me, your ever-loving sister – for Ferryman who shall swell up like a balloon on spring grass if he doesn't have a bit of work soon, and for—' She stopped.

Clovis glanced at her slyly from beneath his forearm. 'For . . . ?' he murmured.

'Yourself, because you are the greatest of all wet blankets recently.'

'Oh I am, am I?'

'Yes, you are.'

'The very greatest?'

'You know you are. I can't think what's got into you.'

'Oh you can't, can't you?'

'Stop that! Stop that silly questioning! You did it when you were eight years old. It's singularly annoying. You *do* it to annoy.'

'Oh, I do, do I?'

Emerald threw a cushion at him, and he dodged it, rolling smartly away and laughing. Finding himself against the fender, he sat up and rubbed his face.

'You know very well "what's got into" me. How d'you think it feels for a man to have his position usurped by a sneaky, one-armed, Irish lawyer—'

'Point of information, Mr Chair: it wasn't your position, it was our father's.'

At the mention of their father they were both quiet. Emerald went back to the dogs, stroking their ears and domed, bony heads.

'I don't believe Father would have wanted you to become what you are becoming,' she said, without turning her face to him.

Evoking their father's name had brought sorrow to the room and it weighed heavily in the air. Clovis put his legs in front of him and, hugging his bent knees, gazed at her sadly. His hair fell oddly to the side. The unsociable and frankly objectionable Clovis of the last three years was changed, as light changes the grey sea to glinting complexity.

'You oughtn't just say things like that,' he said, hurt, and she saw in an instant all the workings of his grief, his loss and failings, and went to her knees, facing him.

'Boy,' she said, and kissed him on the forehead.

He was grateful. 'I miss him tremendously,' he said, feelingly, and with a return to recent form added, 'I'd like to kill the Step with a rusty scythe.'

'You wouldn't.'

'Well, very nearly.'

She tugged his ear. 'Won't you come and ride with me?'

Clovis was nothing if not mercurial. 'I'll meet you in the yard in ten minutes,' he said, jumping up suddenly and striding out of the room.

The dogs, barking wildly, sprang from the chaise longue in his wake, bounding loose-limbed through the doorway.

'Ten minutes is too soon!' she called, but he had gone.

Emerald stood up and dusted off her skirt. There was a framed photograph of Horace Torrington on the mantel. In it, he stood behind their mother who was seated on a chair

in front of a painted backdrop of a garden wearing an excess of white muslin. Her bosom looked immense, as had been the fashion, and her tiny waist was satin-belted. Horace, proudly frowning, looked handsome and upright in a stiff collar, with one hand resting on an ebony cane. Emerald crossed to the fireplace and – knowing the portrait intimately already – leaned her elbows on the mantel to examine it more closely.

The plaited vines on the silver frame and the fine grain of the photographic paper were inches from her unblinking Torrington eyes. Her parents, miniature and still, filled her vision.

'It's my birthday,' she said to her frowning father, but his expression did not change. 'I'm sure you'd like to wish me happy returns and give me a kiss for it, if you could. I should very much like it, too, I can tell you.'

The last birthday of his daughter's at which Horace Torrington had been present was her sixteenth. She had put up her hair, worn her first corset, and been amazed when, after complimenting her very kindly, he had turned away so as not to be seen crying. 'Lovely girl,' he had said. 'It's just the passing of time, that's all, not you.'

Emerald found Florence Trieves in her small study, a room just near the kitchen where were her desk and low, buttoned armchair. Un-swept crumpet crumbs mixed with crumbled fragments of coal on the hearth, for the room was always the last to be seen to by Pearl Meadows and, in spite of her horror of mice, Florence Trieves had a thin but stubborn slovenly streak and almost never swept it herself.

Emerald was anxious to make the most of Clovis's no doubt transient good humour and wanted to be at the stables as soon as she could.

'Can we talk about bedrooms later on? I was wondering if there was any chocolate for a cake. For me. It doesn't matter a bit if not, I like plain sponge just as well.'

Florence, in her habitual black silk dress, was seated at her desk occupied with the accounts. She was a widow. She had been one since Victoria's reign and a great part of her had remained in that era of mourning and restraint. Stepping through the recesses of the Old House in her black silk and buttoned boots, to fetch flour or baking soda from the shelves, she often seemed to fit the place better than she did the New.

She and her husband had been acquaintances of Charlotte's before her meeting Horace, and came into service for them upon their marriage. The exact origin and nature of their relationship were unclear to many but themselves, but to her credit she had become an excellent housekeeper. She had once been, like Charlotte, a beauty; the two of them must have made quite a picture at twenty, in Bloomsbury, before their marriages. Florence Trieves's renouncing of a romantic life – and fashion – had done much to form Emerald and Clovis's expectations of the behaviour of widows, making their mother's swift re-marriage in contrast doubly shocking.

'We can talk about bedrooms whenever you like, Miss Em, but it won't make any more of them habitable.' She had a habit of fiddling with the small watch pinned to her rigid breast as she spoke. 'Miss Sutton will be in the room next to yours and Mrs Sutton at the other end, in the stripes. As to the cake, you're not to worry about it, and I'll not talk to you about it either. A girl making her own birthday cake? The idea is not to be borne.'

Emerald ran off to change for riding much cheered: a surprise cake she had not made herself; a childhood friend on

a train to visit, and no Step until Sunday . . . she felt the childhood thrill of her (whisper the word) *birthday*.

Acid-green new grass had begun to grow between the cobbles of the stable-yard; it was another job for the groom Robert's boy Stanley to get to, but there were so many other pressing tasks to be accomplished at Sterne, and the horses were the very devil to keep clean now their rugs were off. When it rained, the mud caked onto them in hard crusts that cracked as it dried and stuck like flour and water to a table after bread-making. Young Stanley could stand there, picking at it, as Ferryman or Levi – or whichever of the horses it was – went off into a doze, with long ears falling sleepily and nodding head, until the clock softly struck, or Robert barked at him to look sharp, and then he would be back to the present, with all the things as yet undone, slap the horse on the rump and reprimand himself for his vagueness.

With his father off to the station with Mr Edward, it fell to Stanley to get Levi and Ferryman ready. Both father and son were up at five, as was Robert's rule, and worked two hours before breakfast so Stanley had a good portion of the morning for prettifying the horses. Just thirteen years old, Stanley, lacking a female presence at home, was a little in love with Emerald, and oiled Levi's hooves with care.

Edward Swift (like Horace Torrington before him) was very strict about punctuality in all things to do with the horses at Sterne, and wouldn't countenance his stepchildren keeping horses or grooms waiting. Clovis, who had ridden with his father all his life and was a brave and thoughtful horseman, affected a cavalier attitude to the whole business whenever Edward was there; wandering in late and messily dressed, allowing courtesy towards Robert – whom he loved – to slip, and the horses – whom he loved more – to fidget

and misbehave. In his stepfather's absence, however, he reverted to his upbringing and was a pleasure to observe, as Emerald did now, in all his dealings with the stables and their occupants.

'Good man. Thanks.' He smiled to Stanley, and, 'Get up there, stand!' to Ferryman, who struck his metal shoe on the sparking cobbles in his impatience to be off.

Emerald sat quietly on Levi, who arched his black and shiny neck in pride and pleasure. He had been a tenth birthday present from her father as a four-year-old and their partnership was infinitely comfortable. Named Leviathan in anticipation of his reaching 17 hands, he hadn't matured as expected and his nature, runtish, was excessively affectionate; he had the loyalty of the weak.

They left the yard in a clatter, trying to steady the horses who could smell the powerful spring and liked it.

Emerald had never ridden side-saddle but – most comfortably – astride, long before it was fashionable for modern young women to do so. Charlotte had been raised amid and among many occupations and worlds, one of them being horses, and she had an unconventional belief that the side-saddle was a ludicrous contraption, no good to woman nor mount. Emerald had not been welcomed into the local hunt because of her apparently obscene straddling, but if her riding habits, or lack thereof, were one of the reasons the Torringtons were never a part of the local set, they were doubtless not the only one.

Emerald rode in soft, tan-topped, men's boots and a modest voluminous skirt, altered into a pair of giant trousers (sewn by Florence Trieves). On her top half she wore any one of a number of adorably becoming jackets, of green or midnight blue, bracken-brown or pigeon-grey, with neatly fitting waists, velvet collars and button-finished pleats behind, from which

fell gathered, rump-obscuring tails. These jackets were an ostensible extravagance which she enjoyed guiltlessly, owing to their being the rejected halves of conventional skirted riding habits that had somehow lost their mates (perhaps through their unsuitability for some unusually proportioned customer), and could be picked up for a song through small printed advertisements in the local newspaper, that Emerald found amongst the smudgy-penned representations of corsets, dental contraptions and laundry-soap. She also favoured the wearing of a rakish bowler but could not always find it.

Having made her grateful and heated goodbye to Edward, it wasn't until Charlotte heard the horses go out, that she roused herself from her bed and went to the dressing table to attend to her hair.

With hairpins clamped between her lips, she assessed her reflection as a tradesman might assess the life left in his old nag: how many tons its legs might bear yet; how many miles its heart. At forty-eight, her complicated self had at last begun to reveal itself in her features.

Charlotte had always had in her that thing that fascinates – call it charm, or the quality of showing the onlooker a reflection of themselves – whatever it was, it had not always served her well. The best thing to happen to her was, at twenty-seven, to come across – and fall in love with – Horace Torrington; having once learned constancy and the joy of delighting in another human being, she found them again easily on meeting Edward Swift.

She finished dressing her hair and considered her morning: the scenes at breakfast – Clovis's rage and Edward's stalwart kindness; she remembered, too, that her youngest child was so far absent from the day and, frowning, she realised she had not seen much of Smudge the day before either, when she

had first announced her ill-health. With a shake of her head, as if a fly had crossed her vision, she left the room. Charlotte had many good qualities, but was ruthlessly self-serving, and she would have been the first to admit it.

The scullery was scrubbed down; sinks and plate-racks awaiting the washing-up to come.

A leg of lamb in a muslin shroud lay on a marble slab. Tins of mustard, brick-like pats of butter, a bag of raisins, stacks of intensely pink mud-streaked forced rhubarb, bound with string, leant beside other things: a breaded ham, thick glass bottles of milk, wet sausages . . . A large, marbled book, such as one might use as a ledger for petty cash, lay before Florence Trieves on the table, spilling loose pages like spells, handwritten, and straining against its elastic closer.

Having collected all manner of ingredients from the pantry, cupboards and Old House, she stood in the middle of the kitchen with laden counters all around her, tying an apron over her black dress and surveying the resulting cacophony of potential dishes with a determined expression, as if to render their components submissive before beginning their harmonising into a symphony.

Charlotte, having wandered into the kitchen, paused at the sight of so much plenty. It erupted towards her.

'I suppose *all* the cupboards must be emptied, Mrs Trieves?' she asked Florence sourly.

'That way I know where I am to start with,' responded Florence with equal acidity.

A five-pound paper bag of sugar, rolled down some way, stood on the corner of the dresser with a wooden scoop dug into its inviting crystalline landscapes. Charlotte could not resist digging the scoop further into the sugar to feel the small, dry grindings.

'Have you everything planned all the way to Monday?'

'I have. Emerald and I.'

'I envy you cooking it – rather that than talk to the guests.'

'A telegram came.'

'Oh yes?'

Florence Trieves took an opened telegram from her apron pocket and handed it to Charlotte.

'Must there be *no* secrets?' said Charlotte vaguely.

'You know there aren't any.'

Charlotte perused the telegram as Florence undid each of the five buttons of her black cuffs and rolled up her sleeves to the bony elbows. 'Myrtle will be down directly she finishes the bedrooms,' she said. 'It would be this day of all days that Pearl Meadows cries off sick—'

Pearl Meadows was the housemaid, part time, who had beat a hasty and highly inconvenient retreat that morning, pleading illness.

'Oh, dash it all! Deceit!' cried Charlotte, and Florence looked up questioningly. 'Camilla Sutton has influenza – I should be very surprised *indeed* if that were anywhere near the truth, the *harridan* – and has sent Patience with the brother, Ernest, who is a dreadful clot.'

'Camilla Sutton? Do we know her?'

Charlotte was irritable. 'You know we do! They used to come *very* often when Horace was here – alive.'

'Ah. Yes. Well.'

'*Green-eyes*, Florence – *I like* her. Perhaps she doesn't like me any more.'

'Still, Edmund will talk to Emerald and Clovis, and you'll be free—'

'It's *Ernest*, remember? And Emerald and Clovis won't *want* to talk to *him*. Patience is a long toil up a muddy field as it is; he's beyond horror.'

'I seem to recall.'

'He was a weasly, swotty little child – forever catching things in nets and staring. He encouraged Emerald in messing about with inappropriate things. Now she's reading *something* at *Cambridge* and *he's* studying medicine, apparently. He *would.*'

'Oh, I see. A scientist.' This last was said in tones of dreary condemnation.

'With red hair.'

'Lord, yes. And a squint.'

'That's the fellow – *spectacles.*'

'Hardly his fault.'

'You might say that, Florence, but although many may need them, only a certain type of person wears them. I prefer a passionate, squinting man than one who corrects his sight with wiry little spectacles and is in command of himself.'

'His corrected glances will be aimed at Emerald, I imagine, rather than you,' smiled Florence, spitefully.

'Or you!' said Charlotte; then, veering from this thorny subject, 'Will there be cake?'

'There will. Chocolate. With green roses.'

'*Green?*'

'For Emerald.'

'Roses aren't green, dear.'

'Emerald's sugar ones are. Dyed and perfectly sculpted last night.'

'By Myrtle?'

'By me. And candlelight.'

'I should think they'll look most peculiar, and Ernest and Patience Sutton will return to Berkshire with the impression that we're unfit for society.'

'Aren't we unfit?' rejoined Florence.

Charlotte burst, very suddenly, into loud laughter, a bawdy Titania.

'Oh Lord,' she belted, her voice all at once strident, 'that we are, Florence!' And Florence, too, bending forward to allow herself to do it in her corsets, laughed with her, breathily, like a concertina, unused for a while and warming itself up.

'I shall leave you, *unfit* as I am, to your baking,' said Charlotte, exiting the room, and throwing over her shoulder, 'What's for lunch?'

Florence wiped a tear from her eye. 'It'll be early, with all the hullaballoo today, and it's what remains of the pie from dinner.'

'Delicious!' sang Charlotte and floated away.

Smudge leaned from her window into the raw air. There had been a change in the weather and the bruised sky was threatening in all directions.

'Where are my brother and sister?' she breathed. Smudge was content with loneliness, but intermittently the fabric of her surroundings was unpredictable and she craved flesh-and-blood company beyond the spectres of her imagining. Answering her, the trees moved uneasily and she caught the almost un-hearable hoofbeats of the returning horses on the shifting breeze.

The horses emerged from the tunnel of the yews as if they were stepping onto a dimly lit stage from the darkened wings. Clovis reached up to grab a black twig from the tattered tree above him.

'Ah,' he said, 'home,' then, 'Oh!' for an enormous shining car, glaring with chrome and glossy blue paintwork, was parked majestically, glamorously, alarmingly, dazzlingly in the middle of the drive.

'Heavens!' cried Emerald, as both horses started in fright.

Levi jumped backwards, barging into Ferryman who, taking exception, plunged, dashing the gravel.

'Silly,' said Emerald, steadying him with barely a movement or gathering of reins. 'It's just a car, and you've seen plenty of those before.'

Levi rolled his eyes dramatically, looking down his nose at the Rolls-Royce, which seemed to goggle back, the pointed silver lady poking up between its glass eyes like a small and vicious single antler.

'Not any car, Em,' said Clovis, who had exhorted Ferryman to stand square. 'Doesn't . . . *John Buchanan* drive just such an impressive machine?'

'*Clovis*,' Emerald warned.

The horses, having had their fun, suffered themselves to be ridden away to the back of the house, brother and sister locked in silent communication.

'Oh, get on with it!' burst out Emerald finally, Clovis's form of silent communication – insinuating glances and eyebrow raising – having proved too eloquent for her.

'Come on, Emerald, the farmer John Buchanan is well-heeled.'

They were riding close, knees bumping occasionally.

'And what of it?'

'It has come to my brotherly attention that – gobbling up Sterne acres notwithstanding – he holds you in high esteem.'

She was withering. 'Clovis, please, no match-making. I'd rather . . .' she was at a loss to imagine a fate worse than marriage to John Buchanan '. . . sell my hair. So just *cheese* it, as you might say, you uncouth youth. I may as well ask you to marry Patience Sutton!' she finished.

'Pax! Pax! There's no need for that sort of talk. We won't mention it again,' promised Clovis, then, 'What-ho, Stanley!' And he slid off Ferryman, long-legged, and began to lead him

towards his stall. '"Uncouth youth",' he called over his shoulder. 'Wonderful!'

Emerald dismounted, laid her cheek on Levi's damp neck and kissed him. 'Come on, you,' she said. 'John Buchanan will just have to wait for a moment.' And she led him off to his stall.

Some ten minutes later, Emerald, russet-cheeked, hair half-down and smelling delightfully of horse, hauled off her boots by the umbrellas. She considered tidying herself but rejected the notion as potentially misleading. She would gladly bear being seen in her eccentric riding garments if it kept her out of the romantic hot water with John Buchanan.

She strode through the house to find him in the drawing room, opposite Charlotte, perched politely on the low settee. This item of furniture was best suited to polite perching as the seat was broken entirely; it was but an empty promise of a seat. Any person aiming for the cushioned centre found himself on the floor. John had remembered too late having been a casualty of this particular Torrington booby-trap, to everyone's great mirth, once before, but having once committed to the settee he bravely balanced on the frame and kept his eyes locked into those of his hostess.

On Emerald's entrance to the room he lifted his face towards her and was struck by her vitality and the dewy flush of her skin, as well as her clownish trousers. He got to his feet.

'Mr Buchanan,' she said, 'Mother.'

'Yes . . .' said Charlotte, fadingly, 'John Buchanan's here.' And she lightly rose and left the room, looking around her with dim urgency as if searching for something. In the doorway, pausing, she murmured, 'I must see about the hens.'

John Buchanan and Emerald were left alone. This was a very

far from ideal situation and Emerald tapped her stockinged foot beneath the muddy hem of her riding garment.

'Have you hens?' asked John.

Emerald was loath to admit they hadn't any. She felt bound to defend her mother who, in the storm of John Buchanan, had sheltered in the port of invented poultry.

'Robert may have acquired some. And I believe Devlin has been known to keep them.'

John Buchanan stared at her gravely.

'I see you've brought your car,' said Emerald breezily.

'Yes,' he said, adding helpfully, 'I arrived in it.'

In the pause that followed this revelation, running, booted steps were heard, and Clovis raced into the room. Pulling up in the doorway, an unlikely chaperone, he stuck out his hand and said gruffly, 'John!'

John stepped forward to greet him. 'Clovis, how are you?'

'Oh yes, I'm very well, thank you.'

Clovis had the ironic tone of a boy playing the part of somebody tedious in a school production and Emerald winced to hear it, fearing he was in the insulting mood he usually reserved for their stepfather. Clovis, however, reined himself in. 'I'm going to play chess,' he announced, and crossed to the window in his muddy boots, where a board was set up on a cherry-wood table. He sat down and began to set out the pieces.

'I hope he doesn't argue with himself over the moves!' said Emerald, and then in confusion, 'Why don't we sit down?'

They sat – John avoiding the collapsed settee this time and placing himself near Emerald on the chaise. Clovis bent frowning over the chess pieces.

'Has mother offered you –' she glanced at the ormolu clock on the mantel which had never worked, '– anything at all?'

'No.'

Emerald was about to make an offer of tea when John reached inside his jacket and produced a small, navy blue box tied with a thin white satin ribbon.

'Happy birthday, Miss Torrington.'

Behind him, Clovis stared up from his chess with wild, appalled eyes, causing Emerald to look down at her hands, sharply.

'Oh,' she said, 'I'm not sure I really—'

'Please accept it,' he said.

Emerald took the box and placed it on her palm. She imagined a pair of vulgar earrings and was sliced in half by guilt.

'Mr Buchanan,' she began. She looked up into his face. He was the most geometric of men: absolutely symmetrical with no tricky corners or contours to confuse the onlooker. He had a straight mouth and strong brow, dark hair neatly and squarely cut and combed, broad shoulders . . . He was *even* in every way, and on the large side – that is, he was tall, and one had the impression he'd look imposing stepping out of a bathing hut, if he ever were to do such a frivolous thing as to get into one in the first place, for John Buchanan – despite being called the *farmer* John Buchanan by the Torringtons – was a mill owner and single-minded in his pursuit of success. His father was the farmer, and John, on making something of a small fortune, had purchased the tenancy for him in filial gratitude, not to mention sentiment, farming being in steep decline.

This fortune, this generosity, this attraction to Emerald – demonstrated by his rash visit on her birthday, as well as the tedium of his conversation – were what had driven Charlotte to leave her daughter alone in his company for the seeking out of imaginary hens.

Emerald gazed into the square and comfortable planes of his face.

'Thank you, Mr Buchanan,' she said. 'This is an unlooked for and generous present—'

'You haven't yet opened the box, Miss Torrington,' said John Buchanan easily. 'It might be very poor.'

'Still, I feel I must be clear at the outset. If accepting this is going to give the idea, any idea, that I am entering into, well, that I . . .'

Having made a vigorous start, Emerald found the right finish slipping from her grasp. But to her surprise, John broke into a loud, carefree laugh.

'Miss Torrington,' his voice was warm with appropriate kindliness, 'we played as children! Before you were Miss Torrington to me you were Emerald, Emmy, *Little Em* . . . If I come here now, with a trinket, please don't leap to conclusions that cast me in a more romantic light than I deserve.'

Emerald was covered in shame. Her face, not used to blushes, was suffused with heat. Oh, her pride and conceit.

'John,' she uttered.

John Buchanan, in contrast, looked very happy. 'Come! Let's not have this. I have found, in my experience of the fairer sex – admittedly limited by propriety – that they have a tendency to imagine all fellows think enormously well of them.' She was speechless. 'Although, I do, of course, like you most awfully. I mean, I think very *highly* of you . . .' He stressed the word, generously.

Behind him, Clovis sank his head into his hands. Emerald wished she might have been seated on the broken settee, that she could collapse into it and hide under furniture until this humiliation had passed. There was nothing for it but to open the box.

It held a delicate cameo, elegantly wrought and hanging on the most fragile of gold chains.

'It's most delightful,' she said quietly.

'Perhaps your brother could fasten it?' said John. 'I wouldn't want to *misrepresent* myself. Good old Em!' And he laughed again, smacked his broad thigh, and rose to his feet.

Clovis stood, too, and plunged his hands in his pockets, rocking, while Emerald found herself blurting loudly, 'Would you come to supper tonight? I'm having a small party. A terribly small party. My good friend Patience Sutton and her mother—'

'There's no need to tempt me with the list!' said John, and grasped her hand warmly between both of his. 'If there were any fences down between us this invitation would most certainly mend them. I accept. Jolly good and I'll look forward to it. And be off. And thanks.'

He smiled confidently at Clovis, tipped his imaginary hat, and was gone.

'*Clovis, see him out!*' hissed Emerald viciously, and Clovis shot from the room.

'Hold up, old man! I'll see you to your car,' she heard him call and she sank once more down onto the chaise.

'I'm the very last word in dunces,' she said, and flopped back against its unforgiving gilded arm, dashing herself on the forehead with the heel of her hand. The other, tremblingly, sought John Buchanan's piece of jewellery and toyed with it, thoughtfully.

She heard the gutted roar of the Rolls-Royce's engine as it sparked, and moments later, Clovis returned.

'I still don't like him,' he said. Then, '*Good old Em.*' And he laughed, madly.

The sodden sky of earlier had been blasted apart by high and squally gusts and now, duck-egg blue, it smiled sunnily upon the grumpy Torringtons sitting at their lunch.

Smudge's place stood empty. She often took her meals when she pleased, but as Florence Trieves put the pie dish on the table Emerald said, 'Ought we to see if Smudge is feeling better?' and resolved to do just that immediately lunch was finished.

The leftover pie was rabbit, with ham, and would have looked better in a new dish instead of the encrusted messy one of the night before, but Florence hadn't seen fit and nobody felt they should remark on it. There was, more pleasingly, a vast saucepan of white, boiled new potatoes, smothered with parsley, so they wouldn't go hungry – although, 'A serving dish might have been have nicer for those, Mrs Trieves,' as Charlotte observed vaguely.

'It might,' said Florence, and went for the mustard. She would eat her own pie standing in the kitchen. In her widowhood, she distrusted pleasures of the senses, and didn't like to stop for them, perhaps fearing envelopment.

Emerald, following her ride, and having been too miserable at breakfast to have an appetite, was ravenous, and ate hungrily until her mother, sighing, said, 'And what of John Buchanan?'

'What-what of him?' answered Emerald evasively.

'Don't be evasive,' said Charlotte, spotting it.

'I'd rather not go into it, Mother.'

'*Into it*? Into what? You young people have a remarkable way of putting things. Did your meeting with John Buchanan produce something *into which we might go?*'

'Oh, Mother!' Emerald stopped eating. 'What is it you would like to know?'

'In a nutshell?'

'A succinct one.'

'Whether or not he proposed to you.'

'Proposed!' This was Clovis, choking.

'Clovis dear, there's no need for vulgar manners.'

'Ishabod!'

'Nor language. Emerald?'

'You're being ridiculous. He has no interest in me beyond the neighbourly.'

'I see the way he looks at you,' said Charlotte, with an expert's acuity. 'And petrol is expensive. I beg to differ.'

'I begged to differ too,' put in Clovis gleefully, 'until Emerald was smacked sharply on the metaphorical nose by said fellow for daring to infer he was giving her a *love token*.'

'Oh, *Clovis* . . .' groaned Emerald.

'Explain, please,' instructed their mother.

Emerald sighed. 'John gave me a present. I told him I wasn't – well, that he mustn't think – well, *you know* – and then it was just *miserable*, because he stated in no uncertain terms that he wasn't interested in a *romance* anyway. I felt a fool, he looked the jolly nice fellow he no doubt is, and now I'd rather just forget all about it, if it's all the same to you.'

'Well put,' said Clovis. '*Good old Em.*'

Emerald kicked him hard but without effect, owing to her being unshod. He tossed a crust to Lucy and Nell who were lying on his feet and licked his fingers, and then there was a long silence during which they all ate, and kept to themselves.

They were interrupted by Charlotte abruptly pushing back her chair and saying harshly, 'Then I'm to relinquish all thoughts of a match between you and John Buchanan, am I?'

Emerald and Clovis gawped.

'I should say so, Ma,' said Clovis, and Emerald added, 'I didn't know you were entertaining such thoughts!'

'Well, I was. But I shall stop now.' And she left the room – and her cutlery awry.

Emerald, ever loving, ever dutiful, went after her. Clovis, also loving, less dutiful, finished his rabbit pie.

Charlotte reached the bottom of the main staircase, stopped, and drooped, bodily. Emerald, at her side now, was at a loss.

'Oh God,' said Charlotte.

'Mother, please . . . '

Charlotte looked about her, haunted, at the edifying square-ness of Sterne's hall.

'It's a great mistake ever to imagine one is home,' she said brokenly and sank onto the bottom stair.

Emerald was bleak. 'Perhaps your husband will return with good news.'

'You may as well know: it's almost hopeless.'

'Really?' Emerald was aghast. However often she had cried over it, she couldn't quite believe in her childish heart that she might have to live anywhere but Sterne. She had even imagined her husband there – whoever he may be going to be – and never considered he might have other plans. She sat down near her mother on the flagstones, looking up at her.

'We hope against hope,' Charlotte went on, 'but who can borrow against farmland now? And it's too remote to build on.'

'I know,' said Emerald. 'Sterne is too far from anything and no good to anybody.'

'Everybody's leaving the land. The cottages stand empty. Edward is even now trying to beg money from a man, an industrialist, who treats his workers vilely. It's ghastly.' Charlotte began to cry in earnest, with juddering, high-pitched sobs, not the usual, more picturesque expressions of sorrow she showed to her husband. '*My fault. My fault,*' she said into her wet hands. 'I've brought you up to these notions of

permanence, I ought to have been satisfied with wandering, and never having anything of my own, and no love, and no home.' She was becoming hysterical.

'Oh, Mother, Mother . . .' said Emerald and patted her, casting about for a distraction or glimmer to set her parent in a more hopeful direction.

'And then, *then*,' cried Charlotte, 'I had, nestled in my heart, *stupidly*, that you and John Buchanan would love one another. He is so rich,' the word was rough with need as it burst from her, 'so *rich*,' she was lusty with hopeless desire, 'and then generations and generations of us would be set fair. *Set fair*,' she said again, liking the phrase and pounding her fist, which held her tightly balled handkerchief, into the palm of her other hand, 'for a good, safe, future. Just *marriage*—'

But here, Emerald cut her off.

'"Just marriage?"' she said, incredulously. 'It's all very well for you to say, Mother, having married *twice* for love! And John Buchanan may go some way to earning his keep, simply by looking the straight-up, all-white, upright sort of fellow that, *yes*, he no doubt is. And shaking hands with everybody. But very soon thereafter he shows himself to be an utter dolt. How would that sustain fifty years of marriage? And babies. And life.'

Charlotte had some steel left in her for: '"Utter dolt" is surely a little strong, even for you, Emerald, with your exacting standards. The man has, after all, managed to buy a good portion of Manchester since taking up business. And he's not yet thirty.'

'Well, Mother, it's a moot point anyway, as he has no interest in me whatsoever! He made it abundantly clear at our meeting today.'

'It would have been so *nice*.'

Emerald looked upon her with scorn, but softened; her

mother's expression was that of a person watching the very last train home tootle round a distant bend with her luggage on it: wistful, increasingly hopeless, lost.

'I'm sorry, Mother,' she said, and meant it. 'Really and truly, I am. You're quite right: I ought not be so harsh. Perhaps if John Buchanan *were* interested in me I might have *learned* to appreciate his good qualities. I've invited him for supper . . .'

'Really?' Charlotte gave a tiny shiver and appeared to bristle, minutely, all over. She was scenting hope.

She paused, before saying with studied and theatrical carelessness, 'It was an act of real generosity to purchase the farm for his father.'

'Yes, it was.'

She waited again, then, rising to her feet, remarked, 'I hear he's in great demand in town, but not much interested in *fripperies* and the *trappings* of his success – soirées and dances, boxes at the theatre, and so on.'

Emerald was known to have eschewed said hypothetical delights in pursuit of more serious – and attainable – occupations: reading, gardening and something else she could not now recall, which all seemed very tawdry in the light of *things John could afford to do if he liked*.

'Really?' she answered softly.

Charlotte was an old hand at manipulation and knew when to stop. 'Well!' she said briskly, and brushed off her skirts, sniffing. 'I had best to my room, and attempt to regain some dignity.'

'You're always dignified to me, Mother,' said Emerald automatically.

Never having known why dignity should matter so much to her mother, she nevertheless knew that it did, and bestowed on her as often as possible the compliment: *very dignified, Mother*.

'You're a darling,' said Charlotte, patting her head and stepping lightly away from her up the stairs.

'I shall see about Smudge,' called Emerald after her and, 'Yes, why don't you?' was her mother's faint reply.

'Smudge?' There was no answer from behind Smudge's bedroom door.

'Smudge?' cooed Emerald again, before turning the knob. The doorknobs at Sterne were all different, and nobody knew why. This particular one was china and undecorated; others were painted, some coloured glass, or brass, still others were of carved or plain wood. The Torringtons blamed the Victorians.

Smudge was asleep. Emerald sat on her bed and held the hand that lay outside the covers. When she opened her eyes she said, 'Hello, small Smudge, would you like me to bring you something?'

Smudge was blurry. 'Oh, no, or yes.'

'Are you pretending this illness or is it authentic?'

'Authentic, I think.'

'Shall I fetch Dr Death?'

This was not his real name, of course. He wasn't even a Dr D'Eath or Dethe – his name was actually Harris. His nickname had become increasingly morbid and hideous during the course of their father's illness, but was too entrenched to discard. It had, in the last desperate days of his life, become funny once more. They had all, including the weakened Horace, shrieked with laughter at the uttering of the name Dr Death on more than one occasion. Laughed until they cried.

'I don't know. Would he come?'

'Of course. What are your symptoms?'

'My symptoms?' The child's white forehead creased.

'Have you a headache? Are you in pain? Do you have any appetite at all?'

'I'm not hungry very much, but I know the reason for that. I ate a tin of sugar biscuits that I had under my bed.'

Emerald bent down to look. Sure enough, there was an open tin there, revealing a golden interior lightly scattered with crumbs.

'You're not to bring biscuits up here, we'll get mice.'

'We've mice already; we may as well make them welcome.'

'It's no use arguing with invalids.'

Smudge giggled.

'Mother wants you down for supper,' said Emerald, although their mother had made no such statement. At this, the child rallied marvellously.

'Then I will be. With the guests? Topping!'

'Where on earth did "topping" come from?'

'Clovis.'

'Don't say it.'

'Only when I need to.'

Emerald took the biscuit tin and stood up. 'Have you had any other visitors?' she asked.

'What do you mean?'

'Clovis, or Mother, or Mrs Trieves . . .'

'Only animals, but I don't think they like ill people.' All at once, Smudge began to cry. 'They went away again,' she said.

Emerald bent and kissed her.

'You silly,' she said, 'I'll fetch you soup and bread. You're light-headed. The dogs adore you and so does Lloyd. Look! Here he is!'

The brindled cat had crept heavily into the room, with the air cats have of saying, *I understand you're talking about me, but I shan't look at you.*

He affected surprise as Emerald heaved him up and deposited him on Smudge's bed, where he suffered himself to be pinned down and began to purr.

With Lloyd to keep her company, Smudge's tears were very soon over. Emerald left her, and went away to find soup. The kitchen was in uproar. It was a miracle that evidence of it hadn't seeped into the main house. Florence Trieves and Myrtle were hard at it, barely visible among the clouds of flour and puffs of steam, as they flew between the counter and the table – pausing, in heated, fervent disarray to look up and ask: 'What is it?'

An earthenware bowl held a dozen eggs, bright yolks mesmerised by glassy whites. Two anaemic chickens, spatch-cocked, lay broken on a board. The rhubarb had been cleaned, chopped and heaped into three bright pink mountains.

'I was wondering if there might be a little soup,' offered Emerald nervously, as Florence's pointed face and Myrtle's friendly (as a rule), round one looked at her in frank and outraged astonishment.

'*Soup?*' said Florence Trieves, but it might as well have been, *Rabbit's eggs?*

'Ger,' said Myrtle, or similar.

Emerald thought of herself, Clovis and their mother guzzling rabbit pie and boiled potatoes and arguing. Charlotte was now in her room, with swollen eyes but a full stomach, and Clovis back before the fire, probably, amusing himself with mawkish introspection, while Smudge was alone upstairs, ignored, hungry and white as the sheets that covered her.

'Yes, just a bit of soup, or something like it,' she said, 'for Smudge. Stock would do.'

'The ox, Mrs Trieves. The ox-tail,' said Myrtle tentatively (she had once been smacked about the head by Florence Trieves and no amount of subsequent civility could wipe away the memory).

It was true, an ox's tail had been boiled for gelatin that morning and early in the process they had saved a portion of the stock. Emerald was allowed to take some up to Smudge, with soft vegetables floating in its beaded depths, and a hunk of white bread to go with it.

Smudge received the offering graciously, propped up on her pillow.

'I'd love to stay for chattage, Smudgy, but the train's due at four, Pearl Meadows has absconded, and the house is nowhere near ready to receive the Suttons. I must rally the troops.'

'I understand,' said Smudge meekly, 'but don't expect me to eat the carrots.' And Emerald left her once more.

The two hours between one and three were spent in frenzied activity as the household – Charlotte, Emerald, Clovis (scolded to action), Florence Trieves and Myrtle – dashed from room to room, plumping, beating, polishing and straightening the cushions, tables, carpets, handrails and all manner of glass and silver ornaments that hung about the house. A family of mice were discovered in a cushion – what a perfect home for them! – but there were very few spiders; Sterne was not dirty or uncared for, only feather dusters chase off spiders better than they do small rodents and cushion-plumping is a luxury to the over-stretched. With all the mice that the cat Lloyd caught and the many more he let slip through his paws, Florence often regretted they could not roast them, entire, on skewers and suck upon their crispy, corn-fed haunches.

'They eat better than we do,' she said.

But in the kitchen, the ox's massive, meaty tongue lay in splendour upon a vast and flowered platter. It had already been skinned, and a portion of it sliced into razor-thin layers

by Florence's disciplining hand. The slices were almost translucent. They were petals; red, salty, melting, damp. The tongue, nestling in tightly curled parsley, waited keenly for its entrance to the dining room at supper. .

Florence and Myrtle had toiled long and hard with fantastic and imaginative results. As well as the emerald-green roses and glossy chocolate cake, on a high crystal stand, there were bowls of cream; before that, gherkins, as well as various gratins and slabs of pork, forced or minced, with mace, capers, thyme. The rind of bacon soldered leaner components together. There were lemons, sharpening the edges of fat, and chervil.

The house shone about itself proudly.

China bowls and glass vases held small collections of flowers from the garden: hyacinths, lily of the valley and narcissi. The smell of them, miraculous, with wax furniture polish and blue wood-smoke, went all through the rooms and in the air of the halls and stairs, too. A person might walk from a cool corridor full of the scent of lit fires into a bedroom to find the smell of damp flowers from a pot of wild violets and hot starch from the fresh sheets and flat-creased pillow cases.

Flashes of sunlight through the panes found the colours in the faded rugs, but the weather was most changeable; the rooms were just as often thrown into chill shadow, with only their blazing grates to light them.

Halting their activities and all at once, the family realised their sweating, dirt-streaked selves, and with as much hurry as had characterised their housework they set about dressing; the train was to arrive in less than an hour. The women would help one another into their under-garments. Corsets were not routinely worn at Sterne but when guests were expected, vanity more than propriety demanded them.

'Bags I first bath!' shouted Clovis, and was pursued up the stairs by Emerald.

'Let's not queue in the corridor as if we lived in a boarding house,' said Charlotte — who had known one or two of these. 'Can't we use our wash-stands? And yes, Clovis, first bath for you, or you'll be late meeting the train.'

'Tsk-tsk, it would never do to try the patience of Insignificance,' said Clovis, tearing off his collar as he disappeared into the bathroom.

'You aren't at all funny; you just think you are,' Emerald said to the closed door.

2

A DREADFUL ACCIDENT

Lady was a useful sort of pony, part cob, and well up to pulling the brougham if the journey wasn't too long nor the passengers too heavy. The car was impractically small and unreliable in comparison to the proven team of Lady and the brougham, and had been left in its stall next to Ferryman, its black wheels resting on the straw-scattered cobbles, radiator cold. Robert, having returned from his first journey to the station with Edward Swift before lunch, had the carriage ready by the front door from a quarter past three, but Clovis, as usual, was late, having suffered one of his plunges in spirits, and instead of hurrying, he oozed from the house so slowly that Robert had to examine a small split in one of his leather driving gloves to stop himself from shouting at him.

Closed against sudden showers, the carriage rolled away from the house between the yews. Robert would not trot until reaching the lanes, for fear of wrenching Lady's muscles before they softened to walking.

Myrtle began dressing Emerald's hair at quarter to four; hair that was thicker, browner and longer than her mother's but usually piled up hastily, and impatiently stuck with pins. Emerald was never sure she had found them all when she took it down at night. There was so much hair that it literally weighed her

head down, straining her neck when she was tired. The relief of letting it fall down her back, brushing it out in chunks and luxuriant handfuls at bedtime, before putting it into a loose plait for sleeping was one of the pleasures of her life (although she half-expected to find mice in it one day).

While Myrtle worked, Emerald, as slowly as she could to stave off the boredom, powdered her face. She never coloured her lips as her mother did, but she did lightly powder her face and bosom and sometimes, as now, even more lightly rouge her cheeks.

'If you fiddle with my hair much longer, Myrtle, I shall make up my face to look like a clown just to occupy myself,' she said.

'Nearly finished, Miss Em,' answered Myrtle, with her mouth full of pins, but she did not release Emerald for another twenty minutes, by which time her hair did look – she could not deny it – marvellous: improbably shiny, richly looped and piled up upon itself over a small frame, so that its height, in contrast to the creamy face below, gave her womanly jaw a kittenish proportion.

'Myrtle, you're wasted here; you could make a fortune in hair.'

'Yes, Miss Em,' said Myrtle. 'We'll put the comb in it for your party.'

'Or feathers . . .' said Emerald, and got up.

She had two gowns to wear on her birthday, and she stepped carefully into one of them now. It was an old friend, having been worn on her last two birthdays and once at Christmas with a velvet shawl to render it seasonal. She stood at the window, quite as still as she could stand, while Myrtle fastened the buttons at the back. In the main, Emerald preferred clothing she could get in and out of herself, but when she needed to, she enlisted Myrtle.

'It's five. Where *could* they be?'

Myrtle had finished buttoning. 'Unless there's anything else, Miss Em?'

'No, of course. Thank you, off you go.'

Myrtle left her and she stood biting her nails and staring towards the gate. Her room occupied the corner, and not much that happened at Sterne escaped the view from its windows, but the avenue was too dark and there were only the thickening shadows to interpret.

Viewed from the outside, Emerald reflected, she would have made a romantic picture: the young, well-proportioned woman, in the tall window of her old, well-proportioned house, nervously waiting for her guests to arrive as the afternoon sun, having made a fleeting return, glinted on the glass. Looking at the picture one wouldn't imagine the young lady was only waiting for her sulky brother, a childhood friend, the friend's mother and John Buchanan. Put that way it wasn't very exciting at all.

At the thought of John Buchanan, though, who was so very uninterested in her romantically, whose disinterested admiration had been sickeningly familial in its properness, she crossed back to the dressing table, opened a tiny pot, left there in hope by her shameless mother and dabbed her lips with a small amount of red stain. Her face was instantly lit and vital, not least because of the quick naughtiness in her eyes.

'There, to you, stuck-up John Buchanan,' she said, blowing rouged kisses and sticking out her tongue.

Smudge appeared in the doorway.

'Who are you talking to?'

'Myself. I must break the habit.' Emerald turned to her sister.

'Oh, you look beautiful!' breathed Smudge, alight. 'Pity it's only old Patience Sutton.'

'My thoughts exactly, Smudge,' said Emerald, not mentioning John.

'You look better than a girl in a storybook.'

'That's the trouble with pretty clothes, they give you ideas that are certain to be disappointed.'

'Don't say that, Em!' said Smudge, who rebelled against this cynicism. 'You can't *know* what will happen.'

It was then, as if in response – as if the countless mismatched wheels of incident had suddenly, briefly, locked together in faultless mechanism – that they heard the brougham re-enter Sterne. Extraordinarily, Lady was at a very fast trot on gravel, the wheels and hooves were unmeasured and loud, and then there was the spat of running feet on the drive and a shout.

Smudge was the first to get to the window.

'Look at Clovis! He's shouting!'

Emerald picked up her skirt and ran too, and they both left the room, bumping into each other, and raced towards the stairs.

They met their mother on the landing.

'What's happened?' she asked, and all three rushed down together, entering the hall just as the front door flew open.

Clovis, out of breath and very white in the face, with his arms flung wide, announced, 'There's been a dreadful accident!'

The women surged to meet him as Smudge hung back, trembling.

'God! Where?' uttered Charlotte.

'On a branch line!' The answer was peculiar somehow; a branch line? Which one? And where?

'*A branch line?*' echoed Emerald.

They could hear Robert shouting for Stanley, and the muffled frenzy of hooves and wheels on cobbles approaching from behind the house.

'Yes,' said Clovis, 'a carriage came clean off the tracks—'

'What about Patience?' Emerald was horrified.

'No, no, she's here,' Clovis said, and stepped aside.

There, behind him, with a pinched, anxious face and a neat straw hat with flowers on the brim, was the meticulous Patience Sutton. Emerald was flooded with relief and the happiness of reunion, and embraced her.

'Patience! Are you all right?'

Patience looked very shaken. 'Emerald!' she said. 'Yes . . . it wasn't our train, you see, thankfully, but – poor things – it was one on a branch line.' Again, this branch line.

'But where was it?' Emerald glimpsed a tall figure on the gravel behind Patience that certainly wasn't Camilla Sutton. 'And who on earth is *that?*'

Patience was confused.

'That's *Ernest.*'

'Ernest? Where's your mother?'

'We sent a telegram.'

'Really?'

Charlotte, who, in her solipsism had neglected to pass on the news of Camilla Sutton's indisposition, cut in, 'Clovis, was anybody killed?'

'I don't know,' answered he. 'The point is, they need to put people up here, at Sterne. We're to send the brougham and the cart. Here's Robert with it—'

'Put people up here?' said Charlotte. 'Whatever for?'

Clovis, in his haste, was abrupt. 'It happened very near here, you see, the passengers—'

'We didn't hear anything,' said Charlotte, wonderingly.

'No, Mother, of course not! But it was miles from any station.'

Emerald saw that the person Patience had named as her brother Ernest, whom she remembered as slight and rabbit-like

in his mildness, had removed his jacket to help Stanley back Ferryman between the shafts of the cart, while Robert hitched him to it.

'But who told you to send the carriage?' she asked.

'And what *can* you mean, *we are to put people up*?' Charlotte was indignant.

'We met a man on the road. A train guard.'

He was interrupted by Patience, who in a clear voice said, 'I think he was a porter.'

Clovis turned to her. '*What?*'

'I think he was a *porter* not a guard,' said Patience patiently.

'He was a guard,' repeated Clovis.

'No, definitely a porter, on a bicycle.'

Clovis cast her a violent look. 'All right!'

She was unmoved. 'Yes. Yes, he was. I'm sure of it. He had a porter's cap.'

'Well, you're wrong. But at any rate, whatever he was, he was in a lather and he said there had been an accident and we were to send for help.'

'So we came here,' finished Patience, and smiled up at Clovis who, ignoring her, continued, 'We're to get passengers up here from Tibbets Cross and then wait for the Railway.'

'Was it George?' asked Charlotte densely.

'No, Mother, it wasn't *George* – I know *George* – it was another man, an older man. He said the best thing is to—'

'Do you mean older than that fellow who helped us at the station?' enquired Patience, arranging her mother-of-pearl cuff-buttons one by one. 'Oh no, I don't think he was. Was that George? If it was, I rather think this man was very much younger.'

Emerald was distracted from the exchange by the drama taking place behind them. Ernest and the grooms were grappling with horses and vehicles. She couldn't see Ernest's face but watched him place a hand firmly on Ferryman's neck

while the other gripped his bridle. The hunter Ferryman wasn't used to being in harness and was plunging about in the traces, kicking up the gravel.

'I tell you he was grey-haired! But do you think it *matters* what age the fellow was?' Clovis was saying to Patience.

'Clovis,' said Emerald, not taking her eyes from the scene, 'stop squabbling and see to the horse.'

He obeyed her, gratefully, just as Florence Trieves entered the hall behind Smudge, and laid her hands on the child's bony shoulders.

'What's happened?'

'There's been a train accident,' said Charlotte.

'On a branch line somewhere,' put in Emerald.

'And we are to take care of the passengers. Nobody seems to be able to agree on what has happened,' said Charlotte, much perturbed, 'but Sterne is to be some sort of stopping place for the survivors, it seems, while the Railway comes to some arrangement.'

'Great heavens,' said Florence Trieves, her fingers flying up and working the watch on her breast tensely. Then, 'God!' she cried, seeing the men, outside, preoccupied with fighting Ferryman, who was taking ever more serious exception to being walked backwards, and shrieking in a very high-pitched voice for so large a horse.

The women all emerged from the house to watch, Smudge clinging to Florence's skirts in delighted horror.

'Whoa!' cried Robert, as the animal stormed forward.

Clovis was thrown back by Ferryman's great head, and stepped on Ernest's jacket on the gravel. Bending, he picked it up, shook it out, and put it over the horse's head as a blindfold.

'That's Ernest's jacket!' squeaked Patience, but the horse, in darkness now, was disorientated and in another moment between the shafts of the cart at last.

Ernest and Robert set about buckling the straps. Emerald couldn't help noticing that Ernest, although she could still only see the back of him, had broad and straight shoulders, and stood half a head taller than Robert.

'Now, look here, Emerald,' said Clovis, 'we don't need you. I'll go in the cart with Stanley, Robert can drive the brougham; the rest of you can stay here.'

'I don't see why!' Emerald was indignant.

'If you don't mind my saying, Miss Em,' said Robert, turning to her, 'there's no need of either of you. We shall have more room for the passengers if you'll stay put. And we'd best be off, like the porter said.'

Emerald made a noise that wasn't quite, but amounted to 'Hmph!' and Charlotte, mistress of the house, spoke at last.

'Yes, Robert, quite right; you and Stanley can manage. Emerald and Clovis, stay here. Off you go.'

Clovis heaved a violent sigh and turned his back on them all.

'Right then,' said Robert firmly, and touching his cap, jumped up into the cart, hauling Ferryman neatly around into a semicircle so as to face the yews, and slapping the reins on his recalcitrant rump.

Soon both vehicles, cart and carriage, pulled away from the house on their mission at an unprecedented trot. Those who remained, stood in the porch and watched them drive away. The avenue muffled their wheels. The sound of hooves grew fainter. They were gone.

The little group turned to go inside.

'Lord!' said Patience, pinkly. She was cheerfulness personified. 'Rather an unconventional sort of arrival! Hello, Mrs Swift. What a to-do!'

'Hello, Patience dear,' said Charlotte wanly, directing her

nose towards Patience momentarily, and delicately lifting her skirts as she re-entered the hall.

'And here's Ernest,' announced Patience.

'Hello,' said that young man, joining them, in his shirtsleeves and slightly out of breath.

'Yes . . .' Charlotte blinked towards him and her eyes widened. The coquette within, unvanquished by her approaching fiftieth birthday, shook out her feathers. '*Mr* Sutton now, I suppose?' she enquired. 'Or should I call you Doctor?'

'Not yet, I'm afraid.'

'Weren't you needed at the scene of this ghastly event?'

'Apparently not. I offered.'

'Of course you did.'

Ernest seemed not to know how to take this last, and kept silent.

They were all safely inside.

Emerald closed the door firmly.

'They won't return with these survivors in less than an hour,' she said, gathering her thoughts, or trying to.

'I wonder how many people they'll find down there and what state they'll be in,' put in Patience, with enthusiasm.

'Did this railway person say any more than "survivors"?'

'Nothing helpful,' said Clovis. 'It was all rather . . . rushed.'

'Wasn't it?' agreed Patience, and then stopped in her tracks. 'Little Imogen?' she said warmly, noticing the child for the first time. 'I haven't seen you since you were seven years old! I remember you when you were the smudge-in-a-cot!'

Her voice tumbled over Smudge like the shivering glassy fringes on a chandelier. Smudge smiled up at her.

'I like your dress,' she said obsequiously.

The dress was of primrose-coloured muslin, with clinging

lace cuffs half-covering her hand; no trace of the faddish orient for Patience.

'Thank you very much. I like your nightie.'

The family, all at once, noticed Smudge's grubby nightdress and bare feet.

'Heavens, Smudge!' said Charlotte, pink blooms of embarrassment appearing on her neck. 'You can't go about like that!'

'It was the dreadful accident! I had to come down!'

'She did, Mother; don't be cross with her.' Emerald was conciliatory, seeing rage flare in Charlotte against her youngest child.

'Imogen! Go!'

Patience and Ernest affected deafness while Smudge, chastened, began to slink away. An uncomfortable silence ensued.

All their preparations had been in vain. Emerald's birthday celebrations had begun in confusion and disarray. She cast about for something sensible to say, something that would reassure her mother and friends that an hospitable timetable would be re-established, and was about to suggest the library, and tea, when she halted, arrested in movement like a musical statue.

She was obeying a prompt, an instinct left over, perhaps, from an earlier time; the instinct that stops a mouse in its short-sighted tracks when a cat is watching it from a chair; that makes a dog lying by the fire tremble, and whimper, when there is no one near to see.

And as she stopped, there came, of a sudden, a hard gust of wind behind her, striking her through her dress, forcefully, blowing all thoughts of convention from her mind. The heavy front door was closed, but the chill struck Emerald's back, finding its way through the jamb and hinges – through the solid wood itself, it seemed, as a cold wave will sometimes catch one as one leaves the sea and knock the breath from the body.

Halted, she looked around the faces of her friends and family, who, all unnoticing, stood about awaiting the offers of sustenance or rest they had every reason to expect. But the breeze had caused the air to whisper and creak loudly all around and she was compelled to investigate it.

'What is it?' said Clovis as Emerald turned her head to look over her shoulder.

She walked to the door, opened it and looked out into the squally air. Shivering, looking away to her right, far down the drive, she strained her eyes at the emerging vision.

Clovis arrived at her side and followed the direction of her gaze. He gave a low whistle.

'My word,' he said, 'they're here.'

They all hurried to the door, Smudge peering around Florence's skirt.

It was true: a small group of people was emerging from the gloom of the drive onto the gravel, slowly and all together. It was difficult to see how many of them there were.

'They must have missed Robert . . . How queer!' cried Emerald. 'Quick, Mother!'

Florence Trieves and Smudge stayed in the doorway, as Emerald, Charlotte, Clovis, Patience and Ernest moved forward to greet the survivors.

It did make for an odd-looking meeting: the many vibrant colours of the household — party-peacock blues and greens, bright copper — approaching the travelling drabness of the shocked and drifting passengers.

'Can you see the porter?' said Patience, craning, her view obscured by other people's shoulders.

'No,' said Clovis, as Emerald, ahead, neared the first of them.

'Didn't you see the carriage and cart?' she asked them. 'Did the Railway send you up? Are you hurt?'

But none of them answered.

'Have you come from the accident?' asked Clovis. 'We were told to expect you.'

They lifted their faces as one, like a herd of cattle turning their heads in a field to watch one pass by. Shock had brought the group into a mass, as if the experience they had endured had bonded them in strange and bloodless numbness.

'Welcome to Sterne,' Emerald tried again, briskly. 'I'm Emerald Torrington. You must have had the most distressing time.'

Clovis, at her side, glanced down at her and she met his eyes briefly, reassured, and looked back to the shifting passengers. They gazed on her in dazed bedazzlement.

Now that she was nearer to them, she saw that they were not particularly dressed alike, as she had first thought, but only made uniform by dint of their overcoats, scarves, hats and all the other monochrome garb of the journeying. Now she could see them more clearly, snatches of red from a dress, ivy-green on a man's waistcoat – other colours – gradually began to show themselves.

And then, quietly, one of them spoke. She was a pale young woman, ash-blonde hair drawn back from a homely, round face, the skin of which had the same sallow hue as her hair, and there was a gappy, lumped, black woollen muffler bound thickly about her throat, as if to keep her head on her shoulders.

'We've been sent here first,' she said. 'We are ever so grateful you'll have us . . . Will you?'

Her eyes met Emerald's pleadingly, so that Emerald was embarrassed all at once – simply by being Emerald, in all her vigour, standing before this creature.

'Of course,' she said, adding lamely, 'You poor things. Do follow us.' And she turned smartly, took Clovis's warm hand in hers and led the procession back to the house.

The feeble crowd trailed after them as the whole group made their way towards Florence and Smudge in the doorway.

And so, with many exclamations of welcome and comfort, the slow survivors were guided into Sterne.

With Clovis dispatched on Levi to fetch back Robert and Stanley, the women were grouped around the butcher's block in the pantry. It had seemed the best place to have a private discussion.

'Perhaps the wounded were taken off by ambulance,' suggested Emerald.

Fresh blood, pink with rinsing, ran from the block between the women. There were shelves on all four sides, crammed with jars, meats, labelled tins, jugs (covered), terrines and all manner of delicious-smelling foodstuffs.

'It's almost six already! Did anybody say when the people from the Railway might arrive and relieve us of them?' asked Charlotte.

'I'm afraid not.'

'Will they be taken to another train?'

'I don't know, Mother! Ask Clovis when he gets back; he was the one who spoke to the porter.'

'I thought he was a guard.'

'Whatever he was, he was the one who sent them all here,' said Emerald firmly; 'and he, presumably, had some plan as to their removal. We can't leave them in the morning room forever.'

The passengers had been deposited in the morning room with Myrtle, who was under instructions to light the fire – an inconvenience, as the morning room's was the one fire in the house unlaid, it being the afternoon.

('The morning room indeed,' she'd said. 'Why can't they all be put in the barn until the Railway sort out their own

difficulties? Don't see why the family has to be burdened, not with them all so muddled and wandering; it's not reasonable. And me all on my own. I'll wring Pearl's neck on Monday.'

But still, she had heaved the ash *out* and the coal *in*, and lit the slender kindling once more, watched all the while by the gloomy passengers, who stood about her in their overcoats, whispering to one another.

'Have they never seen a housemaid before? *Wallpaper* a shock to them?' raged Myrtle to herself, toiling. But her rage had subsided directly upon leaving the room. In fact, as she attended to her usual, very pressing duties, she found she forgot about the uninvited guests in the morning room altogether.

The Suttons, likewise, had been deposited at the other end of the house – once, that is, Ernest had been dissuaded from examining each and every passenger for injuries. Having not spoken more than a word or two to any one of the family, he was a fountain of verbiage when offered the possibility of in-the-field medical rehearsals. Herded away by Charlotte, he had been forced to content himself with passing between them asking, 'Any faintness? Any pain? Sir? Madam? Light-headedness?', before at last accompanying his sister to the library, at which point Emerald and Charlotte had made their excuses and escaped to the pantry to discuss necessities.

'If we can just give some *appearance* of normality,' fretted Charlotte, twisting her handkerchief, 'until the Railway come.'

'I just wish it hadn't happened on your birthday,' said Florence.

'Tosh.' Emerald picked up a small china jug and sniffed it.

'Lemon cream,' said Florence, with satisfaction.

Emerald lifted the tiny cloth and dipped her little finger into the jug. 'Oh lovely,' she uttered, sucking it.

Florence was smug. 'People don't always think of cloves for lemons.'

'Do you think we might stick to the point, Mrs Trieves?' Charlotte snapped. Her vagueness had all but disappeared. 'My suggestion is this, and it's not a revolutionary one: we will give them *all* cups of tea, Suttons, passengers and all. Surely we can find enough cups.' She remembered her status. 'Not my domain; I'll leave it up to you, Mrs Trieves. And when we have spoken to the Railway we'll have a clearer idea how inconvenienced we shall be, and for how long. Agreed?'

'Tea?' said Florence, tiredly, as it seemed to her the most labour-intensive and least productive substance on the earth. Boiling, steeping, assembling china, carrying things about, and for what? A feeble drink unchanged by passing through the body. She recalled having loved it once; now it was water to her. 'Yes, I suppose,' she said.

'Yes, agreed, Mother.'

'And we all need to keep a very sharp eye on the ornaments and trinkets: I don't want to wave goodbye to the sorry lot of them and half the silver, too, so pass that on to the boy and guests, if you will. And we must at least cling to dignity. Heavens, I wish Edward were here.'

For the first time in the two years of knowing him Emerald, too, almost appreciated her stepfather – the idea of him, at least.

The three women left the pantry to see about appearing normal. Charlotte wrapped her stole around herself, Emerald lifted her old friend the russet tea-gown from the grease on the kitchen floor, and Florence rustled in her dreary black behind, to stay in the kitchen and get the water on for her enemy tea.

Charlotte shuddered as she and Emerald passed the morning-room, its door now firmly shut.

'We must contact the Railway directly,' she said. 'Oh, but first . . . *the Suttons*.'

She said this last word in such tones of ghastliness that Emerald was forced to remark, 'You might be nicer to Patience, Mother; she can see you despise her.'

'Despise her? Whatever do you mean? I very much admire the Modern Female Academic. I'm not sure little Patience quite fits my preconception, but her mind is likely as sharp as a little rat-trap once she stops simpering.'

'Oh, Mother!'

They were interrupted by a shout of laughter from behind the closed door, causing both women to leap sideways like startled ponies.

'What on earth?' Charlotte was pale.

'Dare we look?'

'Lord, I suppose they're going to be rowdy and unmanageable now they're warming up and realising their good fortune.'

'Must you speak so damningly about everybody? They've had a terrible ordeal!' blazed Emerald and, distancing herself from her mother, she opened the morning room door, defiantly generous.

'Everything to your satisfaction?' she enquired gaily, but whoever had laughed was now struck dumb.

They even drew back from her, as if she were going to reprimand them. It was hard to imagine the raucous laugh had issued from this still and staring mass. They seemed beyond speech.

Emerald glanced over her shoulder for support, but Charlotte, predictably, had disappeared; Emerald caught sight of her treacherous back as she darted away around the corner.

She looked about the faces turned towards her. On the drive there had seemed fewer of them, ten perhaps, now there was more like twelve or fourteen – but she couldn't count heads and speak at the same time and she didn't want to appear rude.

'Myrtle is going to bring tea for you,' she announced.

'Thank you,' uttered a man with his hands held out towards the raw fire. He had a woman at his side who might have been his wife, and she spoke next.

'Any word from the Railway?' she said, and another put in, 'They didn't say how long it would be.' And another whispered urgently, 'We really must get on,' to which a few *yeses* and *ayes* were added.

'I am about to telephone them. I shall let you know directly. I do apologise for . . . your delay.' She felt like a railway employee herself, saying it, but she didn't know what else *to* say. She took a step backwards and shut the door again, firmly.

Harsh judgements aside, they were an unnerving lot, and she hoped they wouldn't come *spilling out*.

She reached the hall where her cowardly mother was lurking on the stairs.

'I'm going to my room.'

'What about the Suttons?' hissed Emerald, indicating the library door.

'I've no idea, Emerald: you see to them.'

Emerald was an intuitive young woman. She saw through her mother's glib pretence and attempted to put aside her own dismay at being deserted by her parent to say kindly, 'It's all right, you know, Mother; it doesn't matter.'

'Whatever can you mean?' responded Charlotte irritably.

'All these people; honestly, Mother, the Suttons don't mind.'

Charlotte paused, her hand still on the banister. 'Emerald,' she said icily, 'if you imagine I care a fig for what Insignificance Sutton or her owlish brother think—'

'Here, sh!' Emerald glanced guiltily towards the closed door. 'Come away – go up!'

They scuttled up the stairs and Emerald led her mother firmly to the safety of her bedroom door, where she continued,

in a low voice, 'I do think you care a fig. I think you care a great many figs. Camilla Sutton was part of what you always dotingly describe as your wonderfully conventional child-hood—' She broke off. 'Why didn't she come, incidentally?'

'Oh, she sent a rotten telegram. Something about flu. I shouldn't think that was it for a *minute.*'

'You might have told me. Ernest doesn't look a bit like her. Why would she lie?'

Charlotte had balled her handkerchief again, and now plucked at it, distractedly, a child, fidgeting to get away, forced to respond, and petulant.

'How should I know? Perhaps she despises me. Having no money. Marrying Edward.'

Emerald squirmed under the weight of these confidences. She ought to entertain the Suttons, she must telephone the Railway – yet here she was, once more forced to support her drooping, weak-stemmed, climbing vine of a sun-seeking mother. She drew a steadying breath.

'Ma, Edward is a fine barrister. I should think he is a very respectable person to have married.' Now she found herself defending her stepfather; his absence in a crisis was doing her view of him no end of good.

'Yes, but – well, you know – his arm . . . and nobody knows him. And she's one of the bridge and calling-cards set, and seems to be connected to very high-born types. And I'm . . . well, I'm not.'

'But you never have been, Mother. I'm surprised you should suddenly mind now.'

'I just mind her throwing me over, and then sending out her tedious little spies to see what we're up to, and then we're up to *this* – these people! It's humiliating.'

'Those tedious little spies, as you call them,' said Emerald hotly, 'happen to be my good friend Patience – who may be

as conventional as a box of bricks, but is also perfectly sweet. And her brother, who is——' she faltered, '– too, and another perfectly fine person.'

Charlotte became vague.

'Oh, Emerald, they're divine. I'm going to lie down and think what can be done.'

'Well, Mother, you go on. Only – *please* don't worry. I shall telephone the Railway, all those people will be gone soon, and we'll have the most dignified supper you ever saw. And don't forget, John Buchanan is coming!'

She could have kicked herself for getting her mother's hopes up in the John Buchanan department, but Charlotte smiled her most loving smile at her.

'So he is,' she said and went off into her room mollified. 'Keep an eye on the silver!' was her last instruction, muffled by the door.

Emerald hurried back downstairs to see to the Suttons. *Out of sight, out of mind*, she comforted herself, regarding her parent, but she may as well have been speaking about the poor, shocked passengers, for in her haste to fulfil her duties, like Myrtle, she had clean forgotten them, and altogether over-looked the necessity of telephoning the Railway. She did not stop to consider that the morning room was not large, or that the fire that warmed the passengers might be dying.

Whilst Charlotte remained in her room with her mere dreams of etiquette, Emerald, stalwart, practised it, entertaining Ernest and Patience in the library despite unusual events, displaced passengers and Clovis's sulks. Having obliged by fetching back the grooms, he now felt he had carte blanche to be blackish.

'Can't tell if it's nighttime now, or just *weather*,' he said, flinging himself onto the window seat and glancing askance at the squally afternoon.

The fire, neglected, had sunk down onto itself. Ernest threw apple logs onto it, and wrestled with the coal scuttle as Emerald poured the tea (brought in by Myrtle, who badly needed a change of apron after lighting the morning room fire, but had not yet seen to it).

Smudge had not been able to drag herself away to dress and knelt slavishly at Patience's feet, gazing up at her. Patience stared into the flames and allowed her face to relax the expression of keen enthusiasm she routinely maintained. Exhaustion swept through her tiny frame.

'I must say I'm relieved we didn't die in a train crash,' she said.

Emerald smiled at her. 'I am, too, Patience; it would have quite spoilt my party,' she said, and handed her a cup of tea.

'Thank you. I wonder if anybody *did die!*' said Patience gloomily, wrinkling her delicate brow. The china cup trembled against the saucer.

There came a rumbling sound from near the window.

'Did you utter, dear brother?' said Emerald, fixing Clovis with what she hoped was a granite look.

'I said,' Clovis shook himself violently, like a wet dog and sat up, '"Has that only just occurred to you now?" Whether anybody perished, that is.'

Patience and Emerald exchanged glances. 'We haven't exactly had much opportunity to talk about it!' said Patience and turned her small shoulders pointedly away from him.

'*Brrr!*' exclaimed Clovis, shivering dramatically and making them all jump.

'I should think,' began Ernest in a measured tone, 'that when the railway fellow said "a dreadful accident" he must have been referring to fatalities. Injuries, at least.'

'Yes,' said Patience. 'The porter *did* say "dreadful"; one can only imagine the worst . . .'

Clovis ignored Ernest to continue baiting Patience.

'The *guard* didn't give us any other details, though, Miss Sutton. Did he? You're merely guessing.'

Patience was slapped down, but only momentarily: she was two years older than Clovis and had decided he wasn't to be considered as a potential attachment. There were plenty of older, more serious men who liked her at home in Berkshire and at Cambridge, where she had recently begun to read History, and she had no designs whatsoever on the boy Clovis Torrington. Still, she was disconcerted how often her thoughts hovered tremblingly around his fledgling Romantic looks – even during the years they had not seen one another. When last they had met, she had been a cheerful seventeen and he, at fifteen, boisterous and fair. She did not count his father's funeral as a visit, but even at that sad occasion she had felt an unsettling urge to stroke him, to put her arms around him. At the time she had put it down to sisterly compassion, but now her fluttering pulse gave the lie to that rationale.

History and the heart notwithstanding, the balance of power, Patience decided, remained firmly with her. After all, he couldn't read her mind and wasn't to know how arresting she found him to look at.

She glanced away, saying warmly, 'Oh, well done, Ernest.' The fire was once more throwing dazzling flames into the wide chimney. Ernest sat down.

'You should have seen to the fire, Clovis,' Emerald said tightly. He was belligerent.

'What on earth do we keep servants for?'

Emerald resisted biting him hard on the nose. She had made a promise not to quarrel with her brother in front of the guests but he was so extremely vexing she wasn't sure she could keep it.

'It was awfully good of you,' she said to Ernest sweetly.

'Not at all,' he answered, dusting off his knees. She noticed, sympathetically, that he was a little too large for the chair, which was a button-seated affair, with short mahogany legs like a Dachshund.

Looking at him now, as she did, fleetingly, from beneath her lashes, she found that contrary to her earlier impression, she could easily recognise the boy she had known. The not-unpleasingly asymmetrical face, narrow in childhood, had grown into the aquiline nose and square jaw that in skinny youth had dominated it. The garish hair had darkened to a deep brownish-red, but the eyes, that had been, it's true, before the enforced wearing of a patch, disconcertingly at odds with one another, were still – she risked another glance – frustratingly unknowable. Hidden behind glass, they had been a mystery to her as long as she'd known him; she had never wondered about them until now. Ernest himself affected not to notice her scrutiny but inwardly he smarted beneath her gaze, that, even tempered by soft lashes and quick looks, blazed. 'Oh, lord,' he thought; helplessly, 'She's laughing at me.'

'There's a hiding place in this room, isn't there?' said Patience suddenly.

'You remember!' Emerald smiled, the memory of childhood games of hide-and-seek easing the adult tensions now prevalent.

'I remember there *was* one . . .' Patience glanced about her at the walls and shelves.

The library – panelled and polished – was the most pleasing room imaginable. When Charlotte and Horace had first come to Sterne (Charlotte hauling, wheeling or otherwise trans-porting the squally, lace-bound baby Emerald), the library had been used as a billiard room, and the shelves held a collection

of vile majolica, or were otherwise desecrated. The Torringtons blamed the Victorians and set about fulfilling the room's proper destiny, initially with a hundred-odd favourite books from their previous (suburban, undistinguished) house, and then with a trickle of honoured additions from thrilling visits to auction houses. In later, leaner years, equally satisfying forays into fluff-cornered antiquarian bookshops filled the gleaming room to the brim.

'I think . . . it's over here,' said Patience, rising, and setting down her teacup (that now *somebody* would have to clean and dry and put away). She went over to the window, and the deep recess of its seat, knocking the panelling to the left of it experimentally.

'Wrong!' sang Smudge gleefully.

'I remember hiding in it with you, Emerald – and you, Ernest!'

Clovis turned onto his side so as not to face her and affected deep exhaustion.

'I hid in it all afternoon once, and nobody found me at all,' boasted Smudge, forgetting she hadn't told anyone she was hiding and had not been missed. 'I fell asleep!' she crowed.

Noticing Smudge, crouched barefoot on the floor in her filthy nightgown, all the things she must do before the evening might successfully begin rushed into Emerald's mind, along with the chilling recollection that the morning room was stuffed with strange survivors, her mother was hiding, her brother was a solipsistic fiend, they were a woman down in the kitchen – and *she* had yet to telephone the blasted Railway (who might in all civility have telephoned Sterne, having inconvenienced everybody like this).

'Smudge, do you think you might dress?' she said. 'You can't sit about like that. Off you go, there's a good child; we're all going to.'

'I'm going to look iridescent lovely,' said Smudge, heaving herself up. 'You'll swoon.'

'Oh good: well, off you go.'

With regretful glances at Patience, Smudge left the room.

'What must you think of us?' said Emerald when she'd gone. 'I haven't shown either of you to your rooms, and you must be desperate to – to –' She gestured towards Ernest's disarranged garments. He must have left the house quite well-turned out, but now he was woefully messy; his jacket, having been used by Clovis as a blindfold for Ferryman, might have been anywhere out in the windy night, so he was in shirtsleeves, a missing cufflink causing one stiff cuff to flap about. Manners prevented him from rolling it up. His shoes – brown brogues – were muddy, and both the shirt and the leg of his trousers had long streaks of greenish slime that looked permanent. (Ferryman had been in his field, quietly grazing, when he was called upon to be hitched to the cart and his slobber was thus spring green and staining.)

'I don't know if your things have been taken off the brougham – it's all been so unusual . . . Let's go up. Clovis can chase up Robert about your things – can't you, Clo? How would that be?'

'Capital,' said Patience. 'Lead the way, Em. And don't worry about it all, we'll have tremendous fun despite everything, I'm sure.'

Emerald, with sudden gratitude, kissed her friend's cheek and took her hand.

'Clovis!' she rapped out harshly. 'Stop lolling about like a fat dog, go and find Robert and make sure everything's brought in!'

Patience took her brother's arm and the cheerful threesome left the room.

Emerald imagined the black telephone, standing on its

table under the stairs, was leaning out and craning up at her reproachfully, as they processed up the main stair, peering over their shoulders towards the rooms down the corridor. No sound came from the morning room, but they could not ignore Florence Trieves's carrying voice shouting at Myrtle for more hot water.

Upstairs, it was as if there had been no accident on a branch line. Everything was in order. Patience and Ernest were shown the direction of the bathroom (which had not moved since their last visit, nor been updated) and Patience exclaimed delightedly at everything. To Emerald's chagrin, Charlotte's door remained firmly shut.

'I wonder if you'll like the present I've brought you,' said Patience, bouncing on the balls of her feet as she walked. 'It's such ages since we've seen one another, you might have changed absolutely.'

'I don't think I've changed at all,' said Emerald, knowing herself to be lying, but there was a mist between her and her childhood self, made up of grief and multiple small denials, and she did not care to try to look through it.

'Here's your room,' she said.

It was the room next to Emerald's and had the same wallpaper: large peacocks glancing naughtily over their shoulders at little bowls spilling over with foreign, segmented fruit and grapes.

'How perfect! It's just as I remember!' Patience exclaimed, clapping her hands in delight.

'Supper is supposed to be at eight . . . It's half past six now. Shall we *say* eight, at least?'

'Let's say it.'

'And shall I send Myrtle in to you at – when would you like her?'

'Is she quick?'

'Lightning.'

'And good at hair?'

'Inspired.'

'I don't want to corner her.'

'Oh, footle.'

'Seven?'

'Done.'

'Bye-ee!' said Patience and beamingly closed her door. Ernest was staring at the ceiling.

'You're just this way,' Emerald said, feeling as though she were interrupting him in something.

He fiddled with his sleeve as they walked together towards his room, absorbed in trying to draw the two sides together.

Emerald opened the door, revealing the room's stripes and washstand. She was unaccountably embarrassed to be standing on the threshold with the transformed, unexpected Ernest, so much taller than she and composed by manhood. She hadn't thought about him beyond the obligatory *'and how is your brother?'* in her letters, for years. And yet, if somebody had said the name Ernest Sutton to her, mental pictures would have come tumbling into her mind: herself and a red-haired boy investigating grasshoppers, worms, mould; games with Patience and Clovis; hide-and-seek, blind man's bluff. Sterne had brimmed with childhood then, and easy, predictable, two-armed parents. Now their younger selves had been replaced by her reserve and his startling manliness.

Standing there on the brink of the bedroom, it occurred to Emerald that the medical student Ernest Sutton had most probably seen — she wasn't sure how to put it, even to herself — naked women's bodies. They would most likely have been corpses, but even so, they would still have been unclothed. The thought was a disturbing one. The bed's mahogany curls leered at her, lewdly.

Ernest himself didn't seem to have noticed the bedroom at all, or the fact that he was standing next to Emerald Torrington's unclothed body with only thin air and a few layers of fabric between them. He simply entered the room and, without another word, closed the door in her face.

With his absence from her sight, the spell was broken and she returned to herself, sharply.

'Odd fish,' she said to herself, then, 'Well, he always was.'

She turned away just as Robert and Stanley came into the corridor from the back stairs, all outside boots and shirtsleeves, smelling of horse and bonfire and carrying a large trunk with suitcases piled on the top of it.

'Oh good,' said Emerald. She stood aside to let them pass. 'Is Ferryman over his huff about being hooked up to the cart, Robert?'

'He's eating up nicely, Miss Em, thank you.'

'Glad to hear it.' And she cantered off down the stairs.

As she disappeared, Ernest opened the door to Robert and separated his baggage from his sister's.

'Thanks very much. Good man. What's your name?' he asked.

'Robert, sir, and my son, Stanley.'

Robert was, on balance, an attractive, cleanly shaved fellow, but he had a large pustular boil near his collar. The skin around it was reddened, but it had not yet come to a head. Ernest's fingers were curious to examine it but he kept his hands to his sides. It looked as if it had a great deal of heat in it.

'Perhaps you ought have that boil seen to, Robert,' he said. 'It looks nasty.'

'Been soaking it with vinegar, sir, and milk,' was his reply. 'But it does throb, sir, something harsh.'

'I should think it does.' Ernest frowned at him. 'Make sure the poultice is hot, to draw it out. If it doesn't come to a head

by tomorrow night, come along to see me, would you?' He made a stabbing motion with his right hand and his spectacles glinted. Robert looked alarmed, as well he might. 'I'm a doctor,' explained Ernest.

Father and son, turning their caps in their hands, had been backing out of the room, and now paused. 'Ah,' said Robert.

'Or very soon to be one, at any rate; I'm in my last year of study.'

'Oh, I see, sir.'

'But boils are strictly first-year stuff!' Ernest went on, to reassure them further.

'Well, that would save me taking a trip into the village on my afternoon off, then,' said Robert cautiously, not quite over the impression of Ernest's violent mime.

'Quite.'

'Thank you, sir. Come on, Stanley.' And they both touched their forelocks to him and left.

Ernest unstrapped his suitcase and set about unpacking, murmuring to himself.

'Splendid fellow . . . shame no casualties . . . can't be helped . . . household ailments . . .' He paused, remembering he ought not talk to himself, a folded shirt in each hand, and went to the window.

Looking out into the gloaming, he could see the clean, semicircular edge of the lawn but nothing beyond; a mist had come between Sterne and the county, like the quick drop of a stage curtain.

He felt himself to be absolutely in the present: the milky fog; the close, thick walls of the house; the feeling of the shirts weighing evenly in his hands; all were crystallised in a moment that was, for Ernest, rare in its connectedness.

'This is a most beautiful house,' he said aloud, with warm satisfaction. He had been working very hard in recent weeks,

immersed in the clinging formaldehyde air of varnished laboratories, and had barely a moment to think, certainly none to anticipate Saturday to Monday at Sterne for Emerald Torrington's birthday, which had been sprung upon him by his mother's (quite authentic) influenza.

Emerald Torrington. In childhood he had taken her all as a package, the very *Emerald* of her was assumed – but sitting in the library, covered in horse-spit, with her gazing upon him had been almost intolerable. His maturity gave urgency to her beauty, creamy flesh to the bones of desire. Where once he had been content to be merely in the presence of her untutored glamour, now he could not help but want to have her for his own – however unworthy he felt himself to be. He smiled. *No, Ernest Sutton, she is not for you*, he thought to himself. *Not for we squinty mortals, a girl like that.* (His squint may have been corrected, but his view of himself had not.) And he continued to lay out his things, not minding at all the unusualness of the day so far, and enjoying the prospect of the evening ahead.

In the hall, at last quite alone, Emerald lifted the telephone and unhooked the receiver. Behind her, down the corridor, she could just hear the travellers in the morning room. They were talking and laughing, and the thick noise of them was out of place, somehow, in Sterne's halls and passages, which were used to the family and the dogs.

She pressed the cool cup of the receiver to her ear and the plaited cord lay against her forearm like a dead worm. The line was choked with interference at the best of times, and now the clamorous teatime sounds made it hard to hear anything.

Horace Torrington, with characteristic enthusiasm for all things new and expensive, had had the telephone installed in

the last year of his life. A great proportion of the calls that had been made on the machine had been to Dr Death. Emerald had come to associate the telephone, black as it was, with mourning, and had never relished using it since. The family's delight and wonder at its magical modernity had quickly waned beneath the greater, unlovely wonder that is the decline of the flesh and death itself. Now, Emerald sought a connection, enduring the sadness that the electrical clicks triggered in her heart, and waited for Elsie Goodwin, in the village, to notice her and speak. The line was silent, but at her back, the noise of the passengers surged, as if somebody had opened the door. She strained to listen until, at length, there came the familiar crackle that normally prefaced Elsie's flat, high-pitched voice shout, '*Exchange?!*', but then – then she heard nothing more.

Elsie's greeting, from her home and shop, the Post Office parlour, was not handed down the loose-strung wire miles to rest in Emerald's ear. She could hear nothing but a low hiss, like wind down a long drain.

'Drat it,' she said, as she replaced the receiver, and the sounds of the stranded passengers subsided behind her. She went away upstairs and in a few moments, she had forgotten all about them.

But in the morning room, the passengers wondered what was to happen next. They had been sent here with no proper explanations. They were grateful for the tea and the fire, but their journey had been calamitous, and violent in its interruption, and they should have liked to be getting on.

'I should just like to be getting on,' said a tiny woman, her sickly infant pressed against her breast.

'An accident is a terrible thing to meet with,' uttered a hollow-faced man, the firelight dancing in the sockets of his eyes.

They were unsatisfied. A hunger had come upon them since the accident, born of shock perhaps, an emptiness that the tea had soothed but now returned, voraciously.

'One of us should go and see about things,' said one, and others agreed.

'Yes, one of us should go and see.'

And the crowd by the mean fire, among the strewn teacups, huddling in the corners and on all the seats, nodded their heads and murmured.

'Hungry,' they said, shifting and clutching their garments about themselves.

'Ever so hungry.'

'Hungry.'

It was a quarter to seven. Florence Trieves had sweated through the thick black silk beneath her arms and between her breasts. Her thighs were hot, the damp cotton of her drawers rubbed in grubby wrinkles between them, and her feet had swollen inside her tight boots. She had been marching from kettle to chopping board; from kitchen to drawing room; from slicing to stirring, to delicate, hasty, finger-trembling laying of morsels on precious plates until she thought she'd sob.

'Mrs Trieves?' Myrtle's round, shiny face was enquiring things of her, as it had all afternoon, as it had all day, apart from sudden disappearances, that seemed to last forever just exactly when she was most needed.

'Ma'am?'

'Yes, where have you *been*, Myrtle?'

'Mrs Torrington's hair, ma'am.'

Florence was distracted. 'Oh. Yes.'

'And with Pearl Meadows absent I need to finish taking water up to the rooms, and Miss Em asked me if I'd see to

Miss Sutton's hair, too, and I was wondering if I could lay the table *afterwards*, only I've still got to see to those fires.'

Florence attempted to breathe more deeply than her clothing would allow.

'Yes. Go up now, Myrtle. Take the water, and stay with Miss Sutton if she's ready for you. I'll carry on here and we'll—' She broke off, blankly staring at the wall past Myrtle's head. 'We'll . . .'

'Ma'am?'

'The passengers . . .' The grim weight of the thought of the morning room, packed with strangers in their overcoats, arrested her. 'Ma'am?' Florence felt sweat drip down the inside of one of her thin legs. She gathered herself and set her mind to the task again, speaking rapidly. 'Let me see now: there's the table, fires, wines, rooms, hot water, hair, dressing, hors d'oeuvres, all of supper, and Mrs Torrington's toilette to see to.'

'Yes, ma'am.'

Her voice rose and trembled as she added, 'And this accident . . .' She controlled herself. She always did. 'Well.' There was a silence. 'I should think we can manage that between us.'

Myrtle swallowed. 'Yes, ma'am. And Mrs Torrington *is* nearly finished.'

'Thank you. Well, off you go. Be off upstairs with that hot water.'

So Myrtle went: into the scullery to fill the enamel jugs with hot water and then up the back stairs with them, setting the steps creaking beneath their combined weight.

Smudge had two occasions to dress for: the party and her Great Undertaking. Checking the weather from her window, she noticed that not only was it quite dark now seven o'clock

had come and gone, but there was a smell of thunder on the air. Smudge couldn't have said what thunder smelled like exactly – something like lively coal-dust, perhaps – but knew that she had always known the thick scent of it, as well as that of lightning, which was sharper and apparent to everybody, like gunpowder and lemons. Yes, there was a storm coming, and when she leaned out of the window, high above the gravel, with the path that led along the side of Old House to the kitchen garden and stables tiny beneath her, like a ribbon, she could smell the air charging. She liked to think of the thick electricity in the telephone cables and the thin electricity in the air, thrilling against one another.

She sniffed the darkness bouncing off the wall of mist ahead of her, reflecting – oh so dimly – the lights of the house. The gritty stars above her head were scuddingly obscured as the storm armed itself.

'Yes,' she breathed, 'I'm glad I put on woollen stockings.'

She wore a midnight-blue velvet dress of Emerald's, much too large, and beneath it two pairs of drawers, a woollen vest, chemise and a petticoat of stiff taffeta, with one or two scorch marks from hasty ironing. The dress was too long, so she belted it all with a silk scarf of Clovis's, hoisting the dress loosely over it and feeling very pleased indeed. It was time to go down.

As she was reaching for the doorknob, it turned, slowly, all by itself.

For a moment she thought she had moved it with her intention, but then her mother came in.

'Smudge, my darling.'

Charlotte, having *hogged* poor Myrtle – there was no other word for it – was elegantly and opulently dressed in watered silk, like a sea-nymph. She wore a tiara on the rolled heights of her thick, fair hair. Although the lace at her long neck and the diamonds made Smudge want to touch her, she knew

better and held her hands behind her back. But Charlotte, ever a surprise, enveloped her daughter in bare and scented arms, allowing her stole to slip from her smooth shoulders, and then sat on the bed and took her hand.

'Are you dressed for Emerald's party?'

'Yes, Mother. That's all.' Her mother either did not notice this defence or was incurious.

'You look magnificent.'

Charlotte glanced around the room at the shabby yellow wallpaper, the thick scraped outlines of animals parading, overlapping, towards the window, smudged and complicated by extra units and false beginnings. 'And your gorgeous walls – how clever you are! Would you like to know what I have for your sister?'

'A present? Yes, what is it?'

'Promise you won't tell?'

Smudge was desperate. 'I promise!'

Charlotte, rare vision in Smudge's room, angel of approval, goddess of distraction and important things that did not concern Smudge very often, whispered delightfully in her ear, 'A kitten.'

Smudge was beyond delight.

'What colour?' she whispered, painfully.

'Not unlike you, Smudge: charcoal.'

'Will Lloyd be jealous?'

'Almost certainly he will. All cats are jealous; it doesn't mean we should let them bully us. He has his mice. And he has you.'

'Yes, he does have me. He sleeps here quite often and brings me his kills. I pretend to eat them, just to be polite, and then I throw them out of the window once—'

But Charlotte did not want to hear Smudge's stories.

'Yes, calmly, dear. The kitten came from Bowes farm. I thought we might call it Tenterhooks.'

'For its claws!'

'Will you present her with it for me at supper?'

'Oh yes! May I see it now? Please, Mother?'

'No. Not now . . .You know I don't like you in my bedroom.'
Smudge's time was up. Charlotte became vague. 'I thought a
box would be all right for it, if it weren't for too long. It's
very young.'

She stood up, and with a last kiss, left her. Smudge hugged
herself with delight.

Charlotte carefully negotiated the scullery stairs in her jade
silk slippers and opened the door at the bottom. It was not
a view to which she was accustomed, from the back of the
scullery, by the door to the Old House. She looked past
towers of washing-up, dripping, skinning-over pans, as yet
untouched, and stacks of cups, teapots, milk jugs and trays
– also unwashed – through the wide doorway and into the
kitchen, where Florence Trieves, with her back to her, tensely
worked on some invisible and evidently resistant dish, for
she uttered loudly, 'Ghastly!' and shook her head in
frustration.

Emerald, similarly absorbed, was placing pâté onto a long
dish with a fish-slice, careful not to disturb the jelly shell,
adjusting one bay leaf with the end of her little finger. She
was not dressed for supper, Charlotte saw, but still in her limp
old dress, a little at odds with her immaculately dressed hair.

'Need a hand?' barked Charlotte, to startle them.
Housekeeper and daughter spun around.

'Mother!'

Florence was red-faced. 'Oh, it's you: yes, hold this.'

Charlotte picked her way across the flags, collecting a white
apron from a hook by the scullery door as she went, and slipping it over her head.

'This' was a flap of pimpled skin that Florence was attempting to stitch closed with a thick needle, so that the scented, crumbling forcemeat would not escape the bird into which it had been compactly crammed.

'Good heavens, woman,' said Charlotte, 'you can't imagine that will cook in time; it must be after seven.'

'Ten past,' said Florence through gritted teeth, and stabbed the needle in, drawing the lightly bloodied thread into a long stitch.

Charlotte, pitying her, felt cruelty slip out of her teasing grasp. 'Emerald, you really ought to go and dress. I'm here now. What else may I do to help you, Florence?'

'Nothing, *Mrs Torrington*, that would never do. You're dressed for the party. Your jewels might fall into the soup.'

'What isn't done?'

'What *is*?'

'Are those shabby creatures safely shut away in the morning room?'

'They are.'

'I tried to telephone the Railway,' said Emerald. 'We still haven't heard anything.'

'Rank inefficiency. Where's Myrtle now?'

'With Miss Sutton's hair.'

Charlotte made a spiteful moue. 'Miss Sutton . . .' Emerald uttered an exasperated noise but didn't speak. 'And after *her*?'

'Then laying.'

'The dining table? Not done yet?' She was aghast.

'Not yet.'

'Then I'll do that.' She looked down at the stitched bird. 'May I go?' .

Florence grabbed a stubby knife and sharply cut. 'Yes,' she said. 'Thank you.'

Emerald straightened and wiped her hands on a cloth hanging from her waist. 'Yes, thank you, Mother,' she said with feeling.

In the doorway, removing the apron and patting her hair, Charlotte said, 'Do you ever think we'd be better off if we surrendered?'

'This house?' asked Florence.

'The struggle, yes.' Charlotte ignored Emerald's stricken face.

Florence fixed her with a steady look, the intimacy of the years. 'No, Charlotte,' she said, 'we get along very well.'

'I suppose when Edward returns the question will be a moot one anyway; we shall know one way or another.'

Charlotte, Emerald and Florence stood in a brief but intensely glum silence then, 'Off you go, Mrs Swift,' said Florence.

'Thank you, Mrs Trieves. Onwards!' Charlotte cried, at once commanding and absentminded. She turned on her heel.

Florence opened the oven with her foot, and in the blast of heat that blew from it, hoisted the iron tin that held the little bird, and thrust it inside. 'Off you go and dress, Emerald,' she said; 'you look a sight.' And Emerald went.

Charlotte went into the dining room, closed both the doors and drew the curtains. When she was sure she was unobserved, she darted gracefully about the large room arranging the cutlery and glasses with single-minded accuracy, laying the table with silver and china on damask, all manner of ornaments, and bowls of tight, silk rosebuds bristling down its centre.

'Perfection,' she breathed in the doorway, and glided from the room.

She would stand at her open window to cool down, and, after a good scrub with lye soap, she would rub lavender water into her hands to banish traces of silver polish. No one would know she had degraded herself.

* * *

80

Of the dozen or so clocks at Sterne there were only six that moved at all and three that told the approximate time. It was somewhere past seven. Everybody was dressing or otherwise occupied, and the downstairs of the house was still, the only activity being in the kitchen and among the waiting creatures, the shifting hive of the morning room. It was the precious hour before dinner when the house is quiet and anything might be accomplished.

Smudge slipped down the stairs alone, proud she did not need over-garments for her Great Undertaking, having planned ahead by wearing so many under-garments. She would be warm in any weather and, should calamity befall her, padded, too.

At the top of the stairs she paused, checking the hall and the rooms she could see, with their partly open doors before creeping down, intent. She was most agitated and interfered with when there came, shattering the silence, a loud rapping on the front door. Smudge shrank back up the stairs and waited for the hurrying feet that would attend to it – but no sound of footsteps was forthcoming. The knock came again. Whatever idiot it was had not thought to use the bell-pull. Oh, this was too vexing. She supposed it was the farmer John Buchanan, master of the ill-timed appearance and – even to Smudge – a bit of a stale bun.

She sighed and slunk down to open the door – not before it was rapped upon a third time, loudly and rather rudely, she thought with her child's censoriousness, by what sounded like the metal top of a cane.

She put her hand on the large iron knob and heaved the door open, inch by inch.

Revealed, standing in the porch, with his cane raised to rap once more and an expression of keen enthusiasm – a wide grin, in fact – was not John Buchanan but an absolute stranger.

He was a man of medium build – on the slight side, perhaps

– wearing smartly pointed boots, an air that was altogether sprightly – dapper – and a bushy, vigorously curling moustache.

'I've come!' he cried, then, 'Rather late, I'm afraid!'

Smudge was at a loss. He gleamed at her, staring down his nose and widening his eyes. 'I suppose I may come in?'

Smudge stepped mutely aside, glancing over her shoulder for some adult to save her, but nobody came, only a surging of strangers' voices down the hall, as the noise of the survivors reached her.

'I am so sorry to inconvenience you, but I believe you *were* warned?'

Still, Smudge did not speak.

'My name is Charlie Traversham-Beechers. Is the lady of the house about at all? Perhaps you might . . . fetch her?' Again he showed his white teeth to Smudge.

'Imogen Torrington,' said Smudge at last, and in a whisper. She was a confident enough child in her own realm, but this plainly wasn't it.

The gentleman held out his hand. 'Really? How *do* you do?' he said smoothly, lengthening his 'r' nasally, grasping her fingers in his thickly gloved ones and squeezing.

Just then there was the sound of whistling, and Clovis, hurriedly adjusting his tie, came down the stairs, immaculate in evening clothes – white tie and tails – his hair oiled, the creases in his trousers sharp. He was altogether the most welcome and brotherly sight Smudge could have asked for. She ran to him.

'Hello! Who's this?' said Clovis.

The gentleman stepped forward eagerly. 'Charlie Traversham-Beechers; I believe you were expecting me.'

'If we were, it's news to me,' said Clovis pleasantly, as Smudge retreated behind him to listen.

'I felt sure the Railway had warned you about passengers,' responded the visitor.

'Passen— Oh! You're from the accident!'

'Exactly.'

'How extraordinary.'

'Yes, it was a most dreadful thing.'

Clovis cast his eye over Charlie Traversham-Beechers' attire. 'Where was the accident?' he asked.

'It was on the branch line.'

'To?'

'Just outside Whorley. Some trouble with the points, I believe. Absolute horror. Derailed utterly. Didn't they tell you?'

'Not exactly. Awful.'

'It was. Most of us have been taken care of.'

'Yes, we've a crowd of you around here somewhere . . .' Clovis glanced about, as if to catch them lurking in the shadows. 'We didn't expect any more.'

'Do you have a telephone? Have the Railway contacted you at all?'

'Yes, there,' Clovis indicated the device. 'We haven't heard a thing. I'm so sorry, you must think me a terrible turnip, do come in. I—' He broke off, glancing about him and wondering suddenly what Emerald and his mother would have him do with the stranger, so as not to interfere with their precious dinner arrangements. 'I wonder where old Mrs Trieves can have got to . . .' He lit upon an idea. 'I say, I suppose I ought to introduce you to the other survivors.'

'I suppose you ought. Thanks,' said the displaced person, and the two of them went off towards the morning room, leaving Smudge alone once more.

Tremendously relieved. She contemplated the empty hall for some seconds before recalling her original timetable. She must not be distracted from her plan. She shrugged,

shook herself and scampered off towards the back of the house.

Clovis led the new arrival briskly down the corridor and opened the door to the morning room to find the guests – the *survivors*, that is – hunched around the fire as if they were trying to discover something in the hearth. On his entrance they turned, in attitudes of outrage and distress, and several voices burst out:

'There's no more coal!'

'No more fuel!'

'No more fuel at all!'

Clovis was taken aback. All of them – there appeared to be twenty or more – were surging towards him, crossly, and the complaints piling upon one another were almost a chant: 'We're cold!' 'We're hungry!'

To make matters worse, the new arrival, Charlie Treverish-Beacon or Haversham-Trevor – Clovis was dashed if he could remember his name – turned to him in some astonishment and cried accusingly, 'D'you mean to say these poor blighters have all been crowded in here like this ever since the accident?' And with this startling shift in attitude, he stepped away and into the body of passengers, glowering.

Clovis was amazed and knew not what to say. Traversham-Beechers faced him down. He wore a red waistcoat, of a very rich colour, somewhere between plum and wine; a ruby port-coloured waistcoat, and yet, alarmingly no tie, the absence lending a wildness to his appearance.

'There are women and children here; d'you want them fainting?' he demanded.

Having gained a champion and spokesperson, the little crowd had fallen quiet again, and watched the two men calmly to see what the outcome would be.

'Haven't they had tea?' queried a nervous Clovis, at last glancing about the pallid faces. They consented, grudgingly, that they had and there was an unspoken acquiescence in admitting it; nobody who's been given tea has truly any cause for serious complaint.

The gentleman stepped towards him, neatly, and leaned closer. 'May I have a word?' Clovis, wrong-footed again, restrained himself from backing off. This was all too disconcerting. But the stranger smiled keenly.

'Could we step out for a moment?'

'Of course.' Clovis could think of nothing he'd rather do than get out of that room, which had acquired the fug of a railway station waiting room, of sweating coats and slippery oil-skin, the wet-dog smell of damp wool and old carpet. He would rather have shut the door on the changeable Mr Whoever-he-was along with the rest of them, but hadn't the nerve to do it and feared they'd all come after him if he tried.

'This way,' he said, in a pale voice.

Watched suspiciously by the disgruntled passengers, the young man and the visitor stepped out into the cool air of the corridor, but to Clovis's surprise, once the door was closed behind them, the gentleman let out a big, infectious laugh.

Clovis found himself smiling along with him as he waited to be enlightened as to the joke, and Trevorish-Charlson obliged.

'Let them think somebody's fighting their cause!'

'I beg your pardon?'

'Mollification! They'll leave you alone for hours now!'

'Ah,' said Clovis. The gentleman smiled again, and tapped his nose.

Clovis had quite misjudged this man, he was charm personified.

'They are obviously mostly second- and third-class passengers,' went on the gentleman urbanely. 'They often don't

think to ask, the way *we* might. They don't have the same expectations. Haven't they been perfect lambs about waiting all this time?'

'I suppose . . .' said Clovis, admitting to himself that he hadn't taken very much notice of them. Then, casting around for something to say, 'Did anybody give you an idea when they might come for you all?'

'None at all!' said the other, gaily.

'I believe my sister was going to telephone. You might want to wait in the library; why don't we go along? Can I offer you some refreshment?' (He immediately regretted this last, as seeking out the frenzied Myrtle or Mrs Trieves, in all her subdued distress, for crumpets, or similar stop-gaps didn't remotely appeal.)

'Refreshed simply by being here, old man,' was his new friend's soothing rejoinder and Clovis found he liked him more and more.

He started along the corridor, followed closely by his smiling companion, and there was silence again behind the morning-room door, as the passengers patiently awaited fresh developments.

Emerald had struggled into her evening gown and its various supports and additions with only brief visits from the supremely harassed Myrtle. The dress, of springtime colours, misted green and early rose, fell from two pearled clasps at the shoulder; it was tight under the bust, barely decent above it, and dropped away into the draped silk and embroidered flowers of a long and very narrow skirt, the bottom half of which emerged from a tulip-shaped over-skirt like the clean stem of a flower.

Her toes peeked out beneath, in buckled shoes, dyed to match by gypsies. (They very often camped nearby and

specialised in knives, pans and the dyeing of things.) The buttons down the back had taken Myrtle fifteen minutes to fasten. The dress was quite the most beautiful and infuriating thing Emerald had ever had anything to do with.

'If I didn't like it so much I should burn it,' she said. 'I must stop talking to myself.' And she went down to try the Railway again before the guests assembled in the drawing room.

The air of the hall was cold and as she reached for the telephone, goose pimples raised along her bare arms, furring the down upon them in futile defence.

This time, Elsie Goodwin's voice came hurtling down the line like a corncrake shot from a cannon.

'Exchange!'

'Yes, Elsie, this is Emerald Torrington, at Sterne.'

'Up at Sterne!' shrieked Elsie, for whom repetition was both habit and delight.

'I should like to be put through to the Great Central Railway, please.'

And then, suddenly, the line went quiet. It was as silent as a black pond on a still night as one looks across the water wondering what lies beneath the inky flatness. That is to say, Elsie's voice was no more and there were no crackles, either. Instead, there came a high and carrying gentleman's laugh, issuing not from the telephone, but from the library. A strange gentleman? Emerald, still holding the telephone, leaned out from the shelter of the stairs towards the library door, which, standing partially open, afforded a broad glimpse of the room within.

She could see Clovis's legs and feet sticking out near the hearth. He had his dress shoes on, at least, so she wouldn't have to slaughter him. There, the laugh came again, a big, tenor, *ha ha HA-HA!*

Straining further, pulling the telephone cord taut in her efforts, whilst vainly attempting to keep the receiver clamped to her ear, she managed to see the other pair of legs in the room, those belonging to the owner of the laugh. Then, as if to oblige her, both men stood up. Her view of the two of them, across the hall and through the partially closed door of the fairly generous room, was not perfect, but still, the sight of this stranger made her forget Elsie and the Railway.

He was in profile; taller than Clovis and thrusting his long chin out and up to emit the laugh, with the firelight catching the bottom of his face and gleaming onto the deep red silk of his waistcoat.

A red silk waistcoat? For travelling?

His skin looked yellowish in that light, and his fingers long and of the same oily hue. Emerald, startled by the air of hysteria and secrecy that emanated from both this mysterious stranger and Clovis, found herself recoiling inwardly, whilst at the same time strongly intrigued, compelled, in fact, to know more.

She put the telephone on the table with a light thud and laid the receiver next to it. She found herself tiptoeing towards them. The rest of the house was silent all around her as she approached the door.

'What's the joke?' she asked, at the threshold.

Clovis glanced at her. He was holding a lit cigar; where had he got it?

'This is my sister, Emerald,' he said casually, gesturing her. Even for him these manners were excessively rude.

The stranger looked over his shoulder; his eyes were deeply disconcerting to her.

'It's an absolute pleasure, Miss Torrington.' He approached her with a half bow but his own name was lost in the wet

stub of cigar that he put in his mouth in order to hold out his hand, to shake hers.

He took the cigar from his lips and a heavy curl of smoke stretched, thinning, between his mouth and the cut end, before falling, slowly, down the skin of his chin. Emerald was mesmerised. At a loss, she tore her eyes from him and looked imploringly at Clovis.

'Cigars before supper?' she found herself saying and he let out a little yelp, mocking her. 'Are you one of the passengers?' she asked, turning back to the stranger, who licked his lower lip as if to catch the escaping smoke and eat it.

'Yes, Em, obviously!' said Clovis and Emerald fought the desire to slap him.

She was torn between hauling Clovis from the room to quiz him and her fear that this odious person might pilfer something while they were gone. In the end she did nothing but gaze in confusion at her brother.

'I think we've got off to a bad start, Miss Torrington. I do apologise and take the blame wholeheartedly. Where are my manners?'

He threw his cigar into the fire and Clovis followed suit, straightening his face manfully.

'Your brother and I were having a dashed silly conversation – wasn't it, Clovis? Dashed silly.'

'Beyond it.'

'And you came in as I'm afraid one of us had made a *rather off-colour remark*.' He said this last mockingly.

'Not about a lady,' put in Clovis. They were for all the world like a practised music hall double act.

'Oh Lord, no! Nothing like that. Dash it, Clo, we're digging a worse hole for ourselves!'

Clo?

'I see,' said Emerald. 'I don't want to appear rude, but I

couldn't be less interested. I was just telephoning the Railway, to see if they've made some arrangements to collect you all, so that you might be on your way.'

'I hope,' he murmured, suddenly serious, '*for your sake,* that they have made some arrangements to collect us all, too, Miss Torrington.' Then, amending what might have sounded like a threat – did, frankly, sound like a threat – he added, 'What a thing to happen on a young lady's birthday.'

He said it so smoothly that the word *birthday* seemed to hold a world of unlooked-for intimacy, and Emerald was appalled afresh.

'Oh, come on, though, Em.' Clovis was determined. 'I've already invited our friend to supper, so he won't be going off in any railway wagon tonight. Not tonight, Em; he's dining with us.' And then, with some tiny glimmer of his normal self, he added sweetly, 'If that's all right, Birthday Girl?'

It was, of course, very far from *all right*, but Emerald had been put on the spot and failed utterly to see a way off it. Divided from Clovis she was lost, she hadn't realised how united they were, even in their squabbling, and she felt quite enfeebled without him.

The new friend leaned towards her as he waited for her answer. He teetered forward on his shiny, narrow shoes – although shockingly tie-less, he was very elegantly dressed, as if he'd been on the way to a dinner already – and his face, dropping the sneer she so disliked, was quite charming and open, like a child. She looked from one to the other.

'You look absolutely splendid, by the way,' said Clovis. 'Nice frock.'

'Yes,' echoed the gentleman, 'splendid.'

'All right,' she heard herself say weakly. 'I mean, of course, we'd be very glad to have you.' And she left them.

'Topping! Delightful!' cried one of them behind her, but she was dashed if she could tell which it was.

She collected the telephone again, without much hope of achieving contact with Elsie Goodwin that night, and clicked the loose-hinged cradle several times.

'*Miss Torrington! Sterne!*' came the hoarse shriek, making her jump. 'I have Mr William Flockhart of the Great Central Railway for you. Will you wait?'

'Yes. Thank you—'

'Thank YOU!'

Clovis and his friend had drifted into the hall after her as Elsie Goodwin, unseen in her parlour, went clumsily about the business of making the necessary connections. Behind her, the gentleman said, 'Torrington? Did you say, *Torrington?*'

'Yes,' said Emerald, frowning.

'I didn't take it in before. Extraordinary.' Their guest burst out into delighted, warm laughter. 'I thought so a moment ago but then – oh, it couldn't be!' he exclaimed, and again, 'No, no, surely not! But you are both so like her! Not the colouring, of course, but the chin, the cheek, the brow, the – oh my word, are you the daughter and son of Charlotte Thompson as was – now Torrington?'

'Now Swift,' put in Clovis tightly.

'Yes, we are. You know my mother?' asked Emerald, forgetting the telephone a moment, trying to pin him down.

'Coincidence, eh?' he said, and seemed to search her face minutely, his lips parted breathlessly as he drank her in.

Then, on hearing some sharp sound emanate from the

rounded earpiece in her right hand, she put it to her ear again. 'Hello?' she said, releasing the mouthpiece from her breast. 'Hello?' She rattled the telephone again, but to no avail. 'Oh dear,' she said, 'I believe we've been cut off. And it took me so long to get through in the first place.'

Their new visitor furrowed his brow, elaborately.

'The Railway?' he asked, and as Emerald, wilting, nodded, he leaned a little towards her. 'Yes, they're the very devil to get hold of,' he said, and winked.

Smudge was always nervous when visiting the stable-yard at night, hating the blindness after the shining windows of the house and before the glow from the stables.

Careful lamps stayed lit in the harness room and beneath the clock tower until after evening stable, when Robert, retreating to his home above the harness room, would extinguish them and all would be dark as pitch. (Smudge had seen hot pitch poured from a bucket and slapped oozingly into the cracks of wooden feed-bins and buckets and, true to its reputation, it was the very blackest, darkest thing she had ever come across; black, hot and bitter-smelling.)

A cold wind whipped her skirts about her legs as she entered the yard, the cobbles hugely bumpy under her thin-soled boots. She scampered quickly across the open yard and arrived – with a small trip, banging her knee – at the door to the stalls.

Immediately she was inside, the air was warmer and sweet with hay – life and sunshine fields of grass, now in nets from last year, and being eaten. She could hear the rhythmic grinding of the horses' jaws working on it, the sharper crunch of stray oats, and the occasional clatter of a metal shoe on the herringbone floor. Her fear drained away. She reached confidently to the hook above her, where the halters hung; she

didn't even mind when a fat spider tumbled lightly onto the back of her hand. Brushing it off, she went down the stalls to the last and smallest, which was Lady's.

The horses were curious, watching her. Upstairs, across the yard and above the harness room, she heard Robert laughing, and Stanley's higher voice joining in.

She stopped, stock still and listened, noticing, too, all the other sounds outside: the rush of the wind in the trees like water, surging, and the cry of a small animal as it died.

'Here, Lady, come along,' she said to the pony as she slipped inside her stall. Lady shifted, leaning towards Smudge and sniffing up and down her clothes. 'Good girl; you're coming with me,' said Smudge, trying to keep her voice quiet, but retain the ring of authority.

She led Lady down the line of stables. Levi was lying down, his black tail spread out over the straw, he lifted his nose from curled-up knees to watch her. Ferryman stuck his head out and tried to take a chunk out of Lady's rump, with eye-rolling and faces, but Smudge pushed his head away with her elbow, avoiding the yellow teeth only narrowly.

'Get back, you rude thing!' she said.

Lady's hooves were not too noisy inside, but agonisingly so out in the open yard. They crashed on the cobbles. (Smudge wondered if Mr Darwin had ever noted that his precious evolution had betrayed the horse rather meanly, in not allowing them to develop a tiptoe along with a walk, trot and canter. The cowardly grass-eating things might have been able to sneak past predators and not had to run away so much.) Smudge went on tiptoe herself but it was no use: a stripe of yellow light opened up above her and struck through the air like a broad-sword, as Robert threw the door wide and cried out, 'Hey! Who's there?' in

such a loud and accusing voice that Smudge fairly quaked. Pity the poor burglar that came across *him* at Sterne, she thought.

'Just me: Smudge!' she answered, mouse-like.

'You – and *Lady!* What's all this, Miss Imogen?'

Smudge ducked under Lady's neck and looked up at Robert, silhouetted there above her. Stanley joined him and they both stared down. She had an impression she was floating in a black sea, and they had spotted her from the rail of a ship. She did not want saving.

'Well?'

'The guests wanted a pony,' called Smudge, her voice ringing out confidently. She experienced the thrill of deceit.

'Now? What for?'

'They want to look at Lady, round at the front, because I told them all about her and they are . . .' she faltered, but recovered, 'all determined to indulge me.'

She was pompous, and delighted with herself at it. She could have danced a jig; who would not believe her now?

'I see . . . And why didn't they ask for me?'

'They knew you'd be having your supper, and – I *asked* to do it.'

There was a pause in which Lady snorted, all unknowing.

'Well. How long will you be, Miss?'

Smudge was airy. 'Oh, until they're bored; you know how grown-ups are.'

'I do,' he said shortly. 'Well, mind your toes, you're not in your proper boots. And if I don't see you back here, I'll come up to the house myself.'

'All right, Robert; thank you, Robert!'

Smudge yanked at the rope and went off into the dark. She was not at all scared now, with Robert's authority behind her and Lady at her side, but she waited until he had safely

closed his door, and counted to ten, before she took her across the lawn.

Lady was accustomed to going down the drive and took some persuading before she would plant her hooves on the grass, but once she did, she plunged her head down to eat it, blunt teeth tearing. Lawn grass, manicured and forbidden, was like a drug to the pony, and Smudge forced her to leave off feasting eventually only by smacking her sharply on the stomach.

'Come on!' said Smudge, and they went on together towards the house.

Reaching it, the pony and little girl stood under the magnolia waiting, the white candles of its buds cast no light.

Smudge felt the warm huffs of Lady's breath on her palm as she peered in through the windows.

Nobody was in sight.

She waited until her hammering heart had slowed again. Then – and only when she was convinced she was unobserved – she approached the back door. Holding the end of the rope with one hand, she reached for the heavy ring with the other, turned it, and pushed. Lady startled slightly at the brightness. 'No faint-heartedness, Lady,' said Smudge and led her firmly forward.

The umbrella stand provided Lady with a moment of brief horror, but Smudge would brook no arguments now that they were so nearly at their goal.

The Great Undertaking was within her grasp. This May Day eve was the day that the pony Lady would be immortalised in charcoal. She had only to achieve the sitting of the pony, and it would be done. At the thought of Lady sitting, Smudge's hand flew to her mouth to suppress a yelp. She meant sitting in the way an artist would, not literally; only circus ponies

actually *sat*, on barrels and clowns and so forth, and Lady had too much dignity – and weight on her – for that.

'Sh!' she whispered. 'Come along, Lady; in we go.'

The pony set her first hoof on the inside floor of Sterne.

These, then, were the inhabitants of the house, somewhere between seven and eight in the evening (discounting the majority of the animals who, unless otherwise noted, were either sleeping or surging about people's feet): Robert and Stanley were setting about their supper of bread, cheese and pickles; the pony Lady and Smudge had entered the back hall; Florence Trieves was sweating and snapping at Myrtle in the kitchen; Emerald was in her room, calming herself after her unsettling encounter with the new visitor in the hall; Charlotte was moving about her room, powder-puff in hand, fretfully dusting her pale neck, unaware of the new guest but characteristically resenting the existing ones and ignoring the pitiful scratchings of the kitten Tenterhooks from his little prison beneath her bed. The group of survivors in the morning room were taking off their damp overcoats and waiting, ravenous, for what was to come.

Patience, coiffed and eager, skipped from her room to her brother's and knocked.

'Ernest?'

'Are we to go down?' He opened the door.

'I should think so. Are you ready? Oh, I can see you aren't. I can understand the tie foxing you, Ernest, but a comb? Everyone can manage a comb!'

'I did – *don't*—'

She had taken his hand and was pulling him over to the dressing-table glass. Ernest suffered himself to be pushed onto

a chair while Patience retied his tie for him and dragged the comb through his thick hair, with added dressing to tame it, before she would allow him out of the room. Patience lived in fear of Ernest being ridiculed, although in truth he hadn't faced teasing since his childhood. There was nothing she dreaded more than his humiliation; it was an unendurable pain to her. She had once given a boy a bloody nose for calling him Cock-eyes.

After a few more moments of tussling with tie and comb she released him and they left the room, most smartly and correctly turned out for an evening's celebration. As they descended the stairs, arm in arm, Patience announced, 'We are going to have a grand time, Ernest, aren't we?'

But the voice that responded was not her brother's, but one rather reedier and more strident than that. It was the mous-tachioed gentleman, the guest, the interloper, who, having heard their footfalls on the wooden treads, had leapt from his chair in the library and thrown open the door to cry, 'A grand time indeed!'

The brother and sister paused and looked down upon him – the molishly black serge of his jacket, the snowy-white shirtfront, the shirt itself, shockingly open at the neck, and the cherry gleam of his waistcoat – in some astonishment.

Clovis reeled into the hall after him, laughing, leaving a cloud of cigar smoke behind.

'Charlie Burbisham-Tr – this is Miss Patience Sutton and her brother Ernest. They're—'

'Delighted,' said that gentleman, fixing Patience's bluebell-coloured eyes with his own very black ones. 'Delighted indeed.'

'How d'you do?' said Patience neatly, hiding her shock at both the appearance of this new arrival and Clovis's somewhat wild demeanour, to say nothing of the scandalous clouds of cigar smoke issuing from the library behind them.

Ernest, similarly startled, similarly restrained, held out his hand. The other gentleman held out his, and the white gloves gripped one another firmly.

Patience, dwarfed by the men around her, opened her fan, smartly, and closed it again. All four stood for a moment, unaware that behind them a pony had entered the house by the back door. A clock somewhere was heard to chime.

'Is that eight?' enquired Patience. (It wasn't.) 'So soon?'

'No idea,' said Clovis. 'Shall we go in?' and he led the way.

No explanation of the new gentleman's presence was forthcoming.

'Who on earth is he?' hissed Patience in her brother's ear.

'Friend of Clovis's, looks like,' answered Ernest from the corner of his mouth.

Patience rolled her eyes in an expression that meant, *Oh really? How extraordinary!* And was answered with a silent, *Bizarre!*, from her brother.

They approached the drawing room. Clovis threw open the door and the small group entered, all but the new guest, who darted soundlessly away down the corridor. Without breaking step, he opened the door of the morning room noiselessly and leaned deep inside, whispering, 'Doing my best!' He tapped the side of his nose, sharply, as he had done to Clovis earlier, before shutting the door once more and trotting along to rejoin the others.

No sounds of stilted gaiety reached Smudge, leading Lady up the stairs.

There had been a sticky moment when the pony first heard the hollow boom of her own hooves on the wood and had run backwards, but Smudge, hot with desperation, urged her on.

'Come on!' she said. 'It's not far at all!' Lady had still been doubtful. 'Now get along up the stairs, Lady, there's a good girl.'

So Lady climbed the stairs. The wood wasn't waxed and polished like that of the main stair. Her front hooves found the steps easily, her hindquarters took the rise with ease, but the booming sound was dreadful – still, nobody came.

The landing presented a new challenge. The door must be held open to allow the pony through and then they must go all down the length of the house, past room after room. If only the scullery stairs had been wide enough, they were much nearer her own bedroom. Smudge was giddy with excitement now. Weak fingered, her hand trembled near the doorknob for hateful, frightened seconds. She held it. Her palms were wet though her mouth was dry. She turned the knob with a monstrous click.

The corridor was warm, and the lamps were lit and glowing all down its length in the most inside, house-like way she had ever seen.

She was about to open the door wider when her mother's – her mother's! – door was heard to open, and she closed it again, hastily.

She heard Charlotte's quick tread, another door – even closer – then, as unmistakable as horse's hooves, came the sound of the lavatory flushing. Hysteria rose madly in Smudge's chest, she would laugh, she would fall over laughing, she would die. But Lady, as if she, too, recognised the sound of a pulled chain, lifted her tail and deposited a wet heap of grassy, steaming droppings on the back landing, right at the top of the stairs.

'Oh, Lady,' breathed Smudge, giggles forgotten, 'that wasn't very nice.'

Lady, taking for granted her status as house-pony now,

flicked her ears uninterestedly as Charlotte was heard returning to her room. All was quiet again.

Smudge opened the door wide.

'Now or never,' she whispered, and she led the pony out into the broad corridor.

She heard no sound from any of the rooms, no voices, nothing but the steady muted thud of Lady's hooves planting on the floor. The sweet smell of dung clung to them only slightly as they went. She resisted the urge to trot, imagining a hoof poking through the ceiling below, showering enraged and frightened people with plaster. How cross they would all be; she imagined them looking up, aghast, and shaking their fists at her.

Lady's neatly oiled hooves looked not quite as clean indoors as they did out, but she stepped over the carpets for all the world as if she were quite used to it. Smudge led her past the lamps, past the dull old paintings, the spare room, her mother's room . . . *Leading her pony past her mother's room* — the excitement hit her like a gust of wind, almost knocking her from her feet. She could have screamed with glee, run madly up and down the corridor, whooping, she could have wailed and turned cartwheels in her drawers until she fainted. Her mother's dressing room, the Stripes, Clovis's room . . . They had done it, they were at the corner and around it, her hand was on the door, it was open, her room —how very small it looked — was ahead of her, and then, then, the pony was inside.

Smudge had a job turning, because Lady's hocks bumped into the bed, but she achieved it, and shut the door and locked it.

She leaned against the locked door, weak suddenly. Her pulse and every feeling part of her plunged downwards; she seemed to drop into a chasm. It was as if she were the tightest strung of violin strings, and had been snipped, in an instant, to lie slack and baseless. She was dizzy at what she had done,

feeble and breathless. She struggled with reason and feverish wonder.

Lady seemed to have no idea whatever of her extraordinary situation. She nosed the quilt thoughtfully, but Smudge could see that her thoughts were very tiny.

She stood up straight again, and tightened the knot in Clovis's scarf around her waist. Her equilibrium began to re-establish itself. She had chosen the perfect night for it, nobody would notice the pony with the party going on — grown-ups could only concentrate on one thing at a time. She was achieving her Great Undertaking. She began to smile.

'I had better find something for you to eat,' she said to the pony. 'I don't want you to get bored and draw attention, neighing.'

3

SMELTS AND SMITHEREENS

John Buchanan's blue Rolls-Royce slipped between the two impractically small gatehouses at the beginning of Sterne's drive, just as the first lightning bolt illuminated the gentle crenellations and startled the sharp flints on the ground into relief. The banging of the thunder came a few moments later, like a rolling pin on a metal feed-bin to frighten rats, but John, cocooned on leather seats within the car's consistent growl, was happily protected from the elements. There was no need to fiddle about with the stick for the wipers; the rain began in large, spare drops and the house was easy to make out beyond the tunnel of the drive.

He watched the sweeping beam of his headlights with a thrill akin to acquisition as they smeared across the trees, garden, walls, and into the nighttime secret spaces of Sterne. Powerfully, they took it all in, settling as he stopped, on the porch that would shelter him and the front door that would welcome him.

He turned the headlights off, and the engine, and got out of the car, removing his driving gloves and flexing stiff fingers. He tossed the gloves back into the car and walked up to the house. He was exactly on time.

Standing under the porch, out of the rain that now hit the windows in gusts, like handfuls of stones, John gave the bell a sustained and masterful pull.

He waited a long time, listening to the spaniels barking and flinging themselves about within, before Mrs Trieves, in her interminable black, opened it.

'Good evening, sir.' She smiled – if not warmly then certainly with the intention of welcome.

John Buchanan was jovial as, batting away the leaping dogs, he entered. 'Good evening, Mrs Trieves; I'm expected this time!'

'Come in, sir: let me take your coat. Get down, Nell! You'll find the family in the drawing room – would you like to follow me?'

'I should think I know where the drawing room is, Mrs Trieves.'

'Of course, sir. Then you'll excuse me.'

He hadn't intended to dismiss her, but she darted away, suddenly – as if she had something urgent to attend to. The dogs scampered after her, and he was left alone in the high squareness of the hall. The stair stretched up ahead of him and, in the quiet, the vast fire asserted itself. He could hear the flames, licking.

He thought that if the house were his he would have the place wired as a matter of urgency – wired from top to bottom. He would throw light into those corners, illuminate all with electrical power, as every civilised place was now illuminated. It would mean getting behind all the panelling, of course, but that could be easily removed, and the fiddly plaster, too. He was about to go over to it and give it a tap to check its condition when he heard the sound of a woman's tread on the stairs, and Emerald very soon came into view.

She came down towards him, gleaming, and for the second time that day he was nonplussed, and thought unaccountably of the bottomless settee in the drawing room; he pictured falling through it to loud laughter.

'Hello, John — what weather! Were you caught in it?'

'Oh, not exactly—'

She was wearing his cameo. 'We've had an adventure, have you heard?'

'Heard?'

'About the accident.'

'Accident?'

'The train crash.'

'Heavens!'

'Yes, on the branch line, not far from here.'

'Any deaths?'

'We haven't heard. But they've directed some of the survivors up here to Sterne, and naturally we're happy to help, but the sordid Railway haven't sent anybody up for them and they're rather . . . hanging about the place.'

John cast an eye about the hall. 'Where can you have put them?'

'They're all in the morning room at the moment. Would you like to see?'

He was doubtful; he had not envisaged this and did not like surprises. 'Well . . . I suppose.'

'Come with me.' She went ahead of him, the comb in her dark hair glittering with green and amber as they passed from the hall. He longed to touch it.

Reaching the morning room, she put her hand on the door-knob and glanced up at him.

'If I open the door, they might all start talking to us,' she said.

'Well don't, if you'd rather not.'

'Poor things, I should think they're exhausted.'

She opened the door wide: the morning room was empty. There was not a soul inside it, just the lingering smell of wet, wool coats.

'Where could they have gone to?' said Emerald.

John was as perplexed as she – more so. 'How many are there? Would they have taken themselves off?'

'A good many. I can't think.'

At that moment Myrtle – in fresh apron and cap – darted from the passage that led to the kitchen, and made to speed past them. She was carrying several candles.

'Myrtle, do you know where the passengers have gone?'

Mrytle paused, and ducked her head, hastily. 'Yes, Miss Em; Mrs Trieves has moved them to the study. They kept coming out and getting in the way.'

The study was towards the back of the house, giving onto the hall. It was a gloomy, seldom used room, whose only benefit over the morning room was being further away from the kitchen and the impending party.

'Oh, I see; thank you. I really must see about getting them collected.'

Emerald was anxious, as harassed as he'd ever seen her. He was accustomed to, and admired, a vibrant Emerald, not an anxious one.

'You're wearing my ornament,' he said, to return her to more important matters.

Her fingers went to the cameo at her throat, resting in the hollow made by her collarbones.

'Happy birthday.'

She smiled at him, automatically. 'Thank you, John. Come and meet the others.'

The drawing room was awash with colours which, as water-paints do, seemed to fill the very air. Burnt orange, gold, pink, candlelight's glow and the various figures of stags, birds and unicorns that were represented in chintz, tapestry, cloth and carving, all seemed almost to float, insubstantial, in the

grand size of its pale proportions. The figures in the room: Patience, Ernest, Clovis and the gentleman traveller, were as figures at the ballet; they were no longer prosaic, but infected with grace, absorbed into the house.

Clovis was pulling one of the curtains across the windows against the night, awkwardly, and stopped halfway through the action as they came in. Patience was seated on an upright chair, and stood to greet them. She wore white – or something near to it – but her dress, too, had taken on the colours of the room. Ernest was near a large gilt framed painting; on seeing Emerald he, like John, experienced a falling sensation, and grasped his hands together behind his back more firmly, as if to steady himself. The gentleman traveller was on the broken settee – quite comfortably, it seemed, having miraculously avoided its rotten centre. He sprang up as John and Emerald came in, his black moustache twitching delightedly.

'The birthday girl!' cried Patience.

'This is John Buchanan,' Emerald announced him to the room. 'Clovis, where's our mother?'

Clovis shrugged. He raised a careless hand to John before dragging it through his hair, which stood on end, subsiding slowly over the next few moments.

'Good evening, John,' he said. 'Did you go home at all, earlier, or have you been lurking around all this time we were dressing?'

John was indulgent. 'Good evening, Clovis,' he said amiably.

'You look absolutely divine, Emerald,' said Patience.

'Thank you. John, may I introduce Miss Patience Sutton,' Emerald continued, 'and her brother, Ernest Sutton. Ernest, Patience, John Buchanan.'

They all shook hands and nodded or ducked heads, showing their pleasure in greeting one another with early-evening

shyness; they were all — except their passenger guest — still just at an age where dinner parties felt a little like childhood games wearing their mother's shoes and father's top hats.

'And this is . . . Oh, I do apologise, I've forgotten your name.'

'Charlie Traversham-Beechers, a pleasure to meet you.'

It was ten minutes to eight. They arranged themselves in a loose circle.

'Charlie is an interloper,' announced Clovis cheerfully. 'He ought to be with the other passengers, but luckily I weeded him out.'

'Yes, I do apologise most humbly for my appearance: my tie is in my luggage and I have no idea where that's got to.'

'It must be very discombobulating,' said Patience sympathetically, averting her eyes from the dark hair sprouting from his slightly open shirt.

Charlie burst into happy laughter, and the others found they followed suit, although they had no notion why.

'Discombobulated!' he laughed. 'Yes, that's one way to describe the effect of being in a dreadful train accident, I suppose, Miss Sutton. Discombobulating!'

Patience blushed to the roots of her fair hair. 'I meant the luggage,' she said quietly.

'Of course, of course.'

Ernest went to his sister and stood near her, lending silent support with his presence, as the gentleman went on, 'I hadn't expected to find a house here; I suppose I had no idea what to expect. It's not every day one's railway carriage is flung from the tracks like that!'

'Dreadful . . . And you were separated from the others?' asked Emerald, seeking to discover more.

'Yes, I tagged along with them, or they with me, I suppose, but it was a stroke of luck to find this place, I must say.'

'For us, too,' said Clovis gallantly, but not exactly echoing the feelings of anybody else present.

'Did the porter tell you the way up to the house?' enquired Patience, scenting him out like a rabbit. ('The *guard*,' muttered Clovis, but she ignored him.)

'And did they mention what they might be going to do about you all?' added Emerald.

'And were you on foot, as well? Did none of you see the cart and brougham?' Ernest asked with intelligence. He, of all of them, was the coolest and least affected by the gentleman's bizarre vitality.

'My, my! I'll take you in order.' He spun around on his heels, pointing at them one by one. 'Yes, he did. No, they did not. We all walked, and it was dashed uncomfortable; not a carriage in sight. These shoes were intended for carpets and admiration, not stamping along cart tracks. Those other poor beggars are more used to being foot-traffic, I should think.'

They were none of them any the wiser.

Just then, there was a loud crash from some upper room and all turned their eyes to the ceiling, where the chandeliers trembled.

'Thunder or furniture?' asked Clovis.

'You didn't let any of them upstairs, did you?' asked Emerald anxiously.

'I haven't a clue where they are, Em.' Clovis was unrepentant. 'I was with our friend in the library until just a few moments ago. Mrs Trieves is in charge of them. I say, would you like to borrow a collar and tie? I'm sure I can find one.'

'Borrow. Of course. We should have thought of it!' And he laughed again.

'Wait there. Two ticks,' said Clovis and galloped from the

room, but Charlie Tramerson-Beamer, smoothly smirking, went after him.

It wasn't Lady who had toppled the dressing table, but Smudge, whilst kneeling on it to outline the pony's ears. The fright of it had sent Lady clattering backwards and knocking into the door. These combined noises amounted to the crash heard below in the drawing room. Smudge's legs were now splayed like a deer; one hand holding the heavy mirror, which was wobbling precariously between fallen table and floor, the other gripping the end of the halter rope.

'Good girl, Lady, stand. *Stand*,' she said soothingly, and Lady stood, as Smudge carefully righted the mirror – unbroken; pony and child escaping seven years' bad luck by a whisker – and picked up her scattered charcoals.

'Now, in a moment I ought to go down, so you're to wait here, Lady, and be a very good girl until I return.'

Lady had the look of a pony that might or might not do as it was told.

In his room, Clovis was rummaging through his wardrobe to find something suitable for his new friend to wear about his neck, while Charlotte prowled her room, ignoring the pathetic mews now coming from the box under the bed. In the drawing room, Emerald – rouged and rallying – beamed invitingly at John Buchanan, who strode past her to address Patience.

'We've met before, Miss Sutton,' he said, 'when we were much younger. Many years ago, it would have been. I remember you well, and I don't think you've changed a bit. You would have had another brother with you, though, because,' he turned to Ernest, enquiringly, 'we haven't met, have we?'

'You're mistaken, we have; I'm Ernest,' said Ernest.

'Yes, this is Ernest,' Patience corroborated.

'Ernest? But I seem to remember that *he* was called Ernest – the boy I remember here,' said John.

'Yes, that was me. I remember you, too, John,' said Ernest, to help him out.

'That's rum. I'm afraid I don't remember you at all,' said John, frowning.

'Well, I haven't another brother, so it was most certainly this one – Ernest,' said Patience, a trifle huffily.

'Oh, I see,' said John, generously, with the air of someone who doesn't want to make a row out of a thing, but knows he is right. He prided himself on his memory. He prided himself on a great many things. He was privately perfectly sure there had been another brother, with orange hair and an eye-patch, that these two attractive siblings had either forgotten or decided to conceal from him for some reason, but he couldn't very well accuse the Suttons of lying, so he let it go.

Ernest took off his spectacles to rub his eyes for a moment and Emerald found herself practically leaning forward to discover his face without them. When his spectacles were returned to his face, she was released, and turned back to John. She couldn't think of a polite way of putting, *Yes, Ernest is unrecognisable and changed. He was an undeniably off-putting child and now he is altogether different*, so she said instead, 'I believe it was one Easter, up here at Sterne, that you all met.'

'You're right!' cried Patience, but they were saved from rootling around their collective memories for nuggets of nostalgia concerning painted eggs and games of forfeits designed by her father by the door opening once more. Clovis and his new friend bounced into the room, all smiles, Clovis pointing at the white tie and rigid shirtfront that Charlie was adjusting with sallow fingertips.

'Howzat?' asked Charlie sunnily. 'Howzat?'

Emerald thought perhaps she had misjudged him earlier. He seemed determined to win everyone over.

'You look very smart, Mr . . .' She shook her head, forgetting the name again. 'Very smart indeed; and who would have guessed Clovis would have more than one white tie in his wardrobe? Clo, would you put a log on the fire? It's hard to believe it's—'

A huge clap of thunder – loud enough to penetrate the walls – stopped her mid-sentence, and drew gasps of horror and delight from the guests.

'That's all we need on a night like this!' cried Charlie with relish, and they all crowded to the tall windows, as if expecting to watch a fireworks display. They craned through the glass, eager for more noise, more flashes of the wild electric. Rain lashed the panes. The door opened behind them.

They all turned.

Charlotte, a living painting in the rectangle of the doorway, waited for their welcome.

'Mother—'

'Good evening—'

Charlotte's expression, adoring – either those she gazed upon or herself – altered of a sudden to something like horror. She could not disguise it. Her fingers, which had been resting lightly on the doorknob, a crystal one, gripped it whitely, and she fixed her eyes on the gentleman traveller.

'*You?*' she said.

'Yes.' Their visitor's tone was easy, but his catlike stillness was menacing. 'And yet I feel I ought to *reintroduce* myself – *my* name hasn't changed but yours has, I believe. Mrs Swift now.'

'Yes, Charlotte Swift now,' she murmured, never taking her extraordinary eyes from his face.

Emerald went over to her mother, moved by an urge to protect her, although from what she didn't know.

'Mother, this gentleman was on the train, the one that crashed. Clovis invited him for supper.'

Clovis put in, 'Ma, Mr . . . Charlie said you knew one another.'

All at once Charlotte broke into one of her very vaguest and loveliest laughs.

'We do know one another, Clovis. Charlie Traversham-Beechers is an old acquaintance, although it has been very many years.' She seemed to have no trouble recalling his name.

'Eleven years,' he said.

'Only eleven? I *am* so surprised to see you! And how delightful you ended up here – you must have been guided by the fates.' She laughed again. 'Bad fates for the train; good for stumbling into Sterne! And I'm delighted you are going to dine with us. That is, if it's agreeable to my daughter. It's her birthday, you know.'

She produced a smile for Emerald who, all of a sudden, adored her.

'You look very beautiful, Mother,' she said quietly.

'Nowhere near as beautiful as you, my darling. Your dress is a triumph,' said Charlotte, although she was not now looking at her but at the four men in the room. 'And hello, Patience: and welcome, Edm-Ernest. Welcome all!' She wandered among them, greeting each guilelessly. 'We've had such a time of it – no more than you, of course, Mr Traversham-Beechers. I suppose poor Mrs Trieves has *attempted* to announce supper already? More than once?'

With that, the door opened and Florence Trieves, tidy but for a shred of leek in her hair, and a wild expression, confronted them.

'Dinner is served, Mrs Swift,' she said, and began to

withdraw. She was stopped – that is, she was violently arrested in the process of leaving by the sight of their smartly turned-out visitor, who was himself straining to present himself to her, as if striking a pose to an off-stage drum-roll. Florence froze, staring at him.

'Th—' she began. Then, 'Wha—' And she dragged her eyes from his face to her employer's. The trembling leek dropped from her hair.

Charlotte pinned her with a look. 'We have another guest, Mrs Trieves,' she announced coolly, as all looked on. 'I don't believe you know him.'

There was a brief silence, as loaded as a suet dumpling.

'No, of course. Thank you, ma'am,' said Florence and abruptly left them.

Charlotte turned, beaming, to the room, faltering only minutely as the interloper, Traversham-Beechers, stepped forward and offered her his arm. The others turned to one another, considering the etiquette of who should take whom into dinner, and under cover of their confusion, he said to Charlotte, 'I'm so pleased you're accommodating us – accommodating me.'

She gave him a piercing, fearful look. 'Do I have a choice?' she murmured, for his ears alone.

'Come,' was all he said in response. He patted his forearm.

She slipped her hand through the crook of his elbow, rested her pale fingers lightly on his black sleeve.

'Lead the way, Emerald! Mr Buchanan!' she cried, with studied gaiety.

John gave a small bow to Emerald and took her hand, tucking it firmly into his arm. Emerald was relieved he was taking notice of her at last; she had begun to feel invisible. She was relieved, too, that she should not have to touch Ernest's sleeve, as even thinking of it made the exposed skin

of her arms, breast and neck suddenly, noticeably, feel all the more bare. It was not an unpleasant nakedness, quite the opposite, but for all that, extremely unnerving; the man undressed her without a glance. John's stolid presence was protection, and she grasped his forearm for anchorage, as much as anything.

With two pairs made, Clovis, Patience and Ernest were left in an embarrassed triangle. Clovis stared across at Patience with a look that would have downright frightened many girls but then, having no choice within the rules of decent behaviour, approached her and thrust out his arm. She took it.

'Clovis,' she said.

'Patience,' he responded stiffly.

They did not look into one another's faces, but each was keenly aware of the other's proximity. Clovis could not help but notice that she smelled sweetly of flowers of some sort; she could not help but feel the heat surrounding him, at odds with his ostensible coldness.

Ernest, alone, was without a companion to take to dinner.

'We are in formation. Mr Sutton, would you bring up the rear, and guard us from attack?' asked Charlotte obscurely, and with that the party left the room.

A patter of feet behind them in the passage heralded Smudge's arrival. She tiptoed, hoping vainly to blend in as the adults turned to her as one.

'No hair ribbon?' asked her mother, and Smudge's hand flew to the side of her head where a large, drooping bow was occasionally tied. 'I smell horse. Have you been at the stables?'

Smudge rubbed her blackened hands on her blue velvet skirt under the gaze of her mother, sister, brother and the guests, all sniffing delicately to detect the odour of the stables.

'Yes,' she admitted.

'Go and wash your hands at once,' said Emerald.

'Oh no!' Smudge was appalled. 'Will you wait? Who's going to take me in?' she said, hopping.

'I will, Miss Imogen,' said Ernest firmly, prepared to wait as long as it might take for Smudge to make herself presentable.

'Good, thank you, Mr Sutton,' murmured Charlotte. 'Then, shall we?' And she prepared to leave him.

Just then, the telephone rang.

All stood listening to its harsh tone, echoing from the distant hall, an arresting, modern sound in any case, but jarringly portentous this evening.

They waited.

The telephone continued to ring. At length, Myrtle hurried past them, fiercely out of breath, and pulling her cap straight. Her wake smelled wonderfully of cooking onions and meat.

They reached the door to the dining room just as Myrtle came jogging back, attempting – and failing – to run as if she had no other duty than to answer the telephone.

'Mrs Torrington, ma'am, Miss Torrington; it's the Railway. About the passengers.'

'Oh – I had forgotten all about that,' said Charlotte. '*Must* I talk to them now?'

'Oh Mother, *please!*' said Emerald urgently. 'Perhaps they're coming for them at last—'

'Clovis?'

'Dash it—'

'Would you like *me* to take the call?' said Charlie Traversham-Beechers in an oddly commanding voice. 'I have dealt with the Railway before.'

'No!' said Charlotte sharply. '*Not you.* Emerald.'

Emerald, obeying her mother, started towards the telephone in the hall, but as she reached it, they were all distracted by a loud *click* – not from the telephone, but from the study.

All stared as the knob turned and the door opened, wider and wider . . . Shuffling together, the passengers began to emerge. The room tipped them out like beetles poured from a shoebox. There seemed so many of them, surely there had only been a dozen or so? Now they were at least twenty-five. The family and guests paused and stared as they came, looking, if anything, shabbier, dingier even, than they had on arrival. A few of them wandered aimlessly to the windows, to look at the rain streaming down the rivulets in their thousands splintering the stormy view.

Emerald, distracted, remembered the telephone with a start, and hurried to it. The dingy faces turned to watch her.

'The *Railway*,' they whispered to one another. 'The Railway.'

Guests, family and passengers stood about the hall as Emerald approached the table on which the telephone stood. She picked it up.

Along the pulsing lines in the windy night, up the long, plaited black cord, a hissing, crackling sound came to her, like waves washing over pebbles, moving them to clacking collisions.

Far distant, a feeble voice whispered to her tiredly, *'Hello?'*

'Hello? Is that the Railway?' said Emerald doubtfully.

'Yes,' came the tiny voice, and yet she somehow very much doubted that it was. It sounded for all the world like a child's voice, a feeble child. 'Yes, this is the Great Central Railway,' it said, and a little group whispering by the glass turned their heads to look at her.

The waves washed up over the distant pebbles, back and forth, back and forth, and, at length, a bell vibrated. *Ringing* . . . *Ringing* . . . And then a loud male voice barked, 'Yes, hello?'

Emerald, despite herself, jumped and held the receiver a little away from her ear.

'Go on,' she said.

'Madam, are you calling about the accident on the branch line earlier today?'

'Yes. Yes, I am.'

The voice was extraordinarily loud now, and audible to all of them even over the noise of the storm.

'We have some more passengers for you!'

'More?' Emerald was aghast – as was everybody there, all quite aghast and agog.

'Several more; and they will need to be collected. You missed the group we sent earlier. Why was that?' His tone was strident in the extreme. 'Why, may I ask? They had to make their own way!'

Emerald was shocked at his aggression. What had they at Sterne done to deserve it?

'We – well, we—'

'You are not to miss these. We have sent them up to you. There's no other possible house in the area. They are to be met, do you understand? Met and accommodated!'

'Yes. We'll meet them,' she heard herself say steadily, ignoring the imploring face of her mother.

'Very well. Now, there's no way of reaching you tonight,' said the voice: bossy, tinny, like a loud-hailer at a political meeting instructing people to disband, it rang thinly round Sterne's hall. 'There's nothing at all to be done about these people tonight, do you hear me?'

'Nothing?' said Emerald. The ivory, green and pink contours of her party dress, her rich brown hair, her glistening beaded comb, creamy neck and lifting imperious chin were the focal point for all the disparate people watching her. 'Nothing you can do at all?' she repeated.

'Nothing!' said the voice, even louder than before. 'You'll just have to manage them all until the morning. It is your

duty! Do you know how remote you are? Do you know how far help will have to come? You must make do. Needs must. Can you hear me?'

Emerald bowed her head. 'Yes, I heard you.'

Then the voice spoke rapidly, as if, having been dealt with she had been forgotten already, moving on to some other more pressing problem.

'The Great Central Railway apologises for your inconvenience. Goodbye.' And with a tapping sound, it disappeared.

There was silence.

Then, Elsie Goodwin's voice screeched, 'Oh dear!'

And a click. And silence again.

The guests and family regarded the grouped faces of the travellers, and the travellers stared back, dimly. Charlie Traversham-Beechers was slightly apart; having given up Charlotte's arm for the moment. He was pressed back against the wall, his palms flat to it, his expression glittering with determination or triumph. He was unobserved by all but Smudge, who recoiled from the sight of him.

Emerald looked around them all: Smudge near the stairs; the eager, ornamented figures of her friends and family; the glum, disappointed, shifting strangers.

'Well, that's that,' she said. 'I'm afraid, as you heard, the Railway aren't able to come for you this evening. Perhaps the weather has something to do with it.'

As if supporting her words, the rain outside drummed ever more mercilessly on the house.

The passengers didn't move. In fact, they advanced.

'I'm sorry you can't be on your way,' Emerald went on. 'And I'm sorry for your . . . misfortune.'

Still, they moved slowly towards her.

'There! What more do you want?' Charlie Traversham-Beechers shouted, breaking the spell of their collective

gaze. He had a very commanding tone. 'Later!' he said again.

'I promise,' added Emerald.

Then the passengers, appeased or defeated, slowly withdrew. They returned to the study, jerkily, like the flickering scene of a moving picture run backwards, and the door closed once more.

'Oh my God!' uttered Charlotte, *sotto voce*, and gave a brief, hysterical laugh.

Smudge crept forward and took her fingers.

'But, Mother,' she said, 'they must be hungry.'

Charlotte looked down at her coldly. 'Don't be silly, Smudge; they can't expect to be fed.'

'We ought to see to them,' allowed Emerald, who was trembling slightly from her close encounter with the strangers, and she took a steadying breath.

'Not on your birthday!' said Charlotte.

There was a brief pause as the party glanced at the closed door of the study and examined their consciences.

Then Traversham-Beechers smiled, his voice insinuating itself into the silence like a snake into a sleeping bag. 'That's all very well, but what about the approaching others?' he said. 'Hadn't you better comply? Ought you to send *somebody* to meet them?'

Emerald nodded. 'Someone had better ask Robert to go off with Stanley and see about them. Clovis?'

'I'll nip along to the stables now,' said Clovis, and nipped.

'Well,' said Charlotte in the pause that followed his absence, 'this is all very diverting. But what about dinner? Shall we go in?'

She held out her arm to her moustachioed escort.

At that moment, there was a muffled crash, a splintering crack that resounded, followed by a short scream. The guests

looked around, a little nervously. It hadn't been thunder or furniture that time, but seemed to come from the direction of the kitchen.

The birthday party took their places at the dining table. There was no food to be seen.

Disconcertingly, there was a powerful smell of mock turtle soup that lingered tantalisingly in the cold air, as if from steam only recently dematerialised. The tureen, though, had there been one, was not to be seen. They all wondered where it might have got to.

Minutes earlier, Myrtle, having handed the telephone to Emerald, had scurried back to the dining room to rescue the rapidly cooling soup, thinking to keep it warm in the kitchen until such time as the guests required it. Unfortunately, her fingers were greasy from washing the pan that had held the calf's head as it scalded. The grease on her skin, which had hardened under the cold water, melted again under the hot weight of the gilded tureen of mock turtle soup, and became slick. The brim-full tureen had plunged from her grasp at the kitchen door, plummeted the short distance to the flags – and smashed.

The soup, lumpy and glistening, in impossible, rolling quantities, mixed with smithereens and curlicues of china, poured, wasted, across the span of the kitchen doorway, under the dresser, onto the floor at the foot of the range, and into cracks, troughs and corners hitherto un-thought of. Florence and Myrtle, in silent horror, scooped it hotly into their hands, pushed it about with grey cloths, shovelled it into newspaper, and – disposed of it. This took some time. Florence spared the cringing Myrtle her recrimination. Many worse things had – or might yet – befall both of them. It was very cruel, though, the loss of the soup: the scalding of the head, the chopping

of brains, the pints of Madeira and meticulous rolling of each tiny forcemeat ball had all been for nothing. It was the bitterest of defeats.

Clovis, dispatching the understandably disgruntled Robert and Stanley to seek out the new arrivals, stood shivering and dripping in the doorway of Robert's snug rooms above the harnesses. He envied the remains of the meal that still lay on the scrubbed table. It may have been basic, but it was at least material, as opposed to his thus far hypothetical supper.

As the capable Robert and Stanley made ready to set off into the night, dressed head to foot in oilskins like the crew of a lifeboat, Clovis returned, ravenous, to the dining room. He realised as he took his place amid the small and anxious group, that now there was only themselves, Florence and Myrtle left at Sterne, and nobody else for miles.

The placement of the party ran thus: Emerald was at the end of the table, flanked by Ernest Sutton and John Buchanan; Smudge and the extra guest were opposite one another in the centre, where she eyed his rich cherry-plum waistcoat with wonder; Clovis headed the table's opposite end, with his mother and Patience Sutton to entertain. There was enough room for several invisible persons to have been seated between them all without crowding.

The clock on the mantelpiece did not tick. Time passed silently. The door did not open. Neither Myrtle nor Florence Trieves appeared with any part of supper, no small offering, no *amuse-bouche*, no crust, no crumb, no morsel. Emerald wedged her foot under the sleeping body of the spaniel Nell, for warmth and comfort. Beyond the dining-room walls were domestic toil in one direction and displaced persons in the other, she reflected, allowing her eye to rest on the smoky

depths of the room, on the long candles in the candelabras, and the gold flames that stretched upward into the blue air, quivering.

'Emerald, I hope you won't think I'm speaking out of turn,' said Patience, sweetly, 'but ·I wonder, as we appear to have a . . . gap, if you should like me to fetch your present?'

'Oh!' said Emerald. 'Yes, please.'

Charlotte rose from her chair, mistily. 'Why don't you and I see about a present, too?' she said, and wandered out, with a 'Smudge?' over her slender shoulder.

'Presents, then?' said Patience, jumping up.

Emerald was left, the lone female, with John, Ernest, Clovis and Traversham-Beechers; it was a most unusual situation.

The wines, spirits and liqueurs were lined up like giant, square-cut jewels along the sideboard awaiting the first course.

The butler at Sterne had been Theodore Trieves, Florence's late husband, with a valet beneath him. Since then, three men had been employed in the post of butler with varying success – they were Wiggs, Morton and Stoves – and no valets. With the decline in the Torrington–Swift fortunes there were now no male indoor servants to take on the appropriate duties. If the family drank at all, Edward was the man in charge, aided in the opening by his two-armed wife or stepson. A champagne cup was occasionally taken and hugely enjoyed.

Tonight it fell to Florence Trieves to serve the wines, but it occurred to Emerald that there were a great many duties heaped upon the housekeeper and cook, who was at any rate nowhere to be seen, and she should like to pass this one on to a suitable male. There was none more suitable than her brother, but Clovis was doing something with his collar studs, which were apparently irksome to him, and did not catch her glances. (He'd been wearing collars all his life, he might have become accustomed to them by now.) The farmer John

Buchanan sat stiffly to her left, seemingly paralysed by the delay; he and the stopped clock had something in common, she thought. She would certainly not ask him, it might look as if she were offering him an intimacy, and she'd got her feet wet in that department earlier. Ernest was looking at her, but she was inexplicably filled with embarrassment at the idea of meeting his glance. She found she could not even look in his direction without becoming intensely self-conscious, an inconvenient state of affairs at dinner, where one was absolutely obliged to talk to one's neighbours. She attempted to send the word WINE, via thought waves, to her brother's brain. But it was Traversham-Beechers who read her mind.

'I say – in common with Miss Sutton, I dread offending,' he pronounced silkily, 'but do you think it appallingly rude of me to mention that you've a great many decanters lined up, and no one in sight to dole out the rations?'

Without waiting for a response, he leapt to his feet, weightlessly – it was most intriguing to see. He was at the sideboard in a flash. Clovis at last met Emerald's eye, with an 'oh, dash it why not?' sort of look, and she blinked at him in resentful acquiescence.

'Good idea,' said John, startled into speaking.

Ernest Sutton alone seemed to sit up ever straighter in his seat at this blatant faux pas. *Did nobody else baulk at it?* he wondered, bristling with disapproval. Surely it was Clovis's place to see to the wine, but not *his* place to say so, and so he remained silent.

'Now, what will it be?' sang the gentleman by the sideboard. 'First course. Smelled like soup. *Meaty* . . .' His fingers ran along the bottles lightly, as if along much-loved piano keys, flicking the silver labels on their slender chains. 'La la la,' he said. 'Sherry!'

He grabbed, unstopped and poured, all in a flash, then sat and raised his amber glass to Emerald, winking broadly.

'Salutations and thanks most sincerely,' he said, and drained it.

Where can supper have got to, and what on earth are we going to do with the study full of bodies once the invited guests are fed? wondered Emerald, fixing a hostess's smile on lips that were paler than they had been, most of the rouge having been sucked off them during the course of the fraught and calamitous evening.

Upstairs, Smudge stood, convulsing with excitement, watching her mother's elegant behind wag as she retrieved the boxed kitten from beneath her bed.

'There!' said Charlotte, emerging. The shoebox was bound with twine and studded with holes. A muffled squeak seeped out.

'Tenterhooks,' breathed Smudge.

'Yes. It hasn't been in there too long, I hope. Now, let me see . . .' Charlotte handed Smudge the shifting weight of the box and went about the room picking up scarves and scraps and dropping them again. 'I haven't a letter or card, but a kitten is a nice sort of thing to get, and the Bowes girl was happy to be shot of it and – ah!' She had found a piece of velvet. 'Hold it out,' she instructed coldly. 'No, ridiculous child, there – get your hand out of the way.'

Smudge tried to obey the quick tides of her mother's emotion. She held the box meekly. The kitten's mews reached a pitch.

'Now, may I take it? Can I take it now?' said Smudge. Charlotte kissed her forehead.

'*Darling,*' she said. 'Yes.'

And Smudge ran.

Left alone for a moment, Charlotte paused, wavered, and pressed the back of her hand lightly against her forehead. Her lashes trembled.

God, she thought, *him . . . What can it mean?*

And while she yearned for Edward's strong arm to comfort her, she was profoundly relieved he was not there.

Patience, in her room, was humming as she took the neat package from among the frothy lace and ribbons in the cushioning depths of her trunk. She adjusted the bow and closed the door behind her as, still humming, she started along the silent corridor towards the stairs.

Her pale head bobbed as she descended. *I do hope Emerald is as thrilled by all this as she used to be*, she thought, holding the present carefully and skipping lightly down the polished stair. She passed beneath the oil landscapes – forests on hills and distant temples – and thought back to the time in their childhoods when she, Ernest and her parents had visited Sterne often and, just as often, received the Torringtons in Berkshire. She had always preferred Sterne; it had been the happiest of houses and hardy enough to take the knocks of croquet mallets and tennis balls, pony races on the lawn . . .

Then – of a sudden – she felt herself observed. Looking up, she noticed the figure of a man in the hall beneath her. Her breath caught. Distracted by his expression, which was admiring, her soft shoe slipped on the edge of the stair – glimpsing his face as she lost her balance, it was that man, Traversham – watching her – and she slipped. She gave a scream, her hands flew up, almost – but not quite – releasing the present from her grasp. The stairs were hopelessly slippery and the flags at their foot unforgiving; she must not fall. Patience's white fingers gripped her precious box as one leg shot from under her, the other bumped down and buckled,

and she landed in a slithering heap almost at the bottom of the stairs, bruised but not broken, her head resting lightly against the heavy balustrade.

Her hands shook at the real danger she had glimpsed and she looked up, in hot embarrassment, for the man's reaction.

He was not there. The hall was empty.

Surely he wouldn't walk away from her had he seen her fall? Had she imagined him? Had she mistaken one of those long portraits that hung there, their urbane figures seeming to come forward from the frames?

Patience sat on the stairs, holding Emerald's present and recovered herself. She gave her head a shake, as one responding to an inner voice. Yes: lost in memories, she had experienced that common feeling on emerging from a daydream, that she was observed. She had *not* been observed, except by herself, and she had been foolish – and lucky not to have had a worse accident. Poor Ernest, he would have been delighted at a sprained ankle to minister to.

She stood up. As she did so, the door to the study opened behind her, and three of the passengers – a woman, a child and a young man – looked out. Patience, for the second time in three minutes, gave a yelp.

'Are you all right, miss?' said the woman, whose concerned face peered from beneath a battered straw bonnet.

In a startling moment of recognition, Patience thought it was *her* bonnet – it had the same shape, the same flowers on the brim, but this one was wrecked, not at all the immaculate object in which Patience had travelled. She realised she was staring dumbly at the woman, whose expression remained fixed, inquisitive and concerned.

'Yes. Quite. Thank you,' she said at last, eager to be gone. How could she have thought this small, blonde woman was

wearing her bonnet? She was unlike Patience in every way.
She must be dizzy from her fall.

'Thank you,' she repeated. 'I'm quite all right.'

'Will we be getting along soon?' asked the woman. 'We
can't wait.'

'I hope so,' said Patience, and she set off for the dining
room, hearing the door click closed again behind her and not
at all tempted to look back.

The scene she found when she returned to the party was
a jolly one. There was as yet no supper to be had, but she
was greeted with laughter and the sight of Smudge jumping
up and down crying, 'Hurrah! Hurrah!' as Emerald held
the tiniest of kittens on her palm and looked into its wild
face.

The visitor, her brother, John and Clovis were all seated,
and laughing – and drinking, she noted – while Charlotte
stood at the far end of the room, framed by the curtains, with
a beatific, if glassy smile. The visitor certainly didn't *look* as if
he had just now returned to the room having ogled her on
the stair – he glanced up at Patience only briefly, absorbed in
the presentation of the kitten.

'Look! Look, Patience! It's called Tenterhooks!' said
Smudge, and Patience clapped her hands together too.

'Oh, the darling!' she said.

'Do you think it's hungry?' asked Emerald.

'I should think we all are!' declared the visitor, whose frank-
ness, after the briefest of pauses, was greeted with general
laughter.

'What have you got there, Patience?' asked Ernest. He knew
of course exactly what she had, but was drawing attention so
she might present it. Emerald gave the kitten to Smudge who
clutched it to her neck.

'Happy Birthday, Emerald,' said Patience and handed over the box. 'It's from both of us – and Mother, of course.'

All eyes were on Emerald, smilingly tugging at the bow. 'How beautifully you've wrapped it, Patience,' she said.

'She always had neat little fingers,' said her mother archly.

The box was opened, and inside it there was another, polished walnut with a brass clasp. Emerald opened it hesitatingly, for she knew, suddenly, what she would find.

Several dozen glass slides were arranged in the black felt lining, each wrapped in crisp tissue.

'Oh,' said Emerald.

'Well?' said Patience, eager.

'How generous. How kind,' said Emerald, but she was unconvincing.

Patience's face fell. 'Aren't you interested in your microscope any more, Em?' she asked.

'No. Of course. Of course I am,' said Emerald.

'Emerald hasn't been near it in donkey's years,' said Clovis blithely.

'Oh, I have!' said Emerald, darting guilty glances at Patience.

'All her notebooks and bits and pieces have been banished. She's quite grown out of it, haven't you?' said Clovis.

'Oh, that's a shame,' murmured Ernest, who remembered their heads touching as they bent together over jointed beetles' legs.

'It's a superb present,' said Emerald emphatically, but Patience was not fooled.

'Well, never mind. What a silly. I ought to have kept to rose water.' She spoke as lightly as she could muster but she did not convince, and her bottom was beginning to hurt most horribly from having fallen so hard onto it.

'Patience—'

'It's the thought that counts,' said Patience brightly.

John reached out a big hand. 'May I?' he asked, unwrapping a slide and holding it up to the light. 'Well, you won't go into *real* science, of course.'

'Madame Curie might disagree,' Emerald found herself replying quickly.

'She's a foreigner,' said he, closing the argument.

He crushed the paper and let it fall. Emerald's hand darted out, instinctively, to save the falling ball of tissue from the floor. She flattened it out on the table, remembering as sharply as if he had poked her in the side with a paper knife how, on discovering science had no answer for the question her father's illness presented, she had put away childish things to follow the path of useful womanhood, and nurse him. It was not, as the hackneyed phrase would have it, 'what he would have wanted', no, it was very far from that: it was what he would have dreaded. But there it was. Her beloved father had been ill; her mother had been distraught; her brother arrested by shock; her sacrifice had been required. That had been the end to it. She could not have known that, like an enchanted princess, she would forget so easily everything she had been before. Duty had put a spell upon her heart.

Smudge traced a finger along the exposed glass slide. 'It looks like spun sugar. I want to crunch it up,' she said, her mouth buried in kitten fur.

'And have blood pour down your chin and die a gruesome death,' said Clovis.

'What could they be?' asked Charlotte, looking away restlessly. She knew perfectly well, but frowned with irritation at Patience having run true to form and brought something dull to the party.

Ernest caught her spiteful look and glared. He rearranged his face immediately, of course, but Charlotte had seen him and was distracted from her introspection. There was

manliness in his reserve, she mused, and his hair was not so much red any longer as . . . She sought the right word – something like the stem of a bramble. In the days before her present contentment she would have enjoyed finding the spell that would bind him.

Traversham-Beechers watched Charlotte like a stoat. He rose from his place and approached stealthily. She was breathless at his approach, lest someone should see them and intuit their connection, but standing together by the window, they were unobserved.

'You're unaltered, aren't you?' he whispered, without a glimmer.

'Since last I saw and loathed *you!*' she spat.

'Oh, you weren't so *very* unfriendly then,' he mocked.

'Sit down, get away!' she hissed and so, smilingly, he withdrew.

No matter what the reason for that man appearing at Sterne, Florence Trieves knew that her priority lay with supper.

'Now, Myrtle, are we ready?' she panted, and led the way. She held the baize door open with her back.

'Yes, ma'am, ready.'

'Those blasted survivors safely out of the way?'

'Still in the study, ma'am; not a peep.'

'Well, let's get on then!'

Bearing a platter each, they processed to the waiting diners.

'Ah!' cried the wine-fronted visitor with appreciation, as his nose was touched by butter and delicate fishy things. 'Oh, *yes!*'

The others maintained their good manners, squaring to the table to receive, restrained and eager. Charlotte nestled herself into her seat.

Florence served, and the coral fronds and painted leaves of their small plates were soon obscured by parsley, smelts and

soft, stewed eel. There were sauces. The ravenous guests availed themselves gratefully as Florence circled the table with the sherry decanter. Much shaken, passing by Traversham-Beechers' chair, she widened her eyes in horror in his direction. Charlotte gave her an almost imperceptible wink; the bonds between them strengthened and tugged.

The spaniels Lucy and Nell had woken at the smell of kitten and fish, and were now leaping up and down, banging their heads against the furniture and barking. Emerald hauled the hysterical dogs out, as the kitten, as spiky as a horse-chestnut casing and almost the same size, spat viciously at them.

'Here, hand it over,' commanded Traversham-Beechers, and John plucked up the little cat and did as he was told.

The visitor took it, and the kitten clung weightlessly to his thick fingers. Suspended over the table, it stared blindly into the air around it.

'Don't; it's close to the flame!' cried Emerald as, having shut out the snapping dogs, she regained her place.

'Do you think I would scorch a defenceless animal?' said the visitor, but did not withdraw his hand, swinging the kitten ever so slightly above the stretching flames.

Gradually the guests ceased their feasting. Smelts were forgotten as every look was fixed on the fragile creature hanging above the candelabra, stretching its minute claws to full capacity. The gentleman dared them to interfere, planting in them the desire to be approved of. None there was so weak as Clovis, who began to giggle. Emerald was aghast.

'Stop it!' she said, and the man withdrew his hand slowly, and grinned slickly around them all.

'Footle,' he said, 'nobody likes roast cat.'

He dropped the kitten onto Charlotte's hand. The pads of its paws were hot on her skin.

There was a brief silence and then everybody began to

speak, until the conversation, loosened by sherry, fish and relief, took a solid, self-propelled direction, pleasing everybody present – except perhaps the visitor, who mopped his plate with bread crusts and cast a baleful eye about the table.

Charlotte placed the kitten next to her cheek, enjoying their comparable beauty and the kindness she was demonstrating.

'Poor creature,' she purred and dipped her finger in the fishy wetness on her plate to delectate the animal's rasping tongue.

'I don't know which of you has the prettier eyes,' said Patience obediently, but, being of the wrong sex, was ignored. She shyly glanced at Clovis and, dazzled by him, attempted to cover her perturbation with conversation.

'It's such a shame we shan't see anything of Mr Swift whilst we're here,' she offered.

Clovis was aware they were being observed by Traversham-Beechers, and his mood, as impressionable as soft clay, was influenced by the presence of the subversive stranger like a thumb pot. He felt a restlessness that stirred him, unsatisfied by the pert figure of Patience.

She awaited his response; her polite gaze bridging the gap between their chairs with convention. 'He's in Manchester,' he allowed.

'On business? There must be an awful lot of dissolution in Manchester for him to have to administer the law there on a Saturday!'

Clovis ignored this attempt at levity and continued to stare at her idly, but the visitor, across the table, laughed suddenly.

'Pretty as a picture *and* a first-class wit!' he pronounced.

Patience, remembering the way he had eyed her on the stairs (or she had imagined he had), blushed.

'Perhaps . . . I can tempt you.' Traversham-Beechers cast his eye about the table. His intimate tone ought to have been

too quiet to reach Patience over the wide table, but she heard it as clearly as if he were whispering next to her small ears; everybody, in fact, heard him quite as if he had spoken into their ears.

'Perhaps I can tempt you all.'

He had their full attention in an instant. The conversation spluttered and stalled.

All eyes were once again directed at Traversham-Beechers, who slowly reached into his breast pocket and took from it a silver cigarette box. He held the thing, gleaming, across to Patience, who looked at him askance.

Charlotte released Tenterhooks onto the tablecloth. She wore again something of the expression she had had on first seeing their visitor in the drawing room: wondering and alarmed. Clovis, oblivious, was simply bemused, as were the others.

'Your cigarette case?' said Patience. 'Whatever would I want with that?'

'Not a cigarette for sure, eh, Miss Sutton?'

'Certainly not!'

'No, no, smooth your little feathers; it is what it represents that may interest you – you and Miss Torrington.'

'Me?' Emerald was as perplexed as Patience.

'Certainly, as young women on the brink of . . . so many things, it may interest you in your quest.'

'And what quest might that be?' asked Emerald drily. She did not see herself in a heroic context.

'Why, the bagging of a mate.'

'Oh. That.'

'What else? If you aren't taken with my young host's fallow cheekiness, Miss Sutton, or you, Miss Torrington, with these two other callow creatures,' he nodded towards John and Ernest, 'then perhaps you're looking for maturity?

This case is a solid thirty-five years old. Or for elegance? The case is most slender, and fits invisibly into the most discreet silk-lined pocket, and bears a first-class maker's mark. Or,' he fixed his eyes on Emerald, 'are you looking for wealth?'

The question hung on the air. Clovis had the feeling he was observing a master at work; John was, despite himself, impressed at the fellow's insolence; only Ernest, with clenched jaw, kept his eyes directed at the table and refused to be drawn. He had a fanciful idea Traversham-Beechers' charms were best resisted if one did not look at him. And Charlotte – well, nobody noticed her extreme pallor. Her heart was sinking into her sickened stomach. She had seen it all before.

'If I were, as you say, "looking",' said Emerald shakily, 'I wouldn't, well, I certainly would *not* discuss anything of the sort with *you* – over smelts and trinkets,' she finished emphatically.

'Smelts and trinkets,' he murmured sensuously. 'Very nice, very nice.' And he smiled.

To their horror, and despite themselves, Patience and Emerald together, like a pair of trained ponies, found that they smiled back at him. He glanced from one to the other, lapping up his triumph, as his fingers tapped the small, domed, hard buttons on the front of his waistcoat, lightly. Emerald crossed her legs. Patience shifted in her seat.

Clovis felt the uneasy attraction between them, and was himself discomfited. He had hoped to see Patience embarrassed, but not like this. At the same time, though, he was stirred with the thrill of the chase and could not deny it, even as he disliked the feeling in himself.

'Then see here,' said the stranger quickly, and, with an imperceptible movement, the silver case disappeared completely.

'Where did it *go*!' shouted Smudge, forgetting herself and

leaping up, before plumping back down into her seat and snatching up the kitten, and crushing him to her chest as if to stop herself speaking without being spoken to at the table again.

Even Emerald and Patience had gasped at the disappearance of the cigarette case. John, Clovis and even Ernest laughed with disbelief and sudden innocence, and exchanged childlike, friendly looks.

Charlotte had girded herself once more.

'Steady yourselves, children,' she said coldly; 'it's in his sleeve.'

'Oh, is it?' said the gentleman with a smile, adding mysteriously, 'You won't stop me like that. And I felt sure I saw it . . .' He stood up and reached behind the elaborate cushion of Charlotte's hair. She shivered quickly, all down her body.

'Here!' And with a flash he produced the case again, glinting in the candlelight.

Patience clapped her hands together.

'Oh, do it again! I love tricks!' she said. She had altogether forgotten her discomfort of only moments before, she was so utterly delighted with him now.

Traversham-Beechers looked at Charlotte again. 'Anything for my hostess,' he said, 'who has so very kindly let us *all* in.'

As he said it, they heard a rising whisper, a gentle cry from the abandoned passengers in the study, as if they were a nighttime forest with the wind passing through it. Everyone at the table paused to listen, recalling with distaste that they had eaten their fish course, while the unfortunate passengers were entirely unattended to. Smudge alone didn't notice the sound, the child had the kitten pressed to her ear and, in her innocence, could hear only its purrs.

The following brief silence was interrupted violently by Myrtle's hurried entrance carrying a basket of bread,

which she placed on the table. Seeing it, Smudge was reminded of her responsibility towards the pony Lady; however much fun she was having at the birthday party, she ought not forget her Undertaking. She groaned and leapt to her feet.

'Please excuse me!' She deposited the kitten Tenterhooks onto her chair and sped from the room.

She always ran when going alone through the house and she did so now; along the corridor, through the baize door, into the kitchen, negotiating the chaos there – sorting desperately through it, and finding, in a crate on the floor, a wormy apple, and near it a lumpy crust. Smudge grabbed them, tore open the door to the back stairs and flew up, panting.

Lady had made a good job of chewing the eiderdown and stepped a great many charcoal sticks into the floor, but there was no serious damage done. She dozed now, resting one back leg delicately on the edge of the hoof, her lower lip sagging. Smudge sat at her feet and fed her, regaining her breath with her head leaning against the wall.

The air of the kitchen was thickened to tangibility with steam and coating odours. No more teasing little fishes, no more feeble beurre blanc; it was time for meat.

Florence wiped the sweat from her face, dried her hands on her apron. She should have liked a fresh dress; this one was stiff. She could smell nothing, had been in the thick of it for too long; the roots of her hair, her cuticles, the soles of her feet inside her boots were covered with layers of preparation; the juices and oils of meats and starches were part of her, undetected. Her very tongue was dulled; she wouldn't have been able to taste a pickled onion had one been popped into her mouth.

Joints, knuckles, rolls, twine, sprouts, rabbit, edgings, curls, piles, fronds . . . She bent ever closer. Her fingers worked on figures of eight, spirals, dustings, minute shells and strong-salted pieces, tiny, tinier, tiniest.

Having satisfied herself the pony was no immediate danger to herself or the house, Smudge began the return journey to the dining room. Trotting along the empty upper landing, she did not expect to see, rounding the corner of the stair, a man coming up towards her. She froze in her tracks, hands flung out to stop herself.

He was an enormous man, made thicker and more huge by the carrying of a great sack on his back. He had a cap pulled down over his face, such as a municipal employee might wear, and deep, burning eyes above a thick beard. Behind him were two small children, stick-legged and fearful, clinging to the banisters.

'Excuse me, miss,' he said.

But Smudge did not pause to hear any more from him. She sprinted down the corridor, away from him, and threw herself down the scullery stairs.

'MRS TRIEVES!'

Florence leapt nearly out of her boots. 'Smudge! Miss Imogen! Good Lord! My God!' Her scalp prickled with shock, or sweat, or both.

'I think you need to come and help.' Smudge wobbled with pale fear at the bottom of the scullery stairs, but Florence had other matters to see to.

'Not now! Not now, child.'

'I – I went to see something, and there was a *man*.'

'Oh Lord, *not now!*'

'Myrtle, then?' Smudge was desperate.

'Clearing.'

'Somebody. Emerald . . . *Mother?*' (This last signalled her desperation.) 'Mrs Trieves, they're upstairs!'

'Upstairs? Heavens, that won't do. Come along.'

Through the baize door they went, together, and came immediately upon a small huddle of passengers stealing along the corridor and talking quietly amongst themselves.

'Get back!' Florence commanded violently to the startled group, and, clutching Smudge's hand, ran to the dining room.

'They're out of the study and all over the house!' she cried.

What!, *Heavens!* and other exclamations of dismay came from the group.

'You ladies stay in here,' commanded John, standing abruptly.

He was joined by Clovis and Ernest and they advanced towards the hall.

'Trivering . . .' Clovis had forgotten his dashed name again. 'Aren't you coming with us?'

'Must I?' responded the man lazily, and drew himself to his feet.

'Come along!' cried John urgently, and at last, he joined them.

The gentlemen gone, the door closed, the women were left to themselves. Florence hovering by the sideboard, hesitant.

'Oh heavens,' said Charlotte, fanning herself. 'How vile.'

'I can't imagine what we can have been thinking, neglecting them so shabbily,' said Emerald.

'Footle!' returned her stubbornly unrepentant mother. 'They should all be taken out and thrashed! If only Robert were here,' she cried, dashing her brow with her fist.

Smudge went and knelt by her, touching her dress.

'Oh don't!' she said, flinching, so Emerald took the child's hand. Silently, they listened to the shouts and stamps beyond the dining-room door.

* * *

Amongst the handful of survivors who had released themselves from the lonely study, the mood was not of anger or threat, but more a febrile anxiety. John Buchanan, brandishing a walking stick, had searched the rest of the house, but apart from the man with the children, now returned to the group, there was nobody upstairs.

The hungry souls were seeking rest or sustenance, seeking comfort and communication, seeking, it seemed, the Torringtons, and were now grouped in the hall facing their smartly-dressed captors stubbornly.

'We should like to speak to the lady of the house!' cried a woman.

'We just want to get on! We're hungry. We're so hungry. It was none of our faults!'

'There, there; we'll see what can be done,' said Ernest, wondering, as he looked at her, if she was in fact injured in some way he had failed to discover earlier, or her alarming pallor was simply the after-effects of the accident, and being locked away for so long. 'I really must apologise,' he said.

Although he couldn't speak on behalf of his hosts, he resolved to speak – if not to the unapproachable Mrs Swift, perhaps to Emerald.

'We've waited and waited,' said another woman, and there were echoes of 'hungry' and 'why' all around him, in pitiful polyphony.

'Now, hear this, you people!' came the strident nasal tones of Traversham-Beechers. 'Nothing can be gained by moaning. You and I must wait here some brief, undisclosed time!' They listened attentively. 'We hope our needs will be met. We trust . . .' Here, he paused and of a sudden, there passed over his face a look, briefly – but to Ernest, most powerfully – displayed. A look that very much resembled dread. He went on, '. . . trust God . . .' the word

rang and hung and halted in the chilly air, '. . . will see our needs are met. Until then, we must be patient. Now, in we go!' And with that he gestured the open study door once more.

As all the guests were reunited in the dining room, John announced, 'They are contained!'

'Bravo, John,' said Charlotte.

Emerald let go of Smudge's hand, and addressed them.

'We have begun our dinner,' she said solidly; 'they must have theirs.'

She met Ernest's encouraging glance.

'Hear, hear,' he said.

'Oh, this is absurd!' burst out Charlotte.

'No, Mother, continuing to ignore them is absurd. I won't stand for it.'

'Emerald!'

'Can't you see it doesn't do any good? There are more and more of them already! Some must go into the morning room again, and others into the study. And they must be fed,' she said firmly. 'You're very rude.'

Charlotte cared not a jot for rudeness. She had built her life so that she might avoid third-class train carriages and she wasn't going to wring her hands over those who made use of them now.

'Just the study, please,' she sulkily demanded. 'The morning room is my special room.'

'They are *all your special rooms*, Mother,' said Emerald bitterly, but there broke off, to avoid a public argument.

'How shall we do it?' asked Patience.

The faces, except Tenterhooks', who was lapping up the sauces, and Traversham-Beechers', who was yawning at the ceiling, looked at her expectantly.

'I dislike troubling you with our domestic affairs, but I think I must,' said Emerald, with a glance towards Florence Trieves. 'The maid, Pearl Meadows, is unwell; Robert and his boy have gone to see about these other passengers the Railway are sending. There aren't many of us here at Sterne. Mrs Trieves is all alone in the kitchen, except for Myrtle, and I'm afraid,' the rest of the sentence teetered on the tip of her tongue for long seconds before she sent it out, 'we shall have to go into the kitchen.'

She ignored her mother's gasp at this atrocious notion but Florence cried, 'Oh no, Emerald! I can manage.'

'No, Mrs Trieves. We will help.'

Patience piped up, 'And me! And I, I mean. Show me an apron and the kitchen door.'

'Thank you, Patience.'

'And I,' said Ernest gruffly.

'No!' said Florence, again, feebly.

'And me, Em. I've often helped my mother,' said John.

'I've never helped mine,' said Clovis, 'but count me in.'

'Good!' said Charlotte with sudden violence. 'Then you've plenty of hands for your sordid decks. On your birthday! It's ridiculous. You'll have a riot on your hands if you start trying to please these ghastly people. Smudge will go to her room, unless you're going to reintroduce child labour as well! And I shall go to mine. I shan't expect to be disturbed.'

She turned to the chief amongst their uninvited guests, the insolent Traversham-Beechers.

'*And you will stay here,*' she said slowly and – in that instant – showed every tooth, every claw, she had; the very room shrank away from her.

The gentleman, though, was undaunted.

'Yes, I should think I will dabble about in here for a

while,' he said sleepily, and pulled a long cigar from an inside pocket.

Charlotte turned, sharply, on her heel, held out her hand to a reluctant Smudge, and left them, closing the door behind her.

'Never mind, she'd only get in the way,' said Clovis cheerfully, in an undertone to Emerald.

Their attention was caught by the suggestive, rhythmic, sucking sound of Traversham-Beechers lighting his cigar from a candle. Caught between shock and a brand of anarchic admiration, the five young people watched for a moment, scandalised, then: 'Please,' said Ernest to Florence politely, 'lead the way,' and they set off for the kitchens, leaving the man to his pleasures in a sea of dirty plates.

In the corridor, Myrtle was dispatched to seat the passengers, while the guests set off for the kitchen, with Florence scuttling miserably ahead. They passed the morning room, turned the corner, and the green baize door came into view.

'Perhaps we'll have time for a game or two afterwards, with your cake if you're having one,' said Patience encouragingly to Emerald as they went.

The household had ceased to be surprised at the survivors' increasing numbers, concluding that on this runaway evening they could not be expected to keep count.

'They're like flies,' said Myrtle furiously, as she carried in more chairs, banging them down and glaring at the whole ungrateful hoard. She ushered half of them along the corridor to the morning room and persuaded the other half to stay in the study.

They snatched the chairs from her with powerful fingers.

They sat about the place preparing to feed, their eyes following Myrtle with glinting brightness as they waited, breathless, for their meal.

Emerald, Patience, Ernest, John and Clovis, all in their evening clothes, all together, stared about the kitchen at the piles of half-prepared food.

Florence would have cried if she had been any younger or less disciplined, but she had not cried for years. Sometimes she felt all her tears – of grief and joy – had been shed for Theodore, and her eyes were dry in their sockets, moving slowly towards that oft-contemplated, dusty death. She imagined little sacks that should be filled with lapping tears, hanging shrivelled between her eyeballs and her brain. But yes, if she had had the tears, she would have cried now at all her hard work being squandered in this low crisis. She did not want to be seen in her kitchen – not like this.

She felt as if she were a grand clock with its back hanging open; the face was mother of pearl, diamonds and gold hands, but inside the casing there were only grimy little cogs and wheels to examine. Can it be this, that had seemed so marvellous? Just these springs? Just these tiny screws? She hung her head.

'Aprons, please,' said Emerald brightly, taking strange delight in flying in the face of her mother's wishes. Assorted plates were piled, wobbling and ready to receive. The helpers stood poised to serve. Florence, brandishing a big knife, loomed over the dishes, the weapon held firmly and aloft, but she made several passes before eventually gritting her teeth and plunging the blade through first the pastry of the Boeuf en Croute, then the Fricasseed rabbit, the fowl pudding . . . Her massacre was comprehensive but her portions necessarily

meagre. What had been a feast for eight was a virtual famine for thirty or more. Had there really been so many before?

Plate after plate was carried through, and handfuls of cutlery, and hunks of bread. The hungry visitors, seated on three-legged stools, benches and bentwood chairs, huddled over the desk in the study and the hastily cleared small tables, and gobbled the food before them.

'There are too many of them,' panted Patience; 'they need more.'

So, with the entrée exhausted, they made inroads into the next course. Florence's keen blade found the slippery joints in the Poulet à la Marengo, the tender baby flesh of the veal roll. Still they were unsatisfied. The kitchen resembled a deserted field-hospital at the Crimea after the battle has moved on: bones with shreds of flesh clinging, wet cloths, stained, scraped boards and instruments flung down, as the hoards moved on to demolish the next thing – dessert.

'Wait! God, wait,' said Florence, turning her back on the scene of destruction and closing her eyes.

'Here.' Ernest took the knife from her, as around them the others worked.

Emerald watched his strong hands tuck the tip of the blade between the tender soft rhubarb slices that lay upon the custard of the tart, never tearing them; her own fingers trembled slightly as she held out two fragile plates for the crescents of jelly that came next from his spoon. Patience's slender arm came between them for a moment, reaching for a jug of cream, before darting with it from the room.

'Do you mind if I mention something?' he asked.

'I won't know until you have,' she answered, mentally gazing at an array of desirable and less desirable possibilities.

'Have you really given up your science?'

'My? Oh – the microscope. I suppose I have.'

He slipped a tiny globe of blancmange onto the plate, nestled against the jelly.

'I'm amazed by it – from what I knew of you.'

'Amazed by it? Are you?' she asked. She was nonplussed.

'Yes. Two more.'

She held up two more plates.

'Hell!' cried Clovis behind them, as some lard-loosened disaster hit the flags.

'I think it's a great shame,' said Ernest. Another sliver of rhubarb tart found a home. Another crescent of acid jelly slipped from the rapidly warming spoon. 'Because you are so clever.'

Emerald did not look up. She felt pride creeping into her, unusual and welcome.

'I put it away during my father's illness,' she almost whispered, as unaccustomed warmth touched the hard frost of her restraint.

'Ah,' he answered, equally softly. His fish-slice eased beneath the crumbling pastry, butter wetting the metal.

'Great heavens,' broke in Florence, hot-footing it in from the study and seeing the myriad of desserts. 'Are they each to have quite such a selection?' But she snatched away the plates all the same. Ernest cast Emerald a slow, shy smile; I look a fright, she thought.

She had not thought to change her dress. It was limp, splattered with fat, and altogether ruined. The hem was filthy from treading into the dirt. Strands of hair had escaped from Myrtle's miraculous pinning. Patience, in contrast, had retained, marvellously, the general appearance of freshness; even though on close inspection this illusion did not hold up (there was gravy on her lace cuffs). She and Clovis had assumed something of the pace and pattern of a relay, he down the corridor to the baize door, she on into the

rooms, but the business of fetching plates from the kitchen was quicker than that of distribution, what with different passengers' demands and requirements (some wanted fish, others meat, or only fowl, still more simply demanded all three, not to mention the varieties of taste when it came to fruit, jellies and sugars), and Clovis often had to fly after her to help with the passing round and questions. She was, he couldn't help but notice, unwaveringly charming as she enquired after the well-being of the passengers. She even appeared to enjoy pleasing them, and Clovis found the sight of her – as she darted from one drab person to the next, bright as a gold coin in the shadowy study – was heartening; she seemed to restore him. Once, perhaps fatigued with unaccustomed servitude, she slipped on a well-sucked bone that had found its way onto the floor, the passengers being obliged to balance their food as well as their children and luggage on their laps. Patience's slippered foot shot from beneath her and Clovis – quick as a whippet – was across the room to provide her with a steadying arm.

'Do be careful, Patience.' he said, as not only her face, but all the pinched, white faces in the room paused and looked up for an instant. *What about us?* they seemed to say. *What about asking us how we are faring, we who have had such a dreadful accident, we who are in this state of shock and delay?*

But Patience and Clovis had eyes only for one another as they stood, her arm still resting on his hand, caught in the warmth of mutual concern. 'Thank you, Clovis; how clumsy of me.'

'Not at all,' said he, and he bent to retrieve the offending piece of rabbit. He straightened, grinning at her, helplessly.

There was no sound in the room except for the chewing and breathing of all twenty people.

'I wonder if they've had enough?' whispered Patience in Clovis's ear but he was too delighted by the sensation to reply.

In the empty dining room, Tenterhooks had made a good meal of the remains of the fish. Whatever he had found, here and there, had been consumed with much licking and quivering, although he could barely swallow for purring. Shortly afterwards, the kitten's stomach had revolted, violently, against the unprecedented influx and the table was not now anywhere near as attractive as before the party had been called away. It didn't matter, however, as the dining room was – for the present – abandoned. Even Traversham-Beechers had disappeared. There was no trace of him at all in the room; no stray curl of smoke, no odour of hair oil, lingering. Was he among the passengers, eating his fill? Was he shrouded in a drab woollen shawl with a baby's head in the corner of his arm? Or was he wandering the halls of the house, trailing his fingers over the soft panels? Perhaps he was just resting his flesh and bones until the next time they were needed.

Safely ensconced in her room with Lady, behind her stout, locked door, restored by smelts and grateful for the continued distraction of the demanding survivors, Smudge applied herself to the animal's portrait with renewed vigour. A misguided notion of charcoaling the whole of Lady's side and then pressing her against the wall for a print had been abandoned as too ambitious, and she was now busily occupied in placing her bedside lamp in such a way as to create an accurate shadow outline of the pony and tracing it. The minutes flew by unnoticed, the hours unmarked; she was absorbed in her artistry.

* * *

In the morning room, Emerald, Clovis, John, Ernest, Florence and Patience surveyed the travellers, who had at last finished eating and were glumly licking their fingers, holding the hands of their children, or gazing dully at the fire. Although they were, for the moment, satisfied, their mood had not greatly improved. If anything, there was an increased atmosphere of need; they seemed to suck the very air from the room with their opaque desires.

'Perhaps we might slip away?' murmured Emerald.

The party trooped to the desperately disarranged kitchen, and carried from it plates of whatever they could find back to the dining room, where they seated themselves with their mismatching meats and juices.

Emerald discovered a heap of what she realised was kitten vomit near her place and dropped a napkin over it.

Out of sight, out of mind, she thought, picking up the glass nearest her (that had been John's; the placement was all topsy-turvy) and drinking all the sherry in it straight down. She felt immediately fortified.

'Where's that man?' she demanded, looking around them for their gentleman visitor, but nobody knew.

With no trace of Traversham-Beechers and the dining-room door firmly closed, the little group revelled for a short, thrilling moment in triumph and relief, excited by their adventure in serving. Clovis and Emerald exchanged a friendly look. Had they not met the increasing hoards and fed them? Their mother was absent, in vain and indefensible hiding in her room, but they, the young, were still, on Emerald's birthday, in the dining room.

'It isn't so late,' said Emerald. 'Perhaps we *will* still have time for games, as you said, Patience.'

There was laughter.

'Tuck in!' cried Clovis, attacking his own poor plate of scraps with relish.

Florence, caught between family and servant by the unusualness of the evening, was unsure what to do and now stood, dithering, near the sideboard, from where she might either sit or serve the drinks. Emerald was tussling with a tough pastry crust that normally would have been left stuck to the dish, but now was slathered with mustard and appreciated.

'Florence, Mrs Trieves,' she said, when she could, 'do sit. I think the circumstances demand flexibility, don't you?'

Florence, after a moment's hesitation, slipped into the seat between John and Patience, but kept her hands in her lap. John, who had striven for his good position in the world, was embarrassed and disapproving, having to sit next to the housekeeper, and he began to blush. Covering his discomfort and preserving good manners, he took the plate that Emerald offered for Florence.

'Mrs Trieves,' he said, frowning, 'some bread? There's gravy. Here.' And he fetched that, too.

She was more embarrassed than he, and stared at her plate. 'Thank you, Mr Buchanan,' she said, her sharp-boned face reddening.

Glancing at her, next to him, on the same level, he relented; she was so flustered and upset. Despite himself, he noticed that with her head tilted down as it was, and her hair escaping from the rigid bun in which she kept it, her neck looked remarkably – what would be an apt description? – *womanly*, in the lamplight. Yes, remarkably womanly. Pretty. He instantly brought himself up, cleared his throat, and reached for a glass. Noticing the feminine attributes of a middle-aged housekeeper was the sort of thought he hadn't entertained since discovering his physical maleness at thirteen and fourteen when, in the first flushing fever of connection, he had noted compulsively the fetching shapes of every female form he came across, from

shop assistants to gaunt aunts to sculptures and even, disturbingly, non-human things: the waggling of ducks' downy behinds, the bewitching curves of banisters. Mrs Trieves was not a banister, of course, but, he told himself sternly, she was not to be considered any more than one. And he turned both thoughts and body sharply away from her. It must have been the wine and the bizarre circumstances. Why, she was as old as Charlotte Torrington – but, oh dear, that was a very poor comparison, as that lady was an out-and-out beauty at any age. And with that, lost in confusion, John looked straight up and ahead, and tried hard not to think of women at all – an endeavour doomed, of course, to utter failure; within a minute he was wondering if Florence's ankles were as pretty as her neck. He was saved by Emerald's profile as she nibbled a sprout. Here was elegance, he thought. Here was beauty and suitability itself. He rested his gaze upon her, and wondered if his ignoring of her was having any effect on the indifference she bore him. Sensing his look, she glanced over at him saucily, and he had his answer, feeling confidence return.

'Well, I must say, this has been a rum old evening,' he said happily.

'Extremely,' agreed Patience.

'But I hope you don't mind my saying, Emerald, you've carried it off. Hasn't she?' He appealed to the table. 'Hasn't she been marvellous?'

'Of course I haven't, but—' Emerald's hand flew to her mouth. 'Oh, Smudge! I must fetch her down.'

'Perhaps she'll be asleep?' said Ernest, the Sutton household not having been accustomed to children roaming around in nightdresses at teatime and joining grown-up dinners.

'Not she,' rejoined Clovis; 'not if there's cake in the offing.'

'I promised she could help with the candles.'

Emerald stood, but very soon sat down again, sharply, as the door flew open and Charlie Traversham-Beechers, lightly spinning the knob with dancing fingertips, announced himself nasally: 'Who are the survivors now? Any left for us?'

4

A MOST UNPLEASANT GAME

Arrested in their jollity, faces falling, the group looked at Traversham-Beechers wanly for a moment, and then returned to their suppers.

He went immediately to the sideboard and took a deep ruby claret from amongst the decanters and fresh glasses from the sideboard. They tinkled together onto the muffling cloth as he poured, hurriedly, so that little spots and red splashes flew about their edges, and ran pinkly down to stain the damask.

'Here, be merry and all that,' he encouraged, handing around the drinks and keeping the decanter on the table. As he placed the glasses in front of each of them, their camaraderie dissolved into the air. What had been a friendly group became a tableful of single, separated souls. He sat next to Emerald and drank deeply.

'Well, isn't this cosy? Fancy getting blotto?' he said.

A shocked silence met this suggestion.

'I believe I can return a "nay" to that,' said John, 'but I wouldn't mind a glass.'

'A glass or two! That's the spirit,' said Traversham-Beechers, and topped up all the glasses to brimming. 'A toast to your mother – the beautiful Miss – I do beg your pardon, Mrs Torring— I'm so sorry, *Mrs Swift: Mrs Swift!*'

and he raised his glass, drank, and then asked mildly, 'Where is she?'

'She's – she went off some time ago,' said Clovis, adding to Emerald, 'Don't you think we ought to offer our sainted parent the last of the scraps?'

'Go and seek her out, would you, Clo?' said Emerald, who did not much fancy an encounter with her mother just then.

Clovis left the disturbed and gaudy dining room, the guests, seated anyhow, in grubby clothes and scattered scraps about the table, and went into the chilly emptiness of the corridors and hall.

The cat Lloyd was perched sternly on the newel post and watched him as he passed.

Clovis crept to the study and listened to the muted burble within before continuing. Although he knew the passengers were all satisfied for the moment, he did not quite trust the apparent emptiness of the house and seemed to see them still, from the corner of his eye, as he walked.

Upstairs everything was lit and welcoming as before. He knocked on the door of his mother's room, the biggest, in the centre of the house.

'Who is it?'

The voice was fearful; he had startled her. He went in.

'Just me,' he said.

Charlotte had raised herself up on her elbow. The huge bay window was behind her, its silk curtains half drawn, swagged and tasselled, like the curtains for the boudoir scenes of *La Bohème* at Covent Garden, where Clovis, Emerald, Charlotte and Horace had once sat in the stalls one unforgettable evening, and been bathed and saturated by beauty.

'Are you all right, Mother?' he asked.

She had sunk back onto the bed and sighed, and the question came from his heart.

'Sit here, boy,' she said, and when he did she took his hand.

'The guests are all fed – the accident people, I mean – and the rest of us are having a bite in the dining room. Won't you come down?' He was reminded of the many times he had tried to tempt her from her room in the terrible days that followed his father's death. Clovis had been sixteen when Horace Torrington died; he had looked after his mother as well as he could, and managed very well indeed – until she took another husband. Now he held her hand. 'Ma?'

She did not look at him. 'Is he still here?' she asked faintly.

'Who?'

'Traversham-Beechers.' She said the name dully, in one flat tone. She apparently had no difficulty in remembering his name.

'Where would he go, Mother? Don't you like him? I know he can gas, but I think I do, tremendously.'

She did not answer him. Then, 'What time is it?' She sat up slowly, blinking and patting her hair.

'Not sure. Somewhere near ten, I think. I say, are you warm enough?'

The fire in her grate was all but out. Clovis crossed the room and poked the embers, then took the scuttle and shook coal onto it, with a great deal of rattling and dust flying up.

'Oh, hush! My head!'

'Sorry,' he said cheerfully and went to the window. 'Dreadful night. It'll be a bog out there tomorrow. Are you coming down or not?'

She surrendered to his clumsy affection, and held out both hands to him. Taking them, he raised her from the bed. She laid her cheek against the smooth lapel of his jacket; he had been tall enough for her to do it comfortably since about the time of his father's funeral.

'Darling boy,' she said, 'could you ever hate your old mother?'

Clovis patted her. 'Silly question, Ma; what's up?'

'Answer. I need it. Whatever *happened*? Would you and Emerald hate me?'

Clovis dropped his guard and lowered his head in adoration, his clean cheek lightly touching her hair.

'No, Mother, never. We'd never hate you; you're our very dearest and you should know it.'

She was gay again; it was his reward. 'Then come along, silly, and let's go down. Why on earth would I stay up here when we've guests in the house?'

'Parent delivered, as charged,' said Clovis as he returned, and seconds later Charlotte appeared in the doorway, one arm artfully held aloft as she pushed the door wide.

'Oh, my Lord!' she cried, quizzical and aghast at the state of the room. The table was a study in chaos; a dream-world Caravaggio, a cornucopia of refuse. 'What can have happened!'

'Chimpanzees' tea party,' said Clovis.

The gentlemen hastily got to their feet.

Florence had stood up, too; her appetite had been bird-like. She barely tasted food these past years; it meant nothing to her.

'Have you all lost your reason?' Charlotte asked wonder-ingly, as her eye travelled over the mismatched, filthy table and those around it, all in disarray.

Emerald was not in the mood to be scolded. 'Mother, if you'd been here, you'd know what a time we've had,' she said censori-ously. 'Mrs Trieves has been wonderful, and so has Patience – everybody has. I suggest you get on with it. The rest of us are.'

All present stared directly at the floor, but Charlotte laughed as if her daughter had made the prettiest of speeches. She all but clapped her hands together.

'You poor darlings!' she trilled. 'And your dreadful parent in her room. What must it have been like? How extraordinary

things are tonight! Now, where shall I sit?' And, like an excitable child, she took her place and gazed around her. 'Which course are we on?' she asked.

Florence was still uncertain, and did not meet her eye. 'The second course, Mrs Swift – third if you count the soup we didn't have – but I'm afraid there wasn't very much of it. The passengers had appetites like dogs.'

'So I see; between you you've quite cleared the place,' said Charlotte happily. 'Have our railway guests eaten all the puddings and desserts, too?'

Then they all spoke at once, describing their collective efforts, and the voracious appetites of their displaced houseguests.

'They ate up all the pork—'

'And masses of rabbit!'

'We had to give some of them pewter—'

'And they didn't all have cutlery.'

'Let alone napkins.'

'Napkins!'

'What fun,' said Charlotte, 'but are Robert and Stanley not back? What of the new arrivals?'

'No sign of them, Ma, and no more people, either.'

'What could have become of them?'

As they all talked, conjecturing as to the whereabouts of Robert and Stanley, predicting the abating of the storm, Traversham-Beechers alone said nothing. He sat, in his new place, at the head of the table facing Charlotte, and looked at her. For her part, she behaved for all the world as if she did not see him. 'So, Mrs Trieves, what next?'

'If more do come I don't know what we shall do with them,' Emerald said.

'But there's the cake, ma'am,' said Florence, in quiet, grim tones; 'they're not having that.' She rose to fetch it.

'Oh, cake!' squeaked Patience, and they all set about moving plates from here to there.

'Oh, do call Smudge!' said Emerald.

'I'll see to it.' Florence nodded curtly, as she left them.

The diners had partially cleared the table. Myrtle had run to find plates for the cake and the gas was turned down to low, flickering flames, making the room into a warm cave. The candles still blazed in the candelabras, although meltingly now, smoking and dripping, pouring and spluttering, while the guests spoke in hushed, expectant murmurs as they awaited Florence's return.

Charlotte found her eyes drawn to Traversham-Beechers, his intense scrutiny proving irresistible at last.

'*Marguerite Gautier s'est levée de son lit*,' he said quietly. Even though he was at the far end of the table she heard him, although she had the queer impression that others did not.

In the pantry, Florence took the green cake down from its high shelf. The tall, fluted stand lurched dangerously on its thin neck as she descended the step-ladder.

Myrtle appeared, breathless, in the doorway.

'Fetch Miss Imogen, Myrtle, if she's awake, or we'll never hear the end of it.'

Myrtle darted up the scullery stairs, but returned seconds later with the mystifying news that Miss Imogen would take her cake 'later'.

'She's locked that door again,' she said darkly.

'Who can blame her with the comings and goings tonight? Now here, help me,' said Florence.

The candles were tall, fast-burning tapers. She had piped *Emerald* on it, and the grains of sugar in the writing and the green roses shone like diamond dust.

'Don't light the ones nearest you or you'll never reach the back,' whispered Florence.

Standing over the cake, like conspirators, they had to work quickly. The candles blazed beautifully, but very fast.

'Now, get back,' ordered Florence, as the last one was lit, and she took up the cake.

Myrtle darted ahead to the dining room and Florence went after, the flames flowing backwards in the draught of movement like comets, wildly.

Myrtle threw open the door and they were met with a gratifying gasp, and a small burst of applause.

'Bravo!' cried Charlotte.

Ernest, alone, was not looking at the cake as it made its floating entrance, but down the length of the darkened table to Emerald, to catch her look as she saw it. He had his reward in her fleeting, childlike delight. The candles were still blazing as it reached her, and the collective sighs of admiration brought a little colour to Florence's pale cheeks. She placed the glossy confection in front of Emerald. Her face – her birthday face – was full of joy and pleasure, just as it had been on seeing the nineteen previous cakes presented to her.

Patience began to sing, 'Happy Birthday To You!' The others soon helped her, the pace increasing, with foot stamping from Traversham-Beechers and then Clovis, joining him, and then much laughter at the end.

'Quick! Blow them out or you'll ruin it,' said Florence, producing a sudden knife.

'The green is exquisite, Mrs Trieves,' Charlotte graciously remarked.

'Quick! Blow!'

Emerald leaned forward and took a breath. She blew, and as the little flames roared disobediently, was helped by Clovis and Patience, and the icing was saved, just in time.

The birthday girl – whose dress did not look too tawdry now, in the dim light and candle-glow – stood at the head of the table and plucked out the extinguished candles. An ironic dimple appeared in her cheek.

'What shall I wish for?' she asked, looking about the faces. 'What?'

'An improved disposition,' said her mother sourly.

'Tosh,' said Traversham-Beechers. 'Jewels and furs, gowns and a grand tour . . . cars, horses, bicycles!'

'Your heart's desire,' said Patience (to a pained sigh from Charlotte).

John sought the bon mot. 'A new settee for the drawing room,' he said daringly at last, with a little music-hall mime of rubbing a bruised behind, which was met with much laughter from the family.

He could afford to buy me a hundred settees, thought Emerald grimly, before she could stop herself, *and cushions for them, too.*

'Mrs Trieves?' she said, taking her eyes from John. 'Another cake as beautiful as this one?'

'It might be my best work,' said Florence. 'I'm not sure I could repeat it. What about the departing of that blasted rabble before Sunday?'

'No,' said Charlotte, urgently, 'none of that. Who cares about them? The house, my love, Sterne!'

'Yes, go on, wish for the house. Come on: Sterne.' This was Clovis.

Emerald's dimple had disappeared. She had been planning that as her true wish all along. She stared down at the circle of green icing.

It's perfectly round, like the land we're standing on, but there's no house on it, just my silly name. Perhaps it's an omen, she thought, but did not say it. No father and soon, perhaps, no house either.

The sugar-sparkling letters of the roses and the *Emerald*

moved through the tears that filled her eyes. Her future was a desert and her only desire was to remain where she was. And why? She wasn't even happy.

'All this wishing,' she said hopelessly, 'all this wishing for things that won't come true.'

'If you wish for the best thing, you can't lose.'

Emerald glanced up; it was Ernest. The sight of him was as steadying as a stirrup cup on a frosty morning and almost as heating. *Oh heavens*, she thought.

Taking the proffered knife, she plunged it into the cake, closing her eyes as first the icing, with a snick, and then the sponge gave sweetly to the blade.

'I wish for the *best thing*,' she said warmly.

The metal blade touched the glass at the bottom with a small tap and immediately – before she could even open her eyes again – as startlingly as an axe falling, and to the absolute amazement of everyone – a wild howl went up from Traversham-Beechers.

It was so loud, so feral and wolf-like that the whole party started, shocked, and stared at him.

The man continued to wail, impossibly high and long, like the desperate, lonely cry of animals in far, cold places; the saddest, cruellest sound a human throat could make. His breath held out unnaturally, raising the hairs on the bare forearms of the ladies, running a frisson down the spines of all present, and the wail did not subside until every other moving thing in the room had long since stopped.

Then – at last – it ended. He lowered his chin, licked his lips and, not even panting, said lightly, 'To drive the devil out, don't you know?' And there was nothing to say to that. Any devil would have run screaming from the room by now.

Florence took the knife from Emerald's hand and cut slices for everybody, and they all took up tiny silver forks and tucked

in. Their dinner having been largely purloined by strangers, they hadn't had so much to eat that the cake was spoiled, and that was a blessing.

'Every cloud has a silver lining,' said Patience happily. Next to her, Traversham-Beechers lowered his lids and scrutinised her, as if he would flick out his tongue and grab each of the seed pearls adorning her heaped, fair hair.

As they ate their cake, a faint song from the study started up; rough, soft voices, mixing:

I likes me half a pint of ale . . . I likes a little bit of meat . . .
little bit of fish . . . and half a pint of ale . . .

The travellers, fed but still unsatisfied, had begun to raise their voices once more.

Traversham-Beechers drummed his fingers on the table as he forked cake greedily into his mouth, snatching glances at the women around the table.

'Excellent,' he opined.

The talk floated around him along with the fragments of song.

'You've managed most capably,' John was saying to Emerald, across the table from him.

Katy smiled with a twinkle in her eye,
K-K-K-Katy, beautiful Katy . . .

'It's refreshing to have a little of the unexpected.'

'Oh yes, the salmonella bacteria can kill a person stone dead, though it might surprise you to hear it.'

But I gets much pleasure when I'm playing with me uke —
Keep your ukelele in your 'and . . .

'I don't think I've ever had such delicious icing in my life. It doesn't taste green at all.' (This was Patience.)

Traversham-Beechers reached for the wine and, torn between the red and the white, he chose both, and with unprecedented vulgarity, sloshed them into the glass two handed.

'What does "green" taste like?' he said violently, and before she could answer, drinking, he got to his feet.

He stared for a moment at the tapestry opposite him and then said suddenly, 'I say, what about a game of Hinds and Hounds?'

They all ceased chattering and looked at him.

'Hinds and Hounds?' asked Clovis.

The voices floated to them from the study, softly:

I'm walking down the prom last night as peaceful as can be . . .

'It's a game of my own invention,' he said.

'Tell us.' Clovis was eager, leaning forward on his elbows.

'Well, we need a hind and we need hounds – two sorts. Who'll be the hind?'

They looked from one to the other. Charlie's eye was lingering on the women, but rested at last upon Ernest.

'You!'

There was laughter – Ernest was the least deer-like person among them, at least as tall and broad as John.

'Ernest?' asked Patience. 'Why Ernest?'

'Are we required to run about the house?' asked Charlotte doubtfully.

'Oh yes, like animals in thicket and briar,' said Charlie, and Clovis banged the table and laughed.

The lamps were still low. Charlie leaned over the table, with both palms flat upon it. The candles lit his face bizarrely,

causing his features to change shape, eerily. His nose leapt sideways, his eyebrows jumped.

'You are separated from the herd,' he began, his teeth glowing yellow in the candlelight. 'You are lost and alone, pursued mercilessly. You will be sought by the hounds . . . hunted . . . and shot.'

'But why *Ernest?*' repeated Patience, and was ignored.

'How does it go?' asked Emerald, intrigued at the prospect despite her suspicion of the man.

'Here's the thing: first, a glass –'

He darted to the sideboard, took a clean glass. Then, choosing with care, he opened a new decanter, one of port, and poured the dark liquid until it quivered, swollen, at the top of the glass. The party were mesmerised. The sounds of singing seeped under the door, curling like smoke about them as they watched.

He picked up the glass and carried it, glancing light from the candles as it moved, but never a drop spilt, and placed it in front of Clovis.

'Master of the house first,' he said. 'The hind must be separated from the herd by the tufters. Each of the tufters – that's us,' he winked at the others, adorably, 'must find a way to separate him, before the rest of the pack – us again, we're short on numbers – give chase. Find it, and pass the glass.'

Clovis frowned in confusion. 'Well, how? I'm not sure I follow—'

'Come on!' barked Traversham-Beechers. 'I can't baby you through it! It is an adult game – not child's play – if you can't think of how, then I shall *pass the glass.*'

The others dreaded him doing that, they had no idea how to play, or what they would say themselves, but the idea of his *passing the glass* seemed a terrible humiliation.

Ernest alone seemed unperturbed. He glanced around them

all, mildly, as if indulging their folly whilst thinking of other things. (Much as he had, in fact, in the school playground whenever the chants of '*carrots*' had begun.)

In the silence among the birthday party, the songs from the travellers came again:

But every time that I go out the people stare at me . . .

Traversham-Beechers stared at Clovis. The port sat before him untouched, glassy and dark. '*Clovis,* separate the hind.'

Clovis looked at Ernest, and sought to separate him. 'He wears spectacles,' he said at last.

Relief. It was true. He did. This undeniably distinguished him from the group.

'I'd rather not—' began Patience, but Ernest interrupted her.

'Guilty,' he said, holding up a hand with a small smile, as he thought to himself, *Ah, this is where I am again.*

'Capital. Drink. Pass it on.'

Clovis had to lean down to the table to sip from the glass, and when he had done, he passed it to his left, to Florence.

'Careful,' he said, the port sweet on his lips.

Florence had utterly forgotten her suspicion and dislike of Traversham-Beechers. It was a long time since she had sat at a table to eat at all, and longer since it had been in a dining room. She had forgotten, too, her stiff, black silk dress; she felt almost as if she were adorned like the other women, absorbed into the evening with them, and her gratitude was weak and grasping.

'His ambition is medicine, which is a dull profession,' she said quickly, hoping to be unnoticed, and she too leaned forwards to sip the port and then passed it on. It was sugary and lay thickly on her tongue, burning gently.

Ernest could not find it in himself to answer 'guilty' in regard to his cherished aspirations, so he simply nodded, and began to think of other things (the strength of spiders' silk, penicillin . . .). Beside him, Patience fretted and strained in her anxiety. 'Oh, no!' she said, and, 'But I don't see why!'

Next was John. He had not wanted to be caught out, ridiculed as a parvenu, and had thought of something already. He took the drink, held it and said firmly, 'Mr Sutton is not popular. He had no lady to bring into dinner.'

He admittedly took some pleasure in the statement; it was he whose arm Emerald had taken, and it proved Ernest a poor rival.

Small laughs and 'ooh!'s greeted his remark. John was pleased he had made a splash, drank neatly, and handed the glass to Emerald.

'Not a loving cup, but a dividing one,' she said. She had not liked the game till then, although she was attracted to it. She was clinging to a moral part of herself that naggingly said she ought not take part in such a play. And yet, now, holding the glass and feeling the eyes of the others upon her, and the faint bawdy songs of their rough visitors carrying on the air, she thought: *Ernest doesn't care, it's just a game.*

'Get on with it, Em,' Clovis said, so impatiently that she started.

But she couldn't for the life of her think what to say. The fellow himself seemed interested in something on the wall behind her head.

She regarded him, racking her brains. Charlie Traversham-Beechers began to tap the table, to a rhythm — *tap tap tap-tap-tap, tap tap tap-tap-tap* — and soon Clovis followed suit, then John . . .

'Come on,' they whispered, 'come on . . .'

Emerald did not want to look at Ernest for too long because

it made her blush. As glancingly as she could, she registered his angular jaw, his strong brow. Speechless, she noted the honest stillness of him; his hands; the straightness of his shoulders. The child Ernest would have been easy enough to ridicule (not that she had wanted to) but now this adult was, in every physical way, unapproachable. Around her, the drumming increased.

'Come on, come on,' said Charlie, 'or else pass the glass, *pass it, pass it . . .*'

Hotly, Emerald stared at Ernest; coolly, he ignored her. Her heart beat fast, throbbing inside her. The rawness of her attraction to him mingled with her fear of ridicule, and weakened her. Her blushes seemed to warm every part of her: surely her state was visible to everybody – she winced at the thought. Why wouldn't he look at her? Sitting there so solemnly, in his restraint, his quietness; she longed to shake some reaction out of him; she thought of his ghoulish interest in disease and injury – what sort of a man would surround himself with bruised flesh and diseased organs?

'He's odd – he's just odd!' she burst out violently, her cheeks burning, and felt a stab of cruel delight.

'Emerald!' Patience said sharply, betrayed.

Ernest jolted, faced her suddenly; he was himself, the boy she had known, the man she now desired. She could see she had hurt him. She was flooded with shame.

Amongst the others there was a shout of laughter; this was the most successful barb yet. They all looked to Ernest to see his reaction.

'What do you say to that, eh? What do you say to that?' cried Charlie. 'Odd!'

Ernest affected insouciance with every ounce of himself. Odd? Was that what she thought of him? He fought the urge

to look down, drawing on childhood anguish for his armour; wasn't he a man now?

As a girl she had accepted him, he thought. But perhaps even then she had thought him *odd*; considered him odd as they chased butterflies; considered him odd as they cut up little frogs. At last, as they moved on from him, he permitted himself to close his eyes briefly in defeat. *Odd*.

'Your turn, Patience,' said Charlie. 'Give her the glass.'

Patience, in all the violence of her outrage, could not control herself any longer. If she had felt her better self shrink in this ungenerous atmosphere, now it swelled again, demanded to be heard. She threw out her hand and knocked the glass flying across the table. The thick, ruby-red port sprayed and splashed, pooling on the cloth and sinking in. The glass smashed loudly against the heavy silver candelabra, and was met, at last, with silence.

'*Whatever did you do that for?*' said Traversham-Beechers.

He was genuinely shocked and very dismayed; he was alto-gether flabbergasted.

The others stared at her.

'You're all brutes,' said Patience. 'You're hateful! My brother is a better man than any of you!'

'Oh, bravo,' said Clovis, with studied languor, for Charlie Traversham-Beechers' benefit.

'Certainly better than *you*!' She pointed at him furiously. Clovis raised his eyebrows at her and smiled (although inwardly he shook).

There was another brief silence. Traversham-Beechers and Patience, magnetic poles, were fighting out the tide of the table between them. Like jetsam on the swell, the others might all be washed to shore, or swept away – the mood hung in the balance; the driftwood on the wave.

'Does your sister fight all your battles?' Traversham-Beechers said to Ernest, drawlingly.

'Oh, he was ever a milksop,' said Charlotte, siding with the strongest, as was her nature.

And with that the tide was turned. They might all be swept away now.

Emerald felt entirely confused. Weird delight, shame, shock – all fought within her. She mopped at the port stain with Florence, both dirtying all the remaining clean napkins and not improving it a jot. Ernest appeared the least perturbed of all and concerned mainly for his sister.

'Patience?' he asked quietly. 'Patience,' he said again, 'it's nothing. They were just being silly.'

Patience looked at him with wide eyes, shocked at herself and at all of them. She should have liked to make peace with Clovis, whom she didn't really blame, but his expression was not pleasant. Ernest turned to the table.

'If my hostess doesn't mind, I'd like to take a look at the library – and rejoin you all in a little while. Excuse me, please.'

Charlotte gaped at him. He nodded stiffly, and left the table.

At that, Charlie Traversham-Beechers, who had been momentarily wrong-footed by Patience's rebellion, rose quickly to his feet.

'Really?' he said, and his voice was oddly commanding. 'Then you'll miss the next hind.'

Ernest paused. The singing from the study, which had momentarily abated, floated strongly to them on the air:

With all my might, I nearly balanced over,
But my old friend grasp'd my leg and pulled me back again . . .

'You'll continue playing, then?' he said, and looked around at each of them.

Emerald was staring at her hands, Florence was busying herself with the sodden linen, Clovis was gazing up at

Traversham-Beechers with something akin to adoration. It was Charlotte who met his eye boldly and said, 'You are tiresome, Ernest, for such a young man. Come and join in the fun.'

Ernest was caught between good manners and a strong desire to distance himself from this corrupt revelry.

'The next hind then,' said Charlie, as if it was all decided. 'And that will be Miss Sutton.'

'No,' said Ernest, squaring up to him, as commanding now as his adversary. 'You're a cad; she won't have it.'

'Won't she? She most certainly will,' said Charlie smoothly. '"The first tufter to falter is turned into a hind." Everybody knows that! She passed the glass, do you see? She passed it! It's the rules!'

Ernest appealed to the table. 'Mrs Swift? Come – Clovis? Good God!'

No voice was raised to help him; nobody took his side. All mesmerised – Emerald bewitched.

'It's all right, Ernest,' said Patience suddenly. 'Let's play. I don't mind.'

'You do. I will not.'

'Sit down, Ernest. Really, it's quite all right. You said it: they're all just being silly.'

He could not refuse her and he could not desert her; he sat – and moved his chair closer so that she might take comfort in his presence.

'It's not personal,' said the caddish gentleman. 'It's just a game. And it's your sister's turn. Let's begin.'

He slipped another thick inch of port from the decanter into a new glass.

'I'm first tufter,' he said. They all waited.

He held up the glass still, and spoke in the hasty, cheery manner of one who is getting the ball rolling. 'Miss Sutton

has an inkling she's not quite as clever as the other young ladies at Newnham College,' he said. 'Don't you?'

'Enough! What do you know of her?' cried Ernest, but the others, although not laughing as they had done at him, nevertheless felt the same compulsive delight at the moment. They were hounds now, and their cruelty was bred into them.

Smudge had come down for cake, and to collect Tenterhooks. She was tightly wound with excitement and fatigue as she carefully unlocked her door and crept down the passage. She could hear Myrtle in the kitchen and did not care to come across her, so she took the main stairs and tiptoed past the door of the study on her way to the dining room. The uninvited guests sounded as if they were having what Robert would have called a 'high old time' – she'd heard something like it coming from the doors of public houses before now but never, of course, at Sterne. It was not frightening to her, she trusted that the adults were in control of the situation, but it was certainly exotic.

'Most exotic, I think,' she murmured as she approached the dining room, ready for her cake and to give a birthday kiss to her sister.

Reaching the door, she tiptoed along the wall, at first in instinctive childish secrecy; but then, hearing a game going on, she crept to the threshold to listen.

With the rough songs all about her in the air – louder still as they issued from the morning room, too – through the crack in the door by the hinge, she saw the gentleman stranger hold up a glass, brimming as it was, apparently weightless. The liquid was unmoving, his hand unnaturally still.

She couldn't see all the others, but waited, struck by the

strange atmosphere of the room as the singing voices floated from the rooms behind her.

> *Nearly fainting with fright, I sank into his arms a sight,*
> *Went into hysterics but I cried in vain . . .*

Smudge could only glimpse the faces at the table, but she felt a terror clutch at her, for they were empty, staring, unlike the faces she knew; just as the feeling in the house, suddenly, was unlike any feeling she had ever known before. She could only see the stranger, Traversham-Beechers, clearly, and to her young eyes, he appeared to have a line drawn around him, a line of darkness, that was – as she only so lately had observed – very much like the charcoal smudges that she had made on her wall. Those lines though, were material; dust and finger, plaster and art – this was freakish, of nothing she could understand and nor did she want to. She saw the cruelty in his face, sensed the atmosphere; he was like a magnet, the air was thick with the pull of him.

She took unsteady steps backwards, and she fled. Back this time through the baize door to the kitchens, the fastest way upstairs, past Myrtle at the scullery sink, who did not even turn to see her.

Back in the dining room, unobserved by the child now, seen only by this group of players, Clovis spoke.

'My turn,' he said, and reached for the glass.

The port slopped a little over the brim and he licked it clean – licked the glass itself! – and then, looking straight into Patience's face he said, 'Dashed dull conversation, Miss Sutton, and an ordinary sort of face; a great many other girls are a sight prettier.'

Patience gasped. Ernest took her hand, and if ever he were going to be moved to violence it was now, with Clovis smiling

malignantly across the table and his sister's pale distress. He started up. She grabbed his hand. His fists clenched but Patience held them in her small hands – her need to hold him proving greater than his need to break Clovis's nose – and he remained at her side. The others said not one word.

Clovis felt the flood of approval from Charlie and tasted satisfaction in himself, showing her what she was, proving himself better, and yet a part of him – too small a part of him to be obeyed – stood apart and was appalled. The young lady sat opposite him, insulted.

Charlotte took the glass. She must stay on the side of the hounds, not fall down with the spindly hinds. The cruelty that came with it was an unexpected bonus; she saw her son was entranced by the chit, and wouldn't let him go so easily.

'Our nickname for you – our family's nickname for you, that is – is Insignificance Sutton,' she said.

Again, shock around the table; Patience was frozen now, and Emerald went so far as to say 'Oh!' but not a word of resistance.

Florence took the glass. She was loud. 'When you were children—'

'Stop it!' cried Patience suddenly, and stood up. 'Stop it!' And she turned and ran from the table. Ernest leapt to his feet but—

'There!' shouted Charlie. 'The hind is separated! Pack! After her!' He uttered a piercing halloo as they all found themselves, with no thought or reason, throwing back their chairs in wild haste, and giving cries and yelps of hound-like pursuit, dashing after Patience.

Patience rushed towards the door as if she would escape into the hall, the shouted songs raised louder and louder beyond it as she made to grab the knob, but her way was barred by Charlie, and the others bore down on her. She

broke away and rushed down the length of the room, towards Ernest's sheltering arms, and they went after her – all galloping. Charlie, with his long arms flung out like a puppet's and hands waving madly, rushed around to cut off her escape, while behind him, the other hounds leapt about in ecstasies of barking.

'Stop her! Hold her! She must be worn out!'

She dived behind Ernest into the corner, and he put up his fists in readiness while Charlie shouted, 'Now! She's at bay! Wear her out!'

'Your glasses! Ernest, your glasses!' shrieked Patience, anticipating fisticuffs, while Emerald, Charlotte and Florence fell to barking and yapping.

'Don't come any nearer! I'll strike you, I swear it!' Ernest was addressing the men but was angry enough to lay hands on the women, too, if it came to it.

He glared down at the hysteria – whooping, baring their teeth and claws and laughing – while Patience, pale with frank and open terror, grew weaker, leaning against the wall in the corner. The hounds screeched and shouted, making stabs with their claws and yelping until Patience, pushed past her limit, began to laugh, wildly, mirthlessly, losing her breath, tears starting to her eyes. She panted for air, half-crying, half-laughing, eyes wide and staring about her, the barking ringing in her ears.

'Here's my gun!' shouted Charlie, holding up a long, silver snuffer he had snatched up from the sideboard, and pointing it – past Ernest – at her face, 'BANG!' at which Patience, quite suddenly, fainted.

Ernest, the only one with his back to her, was the last to realise this had happened, and it was their faces that alerted him. Clovis started forward in concern, then stopped himself. Ernest turned in dismay. Patience was lying crumpled on the

floor, bloodless, and the sight of her put an end to the game. Her pursuers fell silent, and stood, staring, as Ernest went to his knees and lifted her up.

'You brutes,' he said, as she had done, and carried her to the chaise under the window.

'She's only fainted,' said Charlie and returned to his place, draining the glass of port and tidying his hair. The rest of them, shocked to silence, were unable, following their behaviour, to show concern but equally, appalled at what had happened, unable to do anything else.

It was a very few moments before Patience recovered.

'Hello,' she said, as people often do on waking, as if they have been away somewhere and are returning.

'Hello,' answered her brother gravely, forgetting his outrage, and relieved.

'What happened?' she asked.

Nobody spoke, because for the life of them they couldn't find an answer.

'Oh, we were playing,' she said, reminded, and propped herself up on her elbows. Looking about her, the memories of the slights and insults came back to her, and showed on her face in a sad frown and blushes.

Emerald knelt by her, and took her hand. 'Patience?' she whispered, but Ernest, at her side, cut her off.

'What were you thinking?' he asked.

'I'm so sorry, I don't know what came over me,' she murmured, but neither brother nor sister responded.

'Shall we go on?' asked Charlie Traversham-Beechers breezily.

'You can't be serious?' Charlotte said, turning on him and voicing all their thoughts as one. 'This has all gone—'

'Too far?' he interrupted her, feeling about his person for a fresh cigar. 'People always say that. And it never has. We

are only reaching the beginning, Mrs Swift. It's your turn next.'

'Mine?' Her face was ashen.

Despite themselves – shocked, concerned as they most truly were – they all looked at him, and at Charlotte, bound to follow this outrageous labyrinth to its conclusion.

'Mine?' she repeated.

Ernest settled a cushion at Patience's back. They sat together, united but ignored, as Clovis, Emerald and Florence found themselves walking, as one reluctant group, back to their places at the table. Sick with the foul taste of cruelty still, they were not quite themselves. And yet, as a reflection in a mirror shows us the truth but is not real, they were exquisitely and intensely themselves. They had to know what this man had to do with Charlotte.

Charlotte herself backed away from the table, her eyes never leaving his face.

'You're cruel,' she said.

'I always was,' was his rejoinder. 'Sit.'

'No.'

'Sit, God damn you.'

Whether there was an intake of breath at this new violation or whether the shock actually drained the oxygen from the room is mysterious, but the candle flames shrank on their wicks, and Charlotte Torrington Swift – née Thompson – as he had commanded, sat.

'No,' she said. 'He will damn *you*.'

'I'll start!' said Traversham-Beechers brightly. 'Shall I begin with a minnow or a salmon? Shall I bid high or low?'

'Do what you will,' she said.

'Here – *Mrs Trieves* – you go first. We're all in this together, as they say.'

He handed Florence the glass. Her eyes were brimming.

She took it — didn't dash it on the table as Patience had done — but with her own quiet rebellion simply passed it on.

'Passing the glass!' mocked Traversham-Beechers.

Emerald took the glass from Florence.

'She is my mother. What am I to say?' she asked quietly, and handed it to Clovis.

'Quite right.' Clovis was terrified, and could only hide in his sister's words.

Traversham-Beechers took the glass from him impatiently. 'She is a whore,' he said coolly.

'God!' cried Charlotte. 'Evil!'

'No, you are evil,' he said. 'You are evil to deceive your husband — two husbands! — to bear children and expect them to be able to live respectable lives when their very souls are stained with your sin. To assume the grand manners of a lady when you are less than a skivvy, less than the smallest chit of a girl selling flowers by the roadside; less, in your moral degradation, than any of the women in this room, or in your *Grand New Life*.' He spat out these last words slowly and then he sat, suddenly, abandoned in his relief, and panting slightly he seemed to shrink.

The others in the room — Ernest and Patience on the chaise, the rest at the table — all were mute, and in that wondering, desperate silence, Charlie Traversham-Beechers began to laugh. It was a giggle at first, a strange, tickling sound that mocked everybody present. It rose in delighted vicious scales and then it stopped suddenly. He wiped his eyes.

'I suppose you'll want to know the whole story?' he said pleasantly to Clovis.

It was a question no son should ever be asked of his mother, and he had no answer.

Charlotte did not move, her eyes were fixed on her enemy.

'Go on,' said Emerald.

'I'll be brief. It's a tawdry tale, and a common one at that. If it weren't your mother's you'd be uninterested, most likely, and think it too distasteful to bother with. Well . . .' He sighed. 'Anyway. You may have heard tell of your mother's carefree days in London before she met your father. Her conventional childhood at Richmond?'

Emerald darted a look at Charlotte. This was familiarity from the mouth of a stranger – what was the truth of it? The ground beneath her feet seemed to shift.

'The childhood's true enough,' he went on, 'or true as she told it to me, but the carefree days weren't exactly that, were they, Mrs Trieves . . . *Florence?*'

Florence was staring into the distance, and did not answer him.

'Not carefree at all. Finding money to pay the rent, borrowing from gentlemen – that was sometimes what you called it, wasn't it? *Borrowing.* Many of them weren't quite gentlemen, were they, Charlotte?'

'You weren't,' she said, ignored.

'Artists – those *thinking, talking, drinking* artists. I say, is whoring any more respectable if you do it amongst intellectuals? I should think . . . not.'

'We were models!' burst out Florence suddenly.

'Hush!' Charlotte cried, fearing his further provocation, but it was too late.

'Ah! Models! Muses! Goddesses, weren't you? Or you were, Charlotte, a goddess to the men you seduced. How they tried to capture your celestial charms – before they bedded you!'

He was too coarse. It was intolerable. John Buchanan, silent up until that point, overwhelmed by cruel passion during the heated game and then, after Patience's collapse, by confusion and shock, now leapt to his feet.

'Enough!' he shouted. 'You ought to go out of this house. How dare you!'

Traversham-Beechers was so unimpressed by this outburst that John's determination subsided like a deflating balloon, and he sat down again.

'I will not go out of this house. I am here to see this through, and I will do it.' He began to speak rapidly, like an accusing barrister. 'In brief, then: Charlotte Thompson, finding herself without means in Bloomsbury, in the year eighteen-hundred and seventy-eight – when that area was not nearly as salubrious as it now is – and, frankly,' he laughed, 'it isn't, very – was forced, and I use the word ironically, *forced* to exploit her only asset: her beauty. Did she exploit it respectably, as other women do, and find a husband? She did not. She removed her clothes for money and had it immortalised in a series of second-rate canvasses painted by love-sick or cynical fools. (I own one or two of them; I wonder if you can surmise to which category I belong?) When I came across her, she – and you, Florence! We mustn't forget you! – was being bedded by men for money. A mistress. A muse. Model. Not usually – not *usually,* eh, Lottie? – a streetwalker.'

He had sunk as low as he could sink – or she had, and he had told of it. Not one of them in the room could look at the other. When Charlotte finally rose to her feet she was unobserved, as every head was bowed.

Her voice, answering him, was dull, and something in her tone laid to rest any doubts, any desperate hopes, her family might have had as to the veracity of his accusations. It was the voice of a woman who had seen all he had spoken of, and more; it was the voice of Charlotte Thompson of Bloomsbury, speaking with the graceless courage of the degraded.

'No, Charlie, not usually,' she said, and left them.

* * *

One by one they left the table. The room emptied. At every opening of the door, the singing grew louder. Snatches of cheerful ditties accompanied the diners from the sordid table. Mocked by the lively strains of 'K-K-K-Katy', they all withdrew: Ernest, with his arm around his sister; Florence to her wrecked and plundered kitchen; Clovis – who could not meet even his sister's eye, let alone the others' – to lay low in some hidden corner of the house.

At last, Emerald and Charlie Traversham-Beechers were the only two left.

He was unconcerned. He pushed through the scraps for morsels and sucked his fingers. Emerald regarded him steadily.

'You shamed us all,' she said.

'You shamed yourselves,' was his smiling answer.

That was true enough.

'How did you know where to find us?'

'I didn't at first. But in my position a great many things are revealed.'

'What *is* your position?'

He met her brave glance and despite herself she wavered; his pupils were black chips, inhuman, from which her fragile soul shrank. She stood up, afraid as she was to turn her back to him, and left the room.

5

ABANDON

Charlie Traversham-Beechers did not have long on this earth. To come upon Sterne so suddenly and violently, with the screeching, bloody crush of a locomotive engine slamming into a siding, had, of course, been no plan of his. In life, he had not known anything of the house at all, only that Charlotte had disappeared from London with Horace Torrington more than twenty years before, love and reform fluttering about her like confetti. He had seen her once or twice since. Those meetings were imprinted on his memory, as well as his greedy, vain efforts to prolong the association; he had once bundled her into a cab outside Whiteleys department store under threat of blackmail for an afternoon of bonbons and impish coercion. In his dank mind she was the light that might save him. The rest of his lonely, dissolute life he had missed her. Her portraits haunted his walls. Every drink he drank was to her, for her and in the hope of forgetting her.

Coincidence is a frail concept, no more satisfying an explanation of this world's workings than the weightier Fate, but in some alchemic combination of desire and violence, a tiny fragile thread in the vast and complex universal weave was broken when Charlie Traversham-Beechers happened to lose his life in a train crash on the branch line near Whorley. Charlie's proximity to Sterne and the intensity of his feelings for Charlotte – a significant material

bond of which he was as yet unaware – as well as the abrupt manner of his death, left his own self dangling, temporarily. It was a circumstance, he had realised with the new found clarity of his position, in which he might remain amongst a crowd of other unfortunates, more or less corporeally, for some little time, and have vengeance upon his life-long love and hate, Charlotte Thompson. Having achieved this most comprehensively he was now left to himself. The guests and family scattered and Traversham-Beechers, the rat on the sinking ship, clung to the wreckage for a while, before seeping about the halls to see what new mischief he might get up to. He examined the house like a dog sniffing a gutter.

Forty or fifty bodies, even if – *particularly* if – they have been well fed and watered, will have needs beyond the capacity of a windowless study and a sparsely decorated morning room. The passengers were finding that the difficulty of reinhabiting flesh was its frequent flushing; efficient but foul. They were increasingly inconvenienced. There were two china pots, which had contained plants, that were put to low but necessary use, as well as the coal scuttle, now brimming.

Despite this squalor, their mood was jubilant. The songs that had begun in sated delight while the family were at their dinner grew louder and bawdier as they sloshed about their temporary home.

> *It does seem so naughty, oh my!*
> *Men are so rough, they'll splash me and duck me!*

They sang and:

> *Come on, out, out!*

And their spirits rose higher along with their songs and chants, until, at last, they burst out of their two despoiled and tiny rooms. Both doors banged violently against the walls as if snatched by a high wind.

It is hard to say which was more powerful, the stench flooding from the room to the hall, or the rush of fresh and pleasing air that caressed their poor collapsing faces. The surge of oxygen filled them with fresh vitality and their well-fed singing grew louder as they issued forth into the larger house.

The howling gale had subsided somewhat, but the rain had only thickened, driving onto the sodden ground.

It was into this rain that Patience Sutton stared from the window of her brother's room, to which they had withdrawn, having left the humiliations of the dining room, to comfort one another. There was no sign at all of any of their hosts, only the rowdy rough songs and shouts, ringing now through every part of the house, circulating through the corners and cornices, along with the drumming of the downpour.

> *Come, come, come and make eyes at me,*
> *Down at the old Bull and Bush . . .*

Ernest stood with his back against the door, as much for security as comfort, although he did not care to admit it. He observed his sister at the window.

'This is desperate,' she said.

'Yes. It's . . .' he searched his heart as well as he could, '. . . profoundly shocking.'

Shocked though he was, by Traversham-Beechers' unmasking of Mrs Swift, he did not think less of Emerald for her mother's weakness, or even for the vicious mood that had infected the

dinner table – all could be put down to the restless, anarchic workings of the night. But he found he could not dismiss the jibe of 'odd'; it stuck like a fishhook in the flesh of his feelings.

'Em didn't mean what she said, Ernest,' said Patience, reading his thoughts.

'No matter. I am odd, I should think.'

'You aren't. Any more than I'm Insignificant.' Patience rubbed her nose. 'Oh look,' she said, 'there's Mr Buchanan.'

He came to the window to see. Sure enough, John Buchanan was running through the rain on the drive below them towards his car, with his jacket over his head. As they watched, he wrenched the door open and flung himself inside. After an amount of rummaging, he backed out again with the starting handle and stumbled through the deluge to the front of the car. A number of vigorous cranks did not appear to start the engine. He ran back, hauled the door open and apparently fiddled about with the starter. Returning to the front of the car he cranked the handle once more.

'I don't think it's working,' said Patience.

'I'll go down,' said Ernest. 'But Patience, keep the door locked. I've an idea those passengers have somehow found a bottle or two of something. It sounds as if they're – abroad.'

'Abroad?'

'They're so loud.'

'Yes, poor things. Don't worry, I shall.' And with that, he exited, not leaving until he heard her turning the key in the solid lock.

He went along the upper corridor of the house without seeing a soul, although a peculiar odour hung in the air – one that, mystifyingly, he associated with formaldehyde.

As he turned the corner of the main stairs he found a good number of the travellers standing about, and others walking quite resolutely towards him. Their expressions were differing but they shared a common look of dazed distraction on their slack faces. They didn't notice him at first. Some were singing —

> Her father killed rats and she sold sprats,
> All round, and over the water —

Others swayed along to the faltering rhythm, or busily stared about themselves at the paintings and doorways of Sterne, emitting murmurs.

Ernest was unsure whether to confront them. On catching sight of him, though, some swung to face him and one cried belligerently, 'Here, mister! How long will it be?'

'Will you put us up?'

Ernest kept his head down, muttering things about 'you'd better speak to your hosts', as he went by. It struck him that he must urgently detain John Buchanan; that his driving away now would leave them significantly worse off in the event of some sort of disturbance.

'Excuse me; I'm so sorry,' he said, as he hurried between them, guiltily noting their extreme pallor, and that many of them, contrary to his earlier observation, were limping.

Reaching the hall, he glanced back up at the dozen on the stairs, only to bump into another poor creature on the way to the front door. It was an old woman with one eye, who glared at him lopsidedly, demanding, 'Where's beds?'

'Excuse me,' Ernest said again, and fairly scampered out, hoping, locked door or no, that they wouldn't go trying to get into any of the bedrooms.

The rain hit him like a bucket of river water. He ran in darkness, instantly drenched, towards the Rolls-Royce.

Reaching John, he shouted over the sound of the rain, already wet through.

'John!'

John turned, both men battered by the downpour.

'Blasted thing won't start!' He was very agitated indeed. 'Here – get in!'

They took shelter in the vehicle.

'I think you ought to come inside,' began Ernest.

'Damn it!' exclaimed John over the loud pelting of rain on the roof. The car was leaking, too – water running down the gleaming maple in the dark.

'You won't get the lamps lit in this,' Ernest said sensibly.

'Damn it!' cried John again. 'I'll not stay under that roof!'

Ernest could see John needed to get something off his chest, so he waited, fretting about the creatures in the house, with the water dripping down his face.

'Whore! Harlot! Whore!' said John furiously. Then, 'Daughter of a whore! I'm damned if I'll have anything to do with her – I'm damned – I—' And he broke off, distressed.

'Ah,' said Ernest, 'Emerald.'

'She can't imagine I'll marry her now.'

'The man is a cad and a villain.'

John ignored him.

'I should have listened to my dad; he knew they weren't right up here.' In his outrage John had returned to the locution of his childhood.

'Oh,' said Ernest. 'Please come inside. The passengers—' But John was in no mood to listen.

'Here! Pull the choke – like this! Help me!' And with that, he jumped out again, and Ernest watched him furiously crank the obstinately unresponsive engine for some moments, before he got back into the car, steaming up the glass with the heat of his rage.

'Did you pull the choke?' he shouted accusingly.

'No,' said Ernest.

'*What!*' Ernest thought he might strike him.

'It's too dark. The spark plugs will be saturated. Let's go in.'

'*In!*' shouted John.

'Would you desert them?'

'I'm not sleeping in that house.' His voice was hard.

'Then you shouldn't have left your car out in the rain,' said Ernest, becoming exasperated. 'With all these people in the house, it would be a great deal better if we could all get along with one another.'

'It's none of my affair!'

'John, be reasonable. The groom and his boy are still not back. There are ladies—'

'Ha!'

'There are *ladies* inside and . . . if something should happen—'

'What might happen?' John was, at last, paying attention.

'We're utterly outnumbered.'

'I see. Come on then.'

And with that, they returned to the house.

Smudge had been very frightened indeed by the scene she had glimpsed in the dining room. She wished nothing more than to take the pony Lady back to the stables, but the rough songs of the passengers were loud enough to reach even her remote bedroom and she did not dare venture out.

She was extremely troubled, too, by the pony herself, whose restlessly scattered droppings had made Smudge's room frankly unpleasant. Like the passengers, she was finding that using rooms in ways for which they were not intended resulted in discomfort, filth and smells. If she opened the window, the wild rain came in; if it was closed, the air was

rank. She tried to distract herself with plaiting the pony's mane and tail, and later, lying on the floor playing tiddly-winks, as the storm continued to rage outside, but she could not look forward to the rest of the night cooped up with anything other than dread.

In the hall, John and Ernest peeled off their dripping jackets. Ernest could no longer see the group on the stairs, and the one-eyed crone had disappeared but, oddly, the singing and talking were even louder than before, disembodied in the emptiness, and the smell of decay still hung in the air. Ernest wondered if perhaps one of their number had an unclean and suppurating wound, knowing such things to give off a stench, but this was more like the smell of many wounds.

John listened. He was a man with a workforce; he knew a mob when he heard it.

'They seem in good spirits now,' he said, 'but I see what you mean. We could be in for a bit of a nasty jar.'

'We need to find the others.'

'Traverall-Beechers —' began John, tentatively, 'he gained order amongst them before. Though I don't like to mention his name.'

'Well, don't then,' said Ernest shortly. 'We can certainly manage without *him*.'

They ran up the stairs, and on reaching Emerald's door Ernest dispensed with convention and knocked loudly.

'It's Ernest. Are you in there, Miss Torrington?' he asked.

'Yes,' came her muted reply.

'Is your door locked?'

John, with a gesture and a nod, set off down the corridor to fetch Clovis.

'Why do you ask?' said Emerald.

Ernest dropped his voice to a discreet level.

'It would be best if you stayed in your room, I think,' he said.

Curiosity evidently overcame her need to hide herself away, for in a moment he heard the key turn and Emerald peered out at him.

'Why?' she asked.

When his sister cried she became pinched and pale. Emerald's face had gone the other way, towards swollen lids and lips, her cheeks were streaked, her hair rather wild. He forgot the passengers. She reminded him of a peony in a rainstorm, only less intensely coloured – perhaps a rose. He was distracted.

'Why should I stay in my room?' she asked again.

'Oh, the passengers. They're out and about. They're rather jolly. We need to contain them, or control them.'

'Well, I can't contribute much from a locked bedroom, can I?' she said, and sniffed. 'Just a moment.'

'I don't think you should—' he began, but it was no use. She shut the door on him and in a moment returned, having splashed her face with water and attempted to tame her hair.

'Ernest,' she said humbly, 'I'm so sorry for – everything.'

'Not at all,' he responded, so stiffly that there was nothing more to be said. Despite her efforts, the comb that had decorated her hair was hanging lopsidedly from a tangled section behind her ear. Ernest extracted it and handed it to her.

'Thanks,' she said, and, dropping it on the desk near her door, followed him, a chorus of distant songs accompanying them.

They met Clovis and John coming the other way, her brother hanging a little behind. John had summoned him from his room as he might have summoned a dog, and Clovis felt the shame of his degraded position very keenly.

'I can't stay in my room,' said Emerald, but John did not speak to her.

'We'd better fetch Patience,' said Clovis, abrupt and inhibited.

There was no need to fetch Patience, however, she had heard the commotion and appeared, having miraculously changed into a sensible serge dress, ready for action.

'Oh, Patience, I'm so sorry!' blurted Emerald, echoed by a rough but indistinct murmur of agreement from Clovis, to which Patience replied briskly, 'Don't mention it. That Trivering-Beeching is the dog, not you.'

A lusty voice behind them – a woman's voice – sang out loudly:

> *Daisy! Daisy! Give me your answer do!*
> *I'm half crazy!*——

But when they turned there was nobody there at all, just the empty corridor.

'Goodness,' said Patience. 'Mrs Swift?' And they went together to see about her.

Clovis, rallying, knocked. 'Mother!'

Silence.

'You ought to come out,' Emerald said gently to the blank panelling in front of her. 'The passengers are all over the house. We need to manage them. Do you know where . . . ?' She didn't say Traversham-Beechers' name, not just because she couldn't remember it, but because the thought of him was so loathsome to her. 'Do you know where the *other* guest has got to? Mother?'

There was no sound from behind the door.

'Mrs Swift?' asked Ernest.

'Yes. Here. Not coming out,' came their hostess's firm reply.

'I think you ought,' said Emerald.

'Well, I shan't,' responded her mother.

The others stood for a moment, each contemplating the

scandalous history of the woman who was refusing to emerge, not to mention how dislikeable she could be.

'None of us likes being here!' burst out John at the stubborn door, unable to contain himself. 'I know I don't care to! I've a mind to leave the lot of you to your trouble; it seems to me you brought it on yourselves!'

'For heaven's sake, man!' said Ernest.

'Go away,' said Charlotte, behind the door.

'Lock your door, Mrs Swift!' said Ernest urgently over his shoulder as they retreated.

Charlotte heard their departing steps. The door was already locked. They had interrupted her in pacing the floor, wringing her handkerchief and tossing her lace-edged garments about the room in an approximation of packing. There was a valise on the bed and an open trunk, dragged from her dressing room, on the floor. Both were full to overflowing. Her jewels were packed, too, what remained of them. She could hear the songs of the passengers, and their occasional shouts, but they barely bruised her self-absorption and she cared not a fig for them. *Let them rot,* she thought. By the stench creeping under her door, it smelled as if they already were.

She paused in her frenetic movement and went to the window, clutching the tasselled edge of the curtain.

She was ruined anyway, but she could still escape. She could slip out during the morning, before her husband's return. At the thought of the stalwart, honourable Edward Swift, with his close-shaven sandy cheek and neatly pinned sleeve, she gave an involuntary yelp. Staring out, she could see only her own pale reflection. She willed Robert, Stanley and the cart to reappear.

'Please come back,' she whispered. 'Please.'

'They aren't coming,' said a cool male voice behind her.

Charlotte spun around to see before her disbelieving eyes Traversham-Beechers, standing in the middle of the room. He twisted the ends of his moustache between his thumb and forefinger – he twirled it – in amusement, contemplating her; it was a gesture she knew well.

It was not Traversham-Beechers, the instrument of her downfall himself, who so dismayed her – he had always been a bully and a pest. It was the manner of his arrival, the impossibility of it, through her locked bedroom door.

'Good God!' she uttered. 'You—' She had been going to say 'must leave', but found her breath failing her. There was no other way but that or the window into the room, and both were securely fastened.

'Packing, Lottie?' he asked lightly.

'Yes,' she said weakly. 'You've done for me.'

'For your reputation, at any rate.'

'What else is there?'

'Everything that you've made here . . .' he mused.

'Gone now.'

'They won't forgive you, then?'

'My family? Would you?'

'If my mother . . .? Good Lord, no,' he laughed, 'I should think not.'

'Oh God, Charlie,' she said, and she sat down tiredly on the cushioned stool by the dressing table. 'Why did you do it?'

'Smudge?' whispered Emerald, knocking and trying the handle with the others standing quietly behind her.

'Smudge?' But there was no answer from inside. 'She must be asleep,' Emerald said, 'and the door is locked, at least,' and they withdrew to see about the singing throng below.

Smudge was not asleep. Only deep-rooted pride prevented

her throwing open her door, revealing the pony and the extent of her own naughtiness. The child was exhausted. Her exhaustion was matched by her desperation to return the pony to the stables and be done with her. But Lady, disastrously, had lain down. No amount of cajoling, clapping or whistling would rouse her, she merely stared at Smudge, condescending in her superior bulk, and lounged on.

Smudge gave up for a while and rested against the pony's stomach, listening to its gurgles and the distant songs of the passengers, but the warm, round swell was too comforting, the well-groomed coat too soft, and she felt the awful urge to sleep. She stumbled dazedly to her feet, near tears.

'No, Lady! We are *not* sleeping!' she stormed.

Lady merely looked at her, as if to say, *speak for yourself.*

'Very well, then, you may – just for a *short* while. And then we're going down, do you understand?'

She went to the window and opened it. The cool fresh night air moved over her, and the fine rain soothed her face.

'You have made a dreadful mess,' she said to the pony. 'I'll be back directly.'

And she hoisted her bottom up onto the ledge. A quick foray over the roofs would smarten her up most effectively. She would deal with the rude horse on her return.

'Goodbye,' she said.

The wind had dropped and, wet though the slates were, Smudge knew the route well. Straddling the sill, she hitched her thick skirts up into Clovis's scarf, knotted about her waist, and then, carefully, stood upright on the sill. She braced one hand flat against the inside wall, while reaching high above herself for the metal piece that attached the stout drainpipe to the house.

* * *

Mere yards away, at the other end of the corridor, Patience, Clovis, Ernest and Emerald were moving, somewhat tentatively, down the main stairs to the hall.

They entered a melee of carousing passengers, at least twenty in the hall itself and several more wandering about, singing and laughing.

The folks, amazed, all thought her crazed,
All along the Strand, Oh,
To hear a girl with sprats on her head –

'We should have taken the scullery stairs!' said Emerald, stopping in her tracks as a coated man brushed her bare arm with his damp shoulder.

Songs and cries, underpinned by babies' wails and women, yelping and encouraging, as well as the shuffled stamping and cracking of knuckles as they began – with awkward abandon – to dance.

'Oh Lord,' said Ernest, 'whatever shall we do with them?'

All at once some of the singing passengers caught sight of them and cried:

'Join us!'

'Here, dance!'

The passengers had formed into ragged lines in the hall and corridor and were executing an odd little morris dance.

'There are so many of them!' whispered Patience urgently.

'*Come on!*' shouted one of the throng to her, holding out a withered hand. 'Dance for the May Day!'

'No thank you,' Patience said politely.

'We don't want them getting any wilder,' said John, but even as he spoke, the songs were turning to shouts, the dancing ceased, or became stamping, and the voices rose in complaint and demand.

'What now?' they shouted. 'What now?'

Ernest turned to Emerald to speak, but saw that she and Clovis had slipped away.

Smudge clung to the drainpipe. The straight, unbroken drop to the ground below fell sheer, clean and bracing behind her. This was always the tricky part, she thought, but her racing heart would keep her sharp. She took a good hold of the drainpipe, shuffled along the sill, let go of the wall inside and, like a lizard, shuffled along until she could lodge her toe between the pipe and wall. The worst was over now. Shinning a drainpipe was an adventure, but not so different from a low garden tree, and manageable in any weather. Her small hands grasped the bracings, her boots clung and strained. The climb up to the wide guttering of the roof had been done many times. There was a brief, breathless moment as she negotiated the overhang of the projecting parapet and, leaning backwards, felt the wet metal, unforgiving and slick beneath her straining fingertips, but even as her thin arms burned with effort, she gained the advantage, used all the strength in her legs for two big ladder-ish steps up, and soon was lodged, high, high above the gravel and stones, on the wide, flowing gutter, leaning, panting, against the cold water-running slates of the roof. She lay back exultantly. The scudding clouds were above her, occasionally lit by the watery moon. Her hair and skin were drenched and her heart sang with freedom and triumph, far from the cries of the passengers and the pony's foul excretions. How comfortable it was to lie back against the roof, her arms thrown wide, and feel her feet braced, strongly in the gutter – the gutter along which icy water rushed, flooding her boots, freezing her toes, reminding her, at last, that she couldn't stay there for ever. This was the easy part; now she would explore. Still leaning

on the roof, she peered through the night to discover the pale stone balustrade of her mother's balcony, some fifty feet along and ten beneath, and made for it.

Charlotte's bed frothed like a rough sea with pantalettes, drawers and petticoats. Charlie Traversham-Beechers pushed them aside like a determined swimmer.

'Come, Charlotte; come and sit with me.'

But Charlotte stayed where she was, on the stool. Her initial shock at his unnatural appearance in her room had subsided slightly, and she was remembering what a pest he was.

'It is very late at night,' he whispered. 'We have hours and hours before morning.'

'Someone will come—'

'Your son? Do you think your son will come to fetch you, now he knows what you are?'

'You're cruel. What do you want from me?'

'I haven't very long. I rather thought I'd enjoy myself.'

And he lifted a garment from the bed (a lace-edged pair of bloomers) and began to tear it into strips.

'Bully!' she cried.

'Not one of them cares for you any longer, Charlotte; not one of them will come,' he said.

She was momentarily distracted by a scuffling sound on the roof above her.

'I wish you'd leave,' she said. 'You've had your fun – you won't get any more from me.'

The child suspended on the wet slates; the woman in the bedroom advanced upon; the dancing hoards in the hall, waving sticks and arms aloft, stamping their feet, juddered Sterne's foundations as the building shouted, '*What now? What now?*' at

the small group clinging together on the stairs: Emerald, Patience, Clovis, John and Ernest; ladies' hands seeking reassurance in the crooks of gentlemen's arms.

'We can't keep them here!' cried Ernest.

'But what can we do?' Patience asked, her slippered feet feeling blindly backwards up the polished steps.

Emerald turned to Clovis. 'Clo,' she said, grasping both his hands, as Torrington eyes met Torrington eyes. 'We must open up the Old House, and put them in it, all of them!'

Clovis, with no understanding why it should be, was instantly convinced of the rightness of her proposal; it was as solid as a well-oiled bolt sliding home. 'Of course,' he agreed, fortified, 'the Old House will take them.'

Florence was alone in the scullery. She had chased Myrtle away when, returning to the kitchen from the dining room in an impotent rage, wanting only to suppress her misery and regain control, the girl had dared to ask her what was the matter. Myrtle, elbows deep in washing-up, had withdrawn hastily into a corner as Florence, maddened, flew at her with a long-handled ladle.

'Get out! *Get out! God!*' Florence screamed, and Myrtle, frankly terrified, had rushed up the scullery stairs, and up again, to the top of the little attic stairs and the safety of her room, where she lay weeping with rage and exhaustion.

'I'll not go down there again tonight,' she promised. 'She's a devil and I hate her.' She had been awake and working for eighteen hours, and in a very short time she fell into a deep sleep, as the suds dried on her arms.

So Florence was alone, viciously upright in her caked dress as she trudged back and forth, trying to regain order, with only her two wiry hands and aching, bony back to do it. She

was trying to ignore the muffled commotion from beyond the service passage, but when Emerald and Clovis came flying through the baize door and into her kitchen she turned.

'You're all right, then?' asked Clovis, wild-eyed.

'Why wouldn't I be?' said Florence bitterly, wiping her hands on a dishcloth.

'We need to open up the Old House, Mrs Trieves, for the passengers. We can't let them run all over the house any longer.'

'Open up the Old House?' Florence was aghast. 'It's nothing but dark in there!'

But they were adamant. Clovis looked about for a candle and, finding a stub on a lower shelf, lit it.

Emerald went to the big door at the end of the scullery, and her white hands gripped the cast-iron bolt and heaved.

'Here, let me,' said Florence, coming to her aid. Together they eased it back.

And upstairs, the scene: the swagged curtains at Charlotte's bed and window; the buttery, glancing intimacy of her boudoir; her travelling dress and bursting cases; the amused scoundrel, lounging on the bed. He was not quite as immaculate as he had been, somewhat tattered; as large as life, if not quite as vibrant, but oh – he was relentless. Charlotte, despite herself, worn down, began to sob wretchedly.

'You have ruined me,' she said.

'You did that before you ever met me.'

'You have distressed my children.'

'They're old enough to know the truth.'

'I'm to lose this house anyway.'

'Why is that? Your husband throw you out when he hears about you, will he?' He yawned then, as if he cared not a sprat, as if he were most awfully tired by it all.

'Most likely, but that's not it; we're stony broke. Runaway, wife – it's all the same. I'm dispossessed and impoverished—'

'As you deserve to be.'

'I have loved this house. My children will lose their home.'

'Do I weep for you? I do not.'

'I'm leaving. The cart will be back soon. Robert and Stanley—' She rose and turned to the window.

'I sent them away, Charlotte.'

'*You?*' she said, facing him.

'Of course.'

'What can you mean?'

He was contemptuous. 'Who do you think got rid of them? And left you defenceless. The *Railway*?'

'Yes. Of course,' she asserted. 'They spoke to Emerald. They told us to expect more passengers.'

'Do you imagine the venerable institution of the Great Central Railway telephoned *you*?' He stopped and sighed, and then he did a strange thing.

A very strange thing indeed.

He began to make a sound that came, as it were, from the small gaping mouth of a telephone. His mouth opened and the crackling, confident, booming voice of Mr William Flockhart of the Great Central Railway issued forth into the room.

'*We have some more passengers for you!*' he shouted in a telephonic rattle, then abruptly changed, as a feeble, far-away childlike voice came from him. '*I have the Great Central Railway for you,*' he simpered, then again, without any human breath, the voice of Elsie Goodwin at the Post Office: '*Exchange! Miss Torrington at Sterne!*' he screeched.

'Stop it!'

She felt her legs give way beneath her at this apparition and sank, liquid with fear, onto the bed, covering her face with

her hands – then uncovered it again immediately, terrified by the idea of what he might do unseen, and was horrified afresh to see that he was advancing – and yet . . . *was it he?*

As she reluctantly watched, he seemed to change; could it be true? One moment sharply outlined against the paleness of her room, it was as if he blurred his edges, wobbling his perimeter like a soap bubble. Smudge, with her child's eyes, had seen something like it in the charcoal outline around him, but this went further. Charlotte now witnessed the unnatural sight of the man becoming both taller and wider; inexplicably, he seemed to alter the shape of his very skull. His head, once round, as sleek as a seal, became brutish, square like a bull's head. Was she mad? Was she dreaming?

Charlie Traversham-Beechers was being replaced.

His wine-coloured waistcoat darkened to flint and, as she watched, darkened further, to black. Her eyes fixed, glassily upon his gold watch chain, as it seemed to thicken, it did thicken – not just in the dilating focus of her fearful eye, but actually, from delicate gold cord to coarse brass links. She dragged her gaze up his chest to his face once more; the freakish squareness of his head had – she felt her gorge rise – changed again, to – could it be? His hair, gleamingly oiled, combed back above his evil ears, became stuck-up and clogged with wool or dust, then more so, piling on, lumpishly, until it became not hair at all, but the thick, felt stuff of a hat, a Railway worker's hat. The peak grew out of his head; at first like a giant fingernail, but then turning black and glossy. The Railway badge, in all its metal solidity, glinted into hard existence. She was transfixed. He came towards her; a porter. A Railway porter. With a kindly wink, he took the cheap watch from his waistcoat with his stubby fingers, and said in a voice thick with local accent and coal-dust, '*There's been a dreadful accident on a branch line, sir.*' Continuing to advance, he smiled.

'You'll have to get down to the crossroads, sir, to collect them. Take them up to Sterne, if you would. The Railway would be very much obliged to you.'

Then, in a flash, faster than the disappearance of steam in a room – a great deal faster than the puff of smoke of a stage magician – the porter was gone and Traversham-Beechers was back.

It was as if he had simply sauntered across the room, as if the porter had never been. He was sitting on the bed across from her – too close – idly plucking a cigar from his pocket and panting a little hoarsely from his efforts.

'Well, here we are again,' he said, a sheen of sweat on his brow.

The watch alone, though, seemed to have forgotten to change back. It hung heavily, swinging on its brass chain, brushing the paisley of the eiderdown ever so lightly with each diminishing arc.

Charlotte, who might have fainted, or dashed around the room distracted, or begun to cry again, did none of these things; she screamed. She screamed as loudly as he himself had screamed at the cutting of Emerald's cake, she screamed as loudly – louder – than Ferryman had screamed, at his most resistant to being put into the traces, she screamed so that the halls and doorways and floorboards of Sterne reverberated with her terror.

Smudge, on the roofs, heard the scream and froze, a brittle twig against the slates, all breath taken from her.

'Mother?' she whispered.

Lady, at the sound, scrambled, at last, to her feet, ears pricked, nervously.

The clamouring passengers in the hall, and the few that had relented and wandered back to the study; John, holding a stick

above his head; Ernest, attempting to speak over the noise; Patience, on the stairs – all were brought to a standstill, as the scream rang out.

Emerald and Clovis stood together facing the yawning blackness of the Old House. Emerald's first thought was that an animal was being murdered somewhere – rabbits had been known to scream like slaughtered babies as foxes' jaws closed about their throats. But there was no denying this was – on the briefest of reflections – her mother's scream.

'God,' said Clovis, and ran back towards the sound.

With Florence running behind, Emerald and Clovis joined the others in the hall, communicating horror with not a word uttered between them, they all advanced up the staircase.

The passengers, arrested, stood below like a silent forest of ragged, misty trees, watching them.

'I'll go,' said John, as they reached the landing, and he strode to Charlotte's door, banging loudly upon it and demanding, 'Who's there? Mrs Swift? Open your door!'

There was absolute silence from within.

Emerald, at his shoulder – with Florence at hers – uttered, 'John . . . open it.'

But the door was locked.

At the sound of John's fist upon the door, Smudge, lodged against the slippery roof, began to hurry, weakly, towards Charlotte's balcony. Her boots slithered on the tiles and only narrowly did she escape tripping and falling, helter-skelter, down the slates and off, into space and the hard ground below. Steadied by danger, more slowly, she resumed her inching journey along the roof.

*   *   *

Seconds earlier, in the bedroom, Charlotte, having screamed, had leapt from the stool to take refuge in the corner, by the armoir, but Traversham-Beechers, not suffering her to go that far, shot across the bed and grasped her wrist firmly.

'Charlotte,' he said, his eyes growing hugely in his head, like spreading ink stains. 'Charlotte, why did you leave me?'

She felt his breath on her face. He had always had bad breath, she remembered, but was surprised at its increased rancidness; it was like a rotting pigeon in a drain. She glanced down at his now slightly peeling and weakened fingers.

'Whatever is the matter with your hands?'

'It's . . .' He looked himself, but before he could go on, John banged on the door with his shout of, *Who's there?*

Charlotte extracted her wrist from the villain's grip slowly, and leaving him, sickening, it seemed, as he contemplated his crumbling nails and softening digits, she crossed feebly to the door and opened it.

John, Clovis, Emerald, Ernest, Patience and Florence surged into the room. Charlotte flew straight into Clovis's arms.

Traversham-Beechers turned to the lot of them and gave a little smile.

'You came,' he said with sad surprise.

Whatever feat of unnatural energy his vile transformational display had been, it appeared to have tired him. He was certainly not bristling with vibrancy as he had only hours earlier.

'How dare you come to my mother's room?' blazed Emerald. 'Leave this instant.'

All stared at Traversham-Beechers, who had not moved from the end of the bed.

'You would come to her aid?' he uttered, slightly wanly. 'This *creature?*'

But there was no need to answer this, as all present had very clearly done just that, and were now approaching, with

familial, righteous rage, the villain standing by the bedpost. But still he was bold.

'You can't contain me,' he said, 'not like those other pathetic victims. They had the idea that I hung on *their* coattails; they hung on *mine!*'

'What can you mean?' asked Emerald, despite herself, intrigued.

'Do you think they *wanted* to come here?' he answered, filled with scorn. 'They know nothing of *you*, nothing of *her*—' he flung at Charlotte, recovering herself still by the open door. '— poor wretches, they would have slipped quietly away from their broken necks and crushed little corpses, had it not been for *my* need, *my* hunger, *my* desire that pulled them here, that gave us all this—'

'This?' echoed Ernest.

'This?' asked Patience.

'—this *opportunity*. Our bodies. And see how they've relished it? For all their complaining, have they not sated themselves? One doesn't appreciate fully the functions of the flesh, be they ever so basic, until they are—' he gazed at his crumpled fingers, sadly, pulled a little flake away, dropped a useless nail onto the flowered carpet, 'finished.' He glanced up, keen as a rat. 'Nearly finished, but not quite. I've force enough in me yet. I won't be sent away.'

'Well, you're not staying up here,' said Clovis stoutly.

'I won't be sent away, I tell you.'

'Won't you?' said Emerald.

'No!' cried Charlie Traversham-Beechers, but his face, like the fellow travellers', from whom he sought to distance himself, had taken on a deathly pallor, a sallow, yellowing quality.

He tugged his evening gloves from his pocket and began to put them on. He appeared to be having difficulty, as if one or two of his fingers weren't strong enough to force themselves

into the snug, white crevices. He started to push a finger of one hand into the glove with the fingers of the other, but it buckled. It was like trying to put gloves onto the collapsed joints of a boiled fowl.

Just then, Emerald barked.

The others turned to her, briefly taken aback. Then Clovis, too, barked. He was quickly followed by Ernest, with the booming bark of a bloodhound, and Patience's high-pitched yap, like a Yorkshire terrier. Soon the whole group, united, were breaking out in a cascade of barks. Even Charlotte, let loose a variety of rabid growls and snaps. Charlie Traversham-Beechers opened his eyes wide, pupils springing nervously from one to the other, and, after a moment, assaulted by the noise, he began slowly to back away as if despite himself, and still fumbling with the evening gloves. He dropped one. The barks grew louder, more frenzied.

'Stop!' he cried. 'These aren't the rules!'

They did not stop. They continued, all seven of them – Emerald, Clovis, Charlotte, John, Ernest, Patience and Florence – all in a pack, barking themselves into a frenzy as they drove him towards the window. Charlotte gave full cry to her howling, snapping like a wolf at a damp little lamb – if she was to be a dog, she'd be a wild one.

Backing away, Traversham-Beechers shrank, crying, 'Stop! Stop!'

Vengefully, they barked their hatred, yapped their displeasure and their mockery, forcing the cowardly, set-upon, weakened villain back towards the large bay window, whose floor-to-ceiling sash gave on to the bowed balcony twenty feet above the drive.

They growled, they howled, they snapped their jaws, and he, holding the sagging fingers of his partly gloved hands in front of him, staggered backwards against the glass. The panes were large, but not large enough to break as he blundered

towards them, and so he turned, scrabbling, as, under the increased volume of the maddened hounds, he bent and, with a final effort, hooking his fingers in the fixings, he heaved the sash up and opened the window wide. Pushing it high above his head, he stumbled, not into the empty air, but with a tangled, tripping, collision, straight into the terrified figure of Smudge, who was at that moment lowering herself from the guttered roof above.

The barking ceased abruptly. Only Smudge's squeaked alarm broke the sudden quiet.

Disastrously, having once made a grab at her inadvertently, for balance, immediately afterwards, the villain took quick advantage of his luck, and held the child fast, and very near to the low and feeble balustrade. It was not meant for leaning.

'Leave off this instant!' he screamed, but there was no need to say anything. At the sight of Smudge, they had of course ceased all attack, concerned only with her welfare.

Traversham-Beechers had not been a violent man in life; nevertheless, the abandon of eternity yawned before him. His humiliation and rage ran uncontrolled as he hovered between the bounds of humanity and the unfettered impulse to flip the little girl off the balcony to her certain death.

'Mother!' screamed Smudge, in mortal extremis forgetting all bonds but the essential.

Charlotte, coolly, and with none of the terror so plainly exhibited by every other person there, stepped forward.

'What do you propose to do, Charlie,' she said, with utter composure, 'murder your own daughter?'

The villain had his hand at the child's neck, and the other braced behind her legs, as if to tip her neatly over. At the sharp intake of breath that followed this stunning question, he allowed his hands to drop, and Smudge, twisting away, freed herself, and ran to her mother's side.

Traversham-Beechers recovered.

'What can you mean?' he asked, aghast, then, shudderingly, '*Whiteleys?*'

'All of you, leave us, please,' said Charlotte sharply, without taking her eyes from him.

Although they would have been very glad to, Florence voiced all their feelings when she said, 'He's not safe.'

'I must be alone with him.'

'I'll stay,' said Florence Trieves grimly.

'But, Mother!' said Clovis.

'You can't!' said Emerald.

'Emerald,' Charlotte was steely, '*children*, do as I say. Out.'

In the face of both her resolve and the prospect of her already tattered character being further despoiled in their eyes, they all turned and obediently left the room.

As they closed the door, Charlotte was preparing to speak and Florence had taken up the poker.

On the landing, Emerald clutched Smudge gratefully, as Patience, Ernest, Clovis and John stood grouped in silent reaction to the scene in which they had taken part, and frank dread at what might be unfolding behind the closed door. They were worn out with barking. Nobody spoke for some moments.

The songs from below had entirely ceased. A strange quiet settled about them.

One or two clocks struck different hours.

The low murmur of voices could be heard within.

'Let's step away a little further,' whispered Patience.

They withdrew to the top of the stairs.

The rain had stopped. The drumming of it was finally absent, and now there was only the creaking house about them, and the dripping on the sills.

'God!' burst out Clovis.

It was Patience – his sister being occupied with Smudge – who took his hand.

After the longest, cruellest wait, they heard the door open and first Florence and then Charlotte emerged from the bedroom.

Silent, breathless; not one of them knew what to say. The two women reached them.

'Well,' said Charlotte with a little toss of her head, her look challenging them brightly, 'shall we all go down?'

Emerald gestured, wordlessly, to the bedroom door.

'He's gone,' said Florence with conviction. 'We can both assure you all that he's gone.'

'Can it be?' uttered Emerald.

'Yes,' said Charlotte. 'He has quite *gone*.'

No further explanation was forthcoming.

'Come along now,' said Florence.

And so, unsatisfied but obedient, they all began to go down, when Charlotte, at the rear, cried, 'Wait!' and all turned to her.

She dropped to her knees, a vision, still, of loveliness in her jade muslin and misty silks. Level with Smudge's gaze, beneath the thick roll of her fair hair, she looked into all their faces and whispered fiercely, 'It wasn't true what I told him! Do you hear me? *It wasn't true!*'

Amid the clearing of throats and averted gazes, nobody but Smudge knew quite how to reply.

'Of course it wasn't, Mama,' she said. 'How could he be my father? I've never even met him before.'

6

THE RESTING PLACE

Charlotte, queenly, stood on the half landing and gazed down at the grim hoards. Holding Smudge's hand, she was flanked by her bedraggled family, her housekeeper, and – slightly distant – the guests. (Most distant of all was John Buchanan, who, despite assisting in hounding out the cad Traversham-Beechers, felt himself too good for this polluted pack.)

The family gazed down on the wan faces beneath. The bedraggled travellers gazed back. It seemed the villain's expulsion had sapped them further: their revels were at an end. Their songs were finished. Distant in their memory were the effects of Poulet à la Marengo and glistening tongue.

'The Old House, then?' Charlotte said. 'Is that the answer to it?'

Emerald saw that her mother had at last reconciled herself to the presence of the travellers, and welcomed it.

'Yes, Mother; they'll be snug as bugs in there,' said Clovis. 'They'll be able to rest. Isn't that all they wanted?'

'I suggest you go ahead, children, and make a start at warming the place up a little. John and Ernest, I wonder if you would,' she searched for the phrase, 'show our guests through to their new quarters?'

She looked down at her youngest daughter's filthy face.

'Smudge,' she said, 'bed.'

* * *

Like sausage meat into a raw casing too small for it, the passengers led by John and Ernest squeezed themselves through the green baize door. The crowd of bodies backed, turned and bustled into the passage, jostling and impatient.

The smell that rose from their garments was no better for not being their faults. The faded stuff of their leggings and mufflers, the skin and flesh of their bodies, had been wetted and dried again. Mixing together, they smelled like the vile depths of a rotting metal bin, neglected by dustmen, covered in the rank secretions that even ordinary rubbish, left long enough, emits. They smelled, in short, of death, poor things.

Clovis retrieved his stump of candle from where he had dropped it on the flags of the scullery, and he and Emerald stepped once more into the cavern of the Old House. Near them were a few crowded shelves – the overspill from the larder, recently plundered – but past that, nobody ever went, not for many years at least.

Their feet stepped over the cracked flagstones and all about them the cold air whispered. Was it the wind outside that made the chill seem so alive? The air writhed above their heads, unseen.

Clovis held his candle aloft and peered into the vast space above, the flame touching nothing but the void.

'Lights!' he shouted, over his shoulder. 'Lights!'

The hoards flowed through into the kitchen. John glimpsed Florence Trieves' snug office, in all its intimate squalor as a man, lantern jawed, pushing to the front, who had not spoken before, fixed him with a look and asked, 'Where will we sleep? Behind the kitchens? Is that what you think of us?'

The breath seeping from his mouth was as sweet as a

fermenting apple. John knew of no existing provision for them, and found he had no clear answer.

'You never fetched the Railway!' came a disembodied woman's voice. And then another, 'This is disgraceful!'

'Yes, please, calmly and slowly,' shouted John with manful authority, herding and chivvying like a stubborn collie.

'On you go!' cried Patience, with Charlotte at the rear, and cheerful.

'What's down here?' shouted a tiny old man, thrusting his toothless face into John's.

'You'll see soon enough.'

The man's head was at a bizarre sideways angle (a childhood injury? A more recent one?) and his eyes blinked rapidly beneath wild grey brows.

'Get on with it, young man; you don't scare me,' he said, saliva spattering his lips, one of his eyes refusing to catch up with the other as he attempted to stare John down.

Ernest ran ahead to the scullery, and set about getting oil-lamps from the highest shelves.

'Here, let me,' said Florence, at his side, both of them standing in the draft from the Old House, pouring through the open door, like a river.

'Thank you, Mrs Trieves,' said Ernest, rummaging hurriedly for matches.

The crowed surged through the kitchen, through the scullery, blindly, and on, past Ernest and Florence, into the Old House – blundering into darkness.

They swivelled their heads about them.

'It's dark!'

'It's cold!'

'I'll not stay in here and you can say what you like – I'll not!' was shouted, and a great many other rising exclamations of rage and disappointment.

Oh, poor and desperate hoards! There would be no feather, no down, no clean cotton, their rest was to be as the stabling of animals.

'NO!'

'If you'll be patient, just one more little while,' cajoled Emerald in the dark, 'we'll have light for you,' while Patience, nervously, trailed behind, emitting compassion like fairy dust among the shambling creatures of the group.

'Are we really keeping them in here?' whispered Charlotte to Clovis. 'Is it remotely habitable?' and the crowd, echoing this reluctance, craned their necks – those that were straight enough for craning – to see.

The woman who had asked Patience if she were hurt when she fell on the stair appeared now, out of the gloom, her face barely visible, and mournful.

'We're blameless! Why would we be punished like this?'

She began to cry – and Patience almost joined her. Anger and distress seethed about the vast building, finding their voice in tears and grumbling, stamping of feet and all manner of disturbing exclamations.

'But when will we be taken?'

'Why is it so dark?'

'It's very late now!'

'So dark!'

'Here!' cried Ernest. He bore a heavy tray of blazing lamps before him, and pushed through the throng, lit up like a beacon. 'Here!' he cried. 'Light!'

Around he went, placing the sloshing lamps, while Florence, with another tray, as yet unlit, went behind. Patience darted after her with lighted spills, picking up her skirts (trying not to think about rats), and plucking at the oily wicks.

'You see!' she said, as haloed lamps were laid and lit. 'Everything will be all right, you'll see.'

Soon there was a brown feathering of the air, and pools of amber and bright gold.

The spaces of the high roof reached above the passengers' heads; the walls of granite blocks surrounded them, solid and tall. The drifting souls fell silent at last, wandering and watching the lighting of the lamps as their new quarters were gradually illuminated.

'And now, a fire,' said Clovis.

The three young men went about the frigid Old House, and out into the rain, too, to the stores, gathering fuel. In no time at all, a waist-high stack of kindling, logs, coal and paper, like a bonfire on Guy Fawkes night, stood ready, and, as Ernest set a match to it, the eager passengers edged closer.

'It's blocked with something.'

John handed him the poker and he jabbed upwards, waving it back and forth like an inept knight after a dragon. With a scraping, scuttling sound, a heap of dusty feathers and rotted birds tumbled out onto the unlit fire, and about his feet, loose heads falling, claws scattering.

'*Ooh,*' said the onlookers.

'They'll soon burn off,' said John.

Small corpses singed as the fire took hold. In just a few moments, clean flames leapt high into the hollow dark of the chimney.

Ernest, John and Clovis, in smutty disarray, heaped the grate with fuel, and heaped and heaped again, until, like a beacon on a lonely cliff, the fire blazed, towering and roaring in the hearth.

Unheated for two hundred years, warmth seeped between the stones of the Old House like blood starting through veins; the snug stones swelled in the walls; the shell became a body. The passengers felt the warmth on the damp membranes of their fragile skins, the cold flesh beneath, almost as warm as life itself.

'Oh heat!'

'Heat!'

'Closer!' they cried, and for a little while, the young men rested.

The passengers pressed on the fire with happy murmurings. They spread, they glowed and softened, their hard bodies warmed to pulpiness.

'Oh, lovely,' they said.

'Good.'

The mice, too, a different colony to those that nestled and played in the velvets and tasselled corners of the New House, made forays from their catacombs and turned their twitching noses to the blaze. With wolfish cries, the lurcher Forth found his way inside from the deluge and lay suspiciously at the indistinct feet of the resting passengers. The very spiders warmed themselves.

Emerald gathered the spaniel Nell in her arms, who had trotted in, wet-pawed from the scullery.

'Look,' she said to John, who stood just outside the fire's warmth, and she held up the pretty dog for admiration. But John Buchanan, proud, preferred to keep to himself.

The fire maintained its pull, and from all parts of the house the other animals came: Lucy, to join Nell; Lloyd, recalcitrant, from some high and watchful place; even the pony Lady, in Smudge's room, let out a whinny, unheard by anyone but Smudge, that tried to tell of her loneliness.

'Shh,' said Smudge drowsily.

Mice and dogs and fetid passengers, all took warmth, bewitched, as their hosts stood by, and caught their breath, and felt the tugging of unseen hands upon their thoughts, coaxing them.

'They need to sleep,' announced Emerald, suddenly and

with decision. All around her the passengers whispered and echoed.

It was becoming clear to her that the feeding of the passengers, the opening of the door, the lighting of the fire, the gathering of souls about it – all were steps along a path that must be trod to its conclusion.

'We must make them beds,' said Emerald firmly.

'Sleep,' they agreed.

'Tired.'

'We must lay them to rest,' said Emerald with warm compulsion, gazing into the fire, 'and we must make them *comfortable.*'

'*Comfortable,*' came a murmured agreement from the passengers. 'Oh, quite comfortable.' And they took up singing again, quietly, one voice joining another.

> *A mother was bathing her baby one night*
> *The youngest of ten, and a tiny young mite*

'Let's fetch linen,' said Patience.

> *The mother was poor and the baby was thin*
> *Only a skellington covered with skin . . .*

'And blankets,' said Ernest, his spectacles reflecting flames, his face, like the others, turned to the fire, his mind possessed by the need to aid the passengers to their rest.

All but Florence and John nodded in agreement – Florence, because she was separated from the others by the shame of Traversham-Beechers' revelations, and John because he was separated by having heard them. The crisis had been averted, he did not care to help his besmirched hosts any longer.

'Not I,' said John, stepping away, averting his face. 'You can all do as you will.'

'John?' murmured Emerald, turning to him (all the others, animal and two-legged, absorbed in contemplating the moving fire, as the sing-song voices softly crooned).

She grasped his hand and whispered boldly, 'John? Do you loathe me now?'

'Loathe you?' In the deep night, while all the house was dim with enchantment, the innocent, daylight conversation in the drawing room – only that afternoon – when he had given her the cameo was of another time and place entirely. She still wore his present, he saw, about her tainted neck.

'Won't you at least help us? Please.'

And grudgingly he relented.

Clovis, Ernest, Charlotte and Patience extracted themselves from the hot circle of firelight to join them.

'We will put their beds on the gallery,' declared Clovis determinedly, looking up the wide black stair to the tilting rail, barely gleaming above him.

'But what will they be?'

'We'll find something. Ernest?'

'Surely.'

He and Clovis set off into the gloom, resolute.

Emerald looked around for Florence. 'Where's Mrs Trieves?' she asked, but nobody had seen her go.

'Patience, come with me, John – would you mind? They must have beds.'

All the figures by the fire turned to her as one, their faces, with the light behind them, black silhouettes.

'And what shall we sleep on?' came their hollow voices.

'Yes, where shall we sleep?'

The moans raised, wailingly; shouts multiplied.

'See about my baby!'

'My mother!'

'She's weak——'

'She's old——'

Emerald felt the urgency of their exhaustion, the fast pull of oblivion that had its hold on each of them.

'Come along,' she said, 'quickly.' And she, Patience, Charlotte and John left the Old House for the New, promising to return.

They went through the house at a run to raid the bedrooms, relieved to be out of the company of the passengers, with John trailing behind them resentfully.

Emerald threw open the bedroom doors.

'All my linen!' Charlotte cried, but she, too, was caught up with the need to help now, and her protests were feeble. 'Strip all the beds,' she commanded, steely.

They knew fresh spoils were to be had in the linen cupboard. They knew where the linen cupboard was – on the upper landing, kept locked by Mrs Trieves – they had walked past it, but its *contents* – the mysterious shelves, labelled in italics (and everything on them white!) – were a foreign land into which they might not go.

'John, fetch Mrs Trieves,' said Emerald. 'We'll see to the bedrooms.'

John was nonplussed. He did not want to speak to Mrs Trieves, whom he now despised utterly, but could not very well refuse. He lumbered down the stairs, unhappily, and paused at her door.

The smell of wood-smoke from the enormous fire in the great hall came to him down the passage. His white gloves were stuffed into his pockets, balled up and safe from the travails of the evening; engine oil and logs. He raised his aching, bare hand to knock.

(*You are needed; the passengers must have bedding*, he rehearsed.)

He did not want to see her. He could not imagine how Mrs Trieves, the housekeeper, could possibly be the same creature so eloquently described by Charlie Traversham-Beechers, gallivanting blatantly about Bloomsbury. What bawdy secrets did she hide beneath the black dress? What delights of the flesh had she indulged, endured or initiated during her low and lusty past?

The survivors were singing again.

Their voices came to him from the great hall, raised in hope and excitement, in comfort and in fun –

> *What could be nicer than this?*
> *A nice old cuddle and kiss?*

No, it was not very nice at all, the thing he was imagining. The thing that Florence had been, that all men wanted and some went so far as to purchase from women such as—

> *All beneath the pale moonlight,*
> *'Oh, what a luverly night tonight . . .*

And certainly *not* 'luverly'. He knocked, and not waiting for an answer, opened the door. Florence gave a scream and faced him. She had been washing. Her hair was long – longer than that – very long, and lay in what could only be described as abundance across her white shoulders and narrow breast.

'Ah!' she cried.

She was wearing nothing at all but her black, tightly laced boots and holding her discarded dress up in front of her. She had just spun around from the wash-stand in the corner where she had been splashing herself with water and rubbing herself

with a big bar of hard soap that now, in her shock, she dropped with a bang to the floor.

The house was filled with some strange magic and all around was chaos, while this . . . woman washed herself.

In that far wasteland of nighttime actions were adrift like seeds of a dandelion clock floating in remote space; did John leave the room immediately, with downcast eyes? He did not. He was, as they say, rooted to the spot, like a staring fir tree.

She recovered herself quicker than he and said, with something akin to outrage, 'Oh what? Shocked are you?'

Startled at her effrontery, he replied, gruffly, 'Shocked at *you*.'

'For washing?' She was bold, and met his eye defiantly, apparently unchastened by the fact the whole household now knew of her monstrous past.

'Not that.' John, too, had recovered and felt his own outrage returning. Why should he be the one wrong-footed? Was not she the one to be ashamed? 'You – you – shouldn't—'

'Shouldn't work in a house with decent people?'

(She was more articulate than he. Had she not seen more of life?) 'Shouldn't wash my own self in my own room?'

'I—'

'Yes? Out with it, cabbage.'

Cabbage? This was the last straw.

'I'll not stand here and be insulted by a . . . by a woman of low morals. I came here, in all civility, to ask –' (He was dashed if he could remember what it was he wanted to ask.) '. . . a thing of you, and you go off shouting like a – like a—'

All of this was unfamiliar to him. He knew he ought to have authority – a man, her superior – but he had never been faced with an angry, half-clothed woman before (outside his

youth and his own family), and as he gathered his thoughts she threw at him, 'Like a fishwife? A slut?'

Far from being silenced by him, she was – oh God – she was advancing.

Her white, bony shoulders, her narrow face, this was not the woman he had passed a thousand times without a second glance; this was not the housekeeper, the skivvy, the *thing* that was somehow past womanhood. She gleamed with the water from washing, she glowed with anger, her long dark hair swirled, like a furiously advancing mermaid, and all John could think of was that he must be in the grip of some dream that she, Mrs Trieves, in all her angular austerity, had been replaced by this harridan, this maenad, this naked abandonment to femininity.

She was feet away from him now, grasping her black dress to her chest still, like a shed skin, eyes blazing, one hand at her throat – her white and slender throat –

'Oh God,' he said out loud.

She stopped. He stared at her, wild-eyed.

'John Buchanan,' she said, in a voice just above a whisper, and the tender softness of her tone both soothed and alarmed him. 'John, you know *nothing* of me.'

He gazed into her eyes (blue!) as she continued, 'Before I was like this . . . I was loved.'

Whatever shocking thing he had thought might issue from her, it was not this. And there was more.

'My husband loved me,' she said miserably.

Her husband? John examined this. Could it be she was not entirely described by her shameful past? That she had other concerns, more poignant? Before his eyes she had transmogrified, from reviled servant to witch to . . . He was bewildered, utterly. She came closer yet, her face dissolving in his vision into sweetness.

'We should have liked a boy,' she said, and kissed him.

From servant to witch to *girl*, then! And John kissed her back. Her face smelled of soap. He had interrupted her washing. It seemed an hour before.

She stopped kissing him, decisively, and looked at him.

'Oh, good God,' she said in shock.

And that would have been an end to it, except that John, as easily as if he had meant to do it all along, and not at all surprised at himself, pulled the black silk dress from her hand and tossed it like a dead thing to the ground.

Her bare flesh, the frail whiteness of her body, pressed against the wood-smoke smelling, coal-smeared shirt and trousers of him and before another word was uttered, before consent or discussion, and with a roughness that was not hateful, and yet had something of violence in it, he took her by the arms and turned her, crushed her, against the door – closing it.

'Oh yes,' she uttered exultantly, and tore at his shirt.

'I've never done this,' he blurted, and with thoughtless passion, he kissed her and grabbed whatever parts of her he could – her hair, waist, thighs – and gripped them, discovering them with hands so unused to discovering anybody and so grateful to be doing it now. Her skin was delightful. He couldn't imagine what possible purpose his fingers had been put to before now that in any way justified their existence.

The door was hard and rattled noisily as they banged against it, but in the headlong rush to heated, gasping – oh wonderful – conclusion, neither thought to move away. And with no consideration of sense and dignity on his part, or any other feelings but wonder and glorious homecoming on hers, they met in deep abandon. They were suffused by intense and unparalleled heat, from core to crust, like the earth cracking and scorched with hot lava; blissful.

There had been a larder, fully stocked but not often cleared,

and among the very many cluttered shelves there was one dusty jar, high up, well-sealed and never looked at, labelled *Florence Trieves, housekeeper, old.* (And that name, latterly, scrawled out and over-written: BAD.) Now she, jolted by the lightning bolts of judgement, and miraculously, had flung against that glass, and rocked and tipped her cramped and smeary jar from the shelf to crash, exploding, on the floor; she had sprung from all its shattered debris, full-blooded, vibrant and demanded to be eaten.

Seated now on the floor in chaotic splendour, the two of them – who might have cried, or blamed, or done any number of harmful cruel things to one another – laughed themselves light-headed.

At length, recovering, Florence caught her breath and said, 'That'll teach you to be so proud, Mr John Buchanan.' To which he – thinking of Emerald as well as the damp and sated creature he had become – could only answer humbly, 'Aye.'

A moment passed.

'Did you mention linen?'

'Yes, the passengers need some.'

Florence gave a sigh and looked about her little room.

'I'm so very hungry,' she said. 'I don't remember ever having been so hungry.'

'Let's see to it then,' said John and helped her up. He saw himself – the self of only minutes before – a bitter, black crow, a hybrid of his father and the pastor at his church, and pitied himself, thinking: *Was that all it was that made me that? The lack of touching a woman? Just that?* He seemed to have a delighted new understanding of every living thing on earth, and be reunited with his childhood self that had rolled in grass and sniffed things fearlessly. That knowledge could restore innocence to him was a marvellous equation.

They made themselves respectable (she in the fresh dress

she had been about to put on when he surprised her, and not the stinking old one) and ventured in agreeable companionship to the larder. They found the last of the bread, and sat on the floor gobbling it. To Florence it was like remembered bread; the faint salt, the stubborn crust and soft interior.

At last they rejoined the others, tearing bedding from the rooms, and if their recent intimacies were not evident to an incurious observer, John Buchanan and Florence Trieves were as unlike their recent selves as fresh green peas from their hoary pods.

Surrendering, then, all of them, to the lost night, the household ransacked every ordered, crisp, fresh thing that was left in that already plundered house.

Like a herd of rampant cattle they charged through the place, whisking up lace, damask, frothy cottons in their arms and depositing them, triumphantly, onto the sooty gallery, where makeshift heaps of broken wheels and carriage springs, sheep hurdles and dank old bales made beds. Beds fit for bodies to be laid out on.

Smudge, in her room, had no interest in the events beyond the scullery door. She had no desire to see the little beds on the gallery; she did not care for the shadowy souls that drifted about, displaced, with their bundles; she did not find it remarkable that even her mother had donned an apron and joined the redoubled efforts of the family to find places for them all to sleep; she was not remotely diverted by the fact that, attached to her normal house, was a vast illuminated cave, thronging with bodies, heaving with movement and reeking of decay. She cared only that, after some little time, the sounds of pounding feet through the house and the occasional cries of *bolsters!* or *curtains!* faded right away, and she was left in peace.

The New House was hers.

There were the familiar sounds of the off-kilter ticking clocks and musical creaks, and apart from the mess, things were just as usual in it. She and Lady were the only living souls – and, thought Smudge grimly, *one of them was on her way out.*

She stood up from her wrinkled bed. She rolled up her sleeves with determination. She braced herself.

'Lady!' she said.

The pony looked up from the crust she had been nosing on the floor.

'Enough is enough,' said Smudge. 'We're going down and I don't care.'

Boldly, she threw the door wide open. Fresh droppings subtly steamed.

There was nobody within sight or hearing of her room. This was her chance.

She took up the leading rope and took the pony out onto the landing, past all the bedrooms again, and the mullioned windows.

Outside, the rain-ragged magnolia flowers were invisible; inside, the flames of the oil lamps flickered and smoked.

They would leave the way they had come: she passed by the main stairs and headed towards the back landing. At the far end of the house, she hauled the door open, stepped over the cold droppings, kicked about by running feet as they plundered the linen cupboard.

She set her foot on the top step.

It was at this point that the thus far obliging pony put her head up, dug in her front feet, and halted.

Smudge stared silently up at Lady. Lady stared down, down the slippery wooden stair.

It was immediately obvious that there was no possibility whatsoever that the pony was going to descend. Further, Smudge could see that refusing to continue was the much

preferable choice. A downward journey would be bound to end in the most grievous calamity imaginable: the headlong crash of frail two-legged girl and large, four-legged pony into a broken heap on the flags below.

Smudge began to quiver.

'Back,' she said, and Lady, knowing what was good for her, obeyed.

Perhaps realising the seriousness of her situation, or simply missing her stall and manger, the animal, who had been the soul of placidity all evening, at last began to get restless. A pony and a pet when at rest, she was unequivocally a horse when agitated. She stamped her feet and threw up her head, yanking the rope in Smudge's small hand, alarming the child and herself until, smartly and heavily reversing, she banged her hock on the bathroom door and reared violently. Coming down, her hooves slithered on the floorboards and wrinkled the thin carpet horribly.

Smudge tried to calm her. What had been most welcome solitude only moments before now felt like desperate loneliness. She had no idea what to do. The pony was rolling her eyes at the terrifying sight of the landing before her, and Smudge was on the verge of panic herself.

She was further startled – and gave a yelp – as, on glancing towards her room, she saw Ernest Sutton standing stock still at the far end of the corridor. He had just gained the top of the scullery stairs. Lady, too, paused in her drama to look. Girl and pony faced auburn-haired young man in silence.

'Forgive my appearance,' he said; 'I've been building a fire, you know, and making beds. I must look a sight, I think.'

This cool ignoring of Lady's presence was comforting to Smudge.

'I thought you were downstairs with us,' he said. He did look very messy.

'I'm not,' said Smudge.

'Evidently. I was just on my way for a muffler.'

Her heart was thumping. She was beginning to think he actually hadn't noticed the pony – perhaps his vision was not as corrected as they had all thought – when he asked, mildly, 'Are you on your way up or down?'

'Down,' said Smudge, 'but Lady won't go.'

'Down the stairs?' he said thoughtfully. 'I can't say I blame her.'

'Nor can I. Hooves.'

'Impractical.'

'Yes. I hadn't realised,' Smudge quavered, a lump rising in her throat.

'Do you think I ought to fetch your sister?' asked Ernest, to which she responded violently, 'Oh no! Please! There'll be the most dreadful to-do!'

Lady, startled by her excitement, jumped about again, dancing heavily on the slender floorboards. Ernest thought for a moment.

His first reaction to the sight of the child and the wretched animal had been to throw his arms in the air and shout, 'Great heavens! A pony!'; he was glad he had curbed it. He could see both Smudge and Lady were bordering on hysteria.

'Imogen,' he said, and checked his watch (a reliable silver affair that was *always* itself). 'It is the middle of the night. Well past it, in fact. This seems to me – regardless of the to-do – that this is the sort of problem we need to help you with. All of us.'

The stubborn child shook her head mutely. She was very tired and about to sob. He made an elegant change of tack.

'Patience loves ponies,' he remarked pleasantly.

'Does she?' replied Smudge, beguiled.

'Her first was a dun named Toffee. She could persuade him to do almost anything.'

He waited, like a confident trout fisherman, for his reward.

'You had better fetch them then,' said she, at last.

'At your service,' he responded, but then, pausing, 'Incidentally, why did you bring her into the house?'

'To make her portrait. In my room.'

'I see.' He took off his spectacles and rubbed his eyes.

Replacing them he said, 'Don't worry, I'll be back directly. I promise.'

He went away down the stairs. Smudge looked about her, forlornly.

7

THE STARLIGHT BATH

In the Old House, the linen, blankets and other bedding were being stacked and moulded into cosy nests and mattresses. The passengers waited, hands stretching towards the fire, pale faces looking up, hopefully, towards the tilting gallery. When Ernest rushed in, shouting, 'Good God, there's a pony upstairs! Imogen is losing control of it!' the family all dashed to the wobbly rail, aghast, while the passengers, in their fog of waiting, merely murmured, 'Delays', disgruntled.

'Oh Lord, I suppose she wanted to make its portrait?' said Clovis.

'Apparently. She's on the landing with it, near the door to the back stairs.'

Beds forgotten, and without an apology, the family ran down the blackened staircase, slipping and tumbling in their haste.

Exhausted stares lingered on them until they were lost from sight.

The group paused in the bright hall.

'Perhaps I had better go up alone to start with?' said Emerald, as they waited, breathless, at the foot of the main stairs. A snort and hoof-stamp from above reached their ears.

She went up, as the others stood about, with 'Whatever

shall we do with it?' and 'How will it come down?' being the general gist of their conversation.

'I didn't mention to her,' said Ernest, 'that the artist Stubbs contented himself with stables as a setting for his equine portraits and demonstrably did quite well with them.'

'She has the other animals' pictures on her walls,' said Clovis, by way of explaining his sister's eccentricity; 'it wouldn't be the same.'

'Forgive me,' said Ernest.

'Not at all,' replied Clovis generously. 'Smudge is quite mad by any normal reckoning, we're just used to her.'

At the top of the main stairs Emerald paused, composed herself, and proceeded. Ernest was not a case for the insane asylum (although her sister very well might be) – Lady and the child were locked in silent battle on the landing. The pony had trodden heavily on Smudge's toe and was now leaning, stubbornly, and gazing at a Venetian landscape, while Smudge, speechless with agony, attempted to shove her off. The pony had become deaf, apparently, and leaned ever more weightily on poor Smudge's foot.

'Oh heavens!' cried Emerald, rushing to her aid. Between them they removed the hoof and Smudge hopped up and down, clasping her foot, with tears streaming down her face.

'She didn't mean to,' she said, when she could breathe.

'Rubbish; she's a brute,' said Emerald and smacked Lady hard on the chest. Lady recognised discipline when she came across it and did not retaliate, but clacked her teeth together in impotent resentment.

'Now, however are we going to get her down?' asked Emerald, and at that, Smudge began to cry again, helplessly.

'I thought you'd know!' she wailed.

'Hush, hush; there, there.' Emerald patted her shoulder

while looking about for inspiration. 'Let's get her to the big stairs,' she said.

At the top, the pony stared down at Charlotte, Florence, John, Patience, Ernest and Clovis and they all stared up at her.

'Oh, *Imogen*,' growled Charlotte, in operatic *sotto voce*.

'Sorry, Mother,' said Smudge.

'Strewth,' said Clovis. 'She looks bigger than usual.'

'I've grown,' said Smudge.

'Not you, the pony!'

'Well, she *is* almost fifteen hands; I'm always telling you.'

'I suppose she won't just come down?' said Patience, ever the optimist, but the stairs were uncarpeted.

'Not a chance,' said Clovis cheerfully. 'Perhaps we could put a sling on her and hang her out of the window?'

'Put a sling on *you*, and *throw* you out!' Smudge exploded, and he didn't tease her further.

'We can gather carpets and rugs and lay them down the stairs to make a ramp,' said Ernest, and this, being an endeavour likely to succeed, was soon done.

The carpets appeared solid enough: a pony might be fooled into believing they provided a slope such as might be found in the natural landscape, but when she placed a hoof upon them they shifted enough to convince the already suspicious beast that she was being led into a trap, and was soon to be set upon by wolves. She teetered at the top of the Persian ramp for some moments before backing off until her rump was pressed against the wall.

'No enthusiasm,' said Clovis.

'None,' agreed Patience.

'Oats,' said Emerald.

'I'll go,' said Clovis, and sprinted away to the stables.

Oats were brought. The pony sniffed them, advanced slightly,

ate them, felt the shifting tapestry ground once more, and refused to go any further. More oats were offered, by hand or scattered on the rugs or, later, shaken in a bucket on the half-landing, but greed proved an insufficient prompt to courage.

'I suppose if we hit her, she'll never go down,' said Florence, who did not like horses and was tempted to beat this one.

'We could get a rope around her behind, and haul her,' offered Emerald, and a rope was brought.

The rain had started again and Clovis was fairly drenched from his two journeys to the stables. While Ernest and Emerald drew the rope slowly around Lady's bottom, Patience gave him her handkerchief for his face. Of all young women, only Patience could be relied upon to have a clean handkerchief on such a night.

Unfortunately, Lady took exception to the rope and knocked a picture from the wall in the ensuing tantrum. The glass shattered and scattered, causing Smudge to cry out in alarm.

The cat Lloyd and both spaniels had torn themselves from the bewitching Old House fire, and had come to watch. They sat looking on smugly from safe vantage points; stairs were child's play to them. Even the new kitten Tenterhooks, with his three-inch legs, could have made the descent given time. He lay curled in the crook of Patience's elbow and slept.

They were, all of them, by now beyond exhaustion, fraught with having to speak calmly and coaxingly to the accursed pony for so long, and not give vent to their frustration. The needs of the host of passengers tugged incessantly at them, like a hunger, a mental toothache, and they were divided between one world and another, neither wholly in the New House, with its earthly calamity, nor physically in the Old, with its other compulsions.

'Could she just become a house-pony?' asked Smudge

sleepily. She had tucked herself into the corner on the half-landing, with her bruised foot, hoping the sight of her might encourage the pony down.

'No, don't be absurd,' snapped Emerald, close to tears herself. She was struck by an idea. 'We must take her down the stairs of the Old House! She'll go down *them*, they are much less steep – and the treads are wider.'

'Aren't you forgetting the little matter of the wall between the houses?' said Clovis.

'We can break it down,' said Emerald, on her mettle.

'My bedroom wall?' said Smudge eagerly.

'Break it down?' Charlotte was shocked.

'Oh Mother, it's only a wall! The men can do it. Can't you?'

'If you wish it,' said Ernest, struck by her beauty.

'You're as mad as old Smudge,' said Clovis cheerfully. 'Let's try it.'

'We can cover the steps with mud and stones. It will be just like the ground outside – we can't possibly do that in this house. She'll go down like a lamb.' Emerald was carried away with her idea and impatient to execute it. 'And if she slithers – then, she slithers! We can bandage her legs up.'

The pony and child were sent to Clovis's bedroom, where Smudge fell asleep on the bed, and Lady looked out of the window, stupidly.

'Come!' cried Florence Trieves. 'Wheelbarrows!' And all seven of them raced from the front of the house into the wild and billowing night.

There was barely a light to be seen. They were engulfed, instantly.

Clovis ran back to fetch lamps, Ernest and Emerald went to the outbuildings and found shovels and picks, hoes – anything that they could use to bring the outside into the house and save the accursed pony.

Charlotte threw open the wide, main door of the Old House. It was thick and softened by lack of use. The travellers turned aghast from the fire to stare as Clovis wedged it open to the air, holding a lamp high and shouting, 'Bring the barrows in!'

'What now?' they murmured, and, 'Confound the Railway: hang them.'

The fine rain had become finer still. The breeze had softened from stiff to spring-like. The tattered clouds rolled and shredded above, revealing the patterns of the stars, late in their nighttime arc, laced above the house like dewy spider's web.

The heaving of wet earth began. Ernest, Florence, Charlotte – with sudden wild enthusiasm for toil – Emerald, Clovis, Patience, all took up tools and worked.

Mud clung to their legs. It sucked their shoes almost from their feet. In places they stood ankle deep in it, then slid, like skaters, across flags coated with water and slime, trip over brick paths and stumble headlong into shrubs and tangling roses.

From dark night to dim house they journeyed, and slapped shovelfuls of soil onto the steps of the great stair. There was a curious satisfaction in it.

Clovis was speedy with his task to illuminate, and soon lamps stood about the place, lighting the kitchen garden door here, the verges there; a pool of brightness by the beds where Emerald had gardened that morning, a watery beam to point out a wall or small tree, and all serving only to exaggerate the vast unfathomable night around them. John and Florence, sworn off one another for ever, so that he might seek a more appropriate mate, took the opportunity to kiss violently under cover of the night and rain.

The mud slathered them all. The women's ruined hems

dragged as they heaved the soil into the wheelbarrows and pushed them, two together to the door of the Old House.

'I'll fetch sacks to hold it to the stairs,' said Clovis, rivulets streaming down his face and into his mouth.

'Yes, for gripping!' shouted Patience across the gravelled paths.

John, Clovis and Patience had set up a loose chain to the house, and were carrying the earth inside. The barrows rattled and jumped over the cobbles and ploughed through sodden earth.

The soothing rain poured down; the leaden, sucking earth ensnared them. They were washed into the seething night, like ragged night-birds, like fallen leaves; like spirits.

'Ooh,' and 'See?' moaned the travellers as they watched the household go in and out of the Old House, and in and out again; flinging shovelfuls of mud onto the stairs of the great hall.

In the border, Ernest and Emerald toiled together, clothes sticking to them, he breaking the compacted earth, she heaving it up.

'This is madness!' she cried, blood pounding around her body, palms wet and slippery on the handle of the shovel, and hair blown into her face as she worked.

And he, bringing the pick down, working its point into the soil so that she might take it up, glanced up at her and replied, 'Yes, it's marvellous. Magnificent.'

And in the churning mud of the border, Emerald slipped and tottered and fell into the ooze. Her hand smacked down onto it, and deeply into it, almost to the elbow.

'Here.' Ernest's hand came out to save her and, as she hauled at his arm, he too reeled and fell into the mud with a smack

— at least the side of him, and all of one leg. Mud slapped and slopped about them. She began to laugh, as for brief moments it was as if the bed would swallow them, as if they would never raise themselves from its rich earth, buried like bodies in a graveyard, for ever.

'Oh, heavens!' cried Emerald, as they struggled together. 'Help!'

They knelt, gripping hand to arm.

Clovis had left the lamp several feet away, and in its watery beam only their teeth and eyes gleamed; pale cheeks, mud-streaked; daubed hair, sleek. Emerald tasted the mineral grit of earth on her tongue; her hands gripped Ernest's forearms as they fought for stability. She felt the heat of his body, close to her, inside his ruined clothes, and caught the faintest smell of lemon. She looked up at him; he down at her. They gripped one another firmly, knees sinking ever further into that primeval herbaceous border.

His glasses had fallen from his face. The lamp-light shone upon him. She had forgotten altogether about the colour of his eyes. She placed her mud-coated hand against his cheek, touched the edge of his ear, and felt all the wavering, fearful centre of herself rejoice.

'You're an angel,' he said.

'No—' Thinking of her mother, suddenly, she said, chok-ingly, 'none of us are that.'

'You are *Emerald*, then,' he said, and muddied his lips kissing the fingers of her chilled hands.

Emerald was drenched and dancing with delight, as the stars shone down, like showering sparks around them.

I cried in that flower-bed this morning, too, she thought and laid her cheek against his bowed head.

The breeze had dropped to a whisper. The rain – oh miracle! – had utterly ceased. Emerald began to shiver.

'Shall we send out a dove?' said Ernest, then, 'Ah, I've dropped my spectacles somewhere.'

Together they groped in the mud until they were found.

As Smudge slept on, the men, joined by an exultant Ernest, assaulted the wall from the great hall side, crowded onto the gallery and upper steps, with picks and the utmost violence.

Blackened like miners by the wet earth of Sterne, they set about destroying the plaster and lath and, dry as bone, it fragmented beneath their blows. Dust and paint chips flew up in clouds, with horse-hair, and soon, very soon, the queer sight of Smudge's little bedroom, like Tinkerbell's boudoir, only bare and shabby, came into view.

Below, the white hoards of travellers watched, silently and in awe, this violent life distracting them even if only briefly from their arrested journey.

The noise woke Smudge, who left the pony and came to her bedroom doorway to watch.

'Oh,' she said, 'there's the Old House!'

From her side the view was even odder: through the hole the enormous old place opened up like the wide underwater world seen through the porthole of a ship from a snug cabin; the long gallery banister, the rows and rows of beds, the chalky passengers far below, staring up at her, the leaping shadows thrown up by the fire; this really was the most rare of adventures.

'Hello!' she called to them. 'Hello! Hello!'

'Here, clear that away,' said Clovis, kicking the broken pieces away from the gap – now some six feet wide – so that the pony might step through.

Patience hovered behind the men on the gallery, squeaking and exclaiming concernedly. Florence and Charlotte were next

to her, and Emerald was gazing on the miracle that was Ernest, as she relived their embrace in the flower-bed.

'I think it's time to give it a try, don't you?' said Clovis.

While Smudge and he went to fetch Lady, Emerald and Ernest ran to the stables to fetch Levi, who was to stand by the door as encouragement to the pony, and Patience, Charlotte and Florence placed themselves about as human barriers to prevent her rampaging over the gallery and laying waste to the rows of beds they had so painstakingly constructed there.

As Smudge brought Lady into her bedroom, and the pony saw there was a hole where once the wall had been, she stopped and stared.

'Stupid animal,' said Charlotte.

'Ought not somebody else lead her down?' queried Patience fearfully.

'No!' cried Smudge, appalled. 'She's mine!'

At the sight of Smudge's stricken face, Charlotte murmured, 'Imogen would like to do it,' and slowly, she approached them. 'Smudge?' she said softly, holding out her hand.

'I'm sorry, Mother,' said Smudge.

'It's quite all right. These things happen.'

With that, she took a hold of the pony's headcollar, while Smudge took up the rope, and they led her through the gap.

The child stared around her. The household, mud-coated, encouraged her, kindly; the great group of travellers stared up with hollow eyes, not breathing.

Emerald, with the horse Levi, shiny and immaculate, appeared at the open door, but despite his love for Emerald, he gave a start at the sight of the crowd of pale watchers. He did not seem to like the look of them at all. She made do with just his head and shoulders and forelegs inside, and once he saw Lady, high above, on the gallery, he appeared to realise

the situation, gave a low whinny of greeting to the pony, and stood solidly to wait for her.

Smudge stared down at them all bleakly.

'I think she may be more willing if I ride,' she said in a small voice.

'You may be right,' said Charlotte steadily, and she bent and hitched up her skirt, tying it firmly in a knot so as not to trip over it on the stairs. Lady stood stock still as Charlotte helped Smudge up. The stairs, hidden beneath wet mud, heaped with stones, sloped steeply down to the ground.

'*Down you come,*' said a soft, breathy voice from below.

It was an encouragement from among the grouped survivors.

Other souls took up the whisper. 'Down you come, child. Down.' And then subsided into silence.

'Ready?'

Smudge nodded. Tremblingly, tentatively, she touched Lady with her bare heels. Lady took a step towards the top stair. She lifted one back leg high up and waved it, gropingly. The front legs wobbled. One front hoof stepped forward. The hind came down, a slither, a stumble – a gasp from everyone assembled – and then she steadied herself once more.

The first half-step was accomplished, but the hind legs were still on the gallery, and the front two were below, unevenly splayed.

'Lean back,' murmured Charlotte.

Smudge leaned.

'Come on, Lady, good girl,' said Charlotte. 'Leg on, Smudge, pretend it's a bank, out hunting.'

Smudge obediently squeezed with her legs – although her thighs were weak and shaking with fear.

All eyes on the gallery were fixed on the pony's hind legs,

holding their breath to see if, when they left the stability of the landing, they would lose their footing.

Tears started into Smudge's eyes. She gritted her teeth.

The pony slipped down yet another step with a foreleg, trying to avoid the moment when all four were on the slope but, stretching too far, she was forced to catch up with her back legs. She slid her back feet forward in tiny, slithering, skating movements until, at the edge, she simply ran out of wood and a hoof dropped the inches into the built-up squelching slope below.

'Walk on,' said Charlotte, brightly.

Below them, Levi lifted his nose and huffed comfortingly. Emerald leaned against him, grasped Ernest's hand in breathless anticipation.

Lady took another slow step. Her hooves found mud, rocks, steps themselves. With slithers and jolts, and legs bent at angles, she made her slow progress. Her hocks trembled. She threw up her nose, eye-whites showing. Smudge slipped a little on the smooth coat, leaning back further for balance, her small fingers twisting in the long mane, white-knuckled, her mother's hand firmly holding her hip.

Finding hoof-holds in the mud, heaped sacks and stones, it seemed the pony had begun to seek purchase with equanimity and even, from what they could judge by the set of her ears, cheerfulness.

'Good girl,' said Charlotte.

They were more than halfway down the staircase.

They stumbled.

With a great scooping slide of a back leg, her weight toppled and Lady almost sat down on the stairs, as the child fell sideways and grabbed at her mother's shoulder.

'Oh!' cried the watchers beneath them. 'Oh!' cried the

watchers above, as the pony's front legs, unbalanced by the weight of her back end, buckled.

Both knees crumpled, as if to somersault, and Charlotte, losing her footing, too, on the slithering mud, screamed. Her scream was not for the fall, though, but for a different reason.

As the pony began to tumble she caught sight – through locks of hair, half-hidden in the bleary soil-heaped lumps of the ground below – of the white face of Charlie Traversham-Beechers, buried in the mud. Its eyes were open, staring at her. Even as she screamed, the pony's flailing metal hoof came down upon the face, flat. And gripped, halting. And stood – still. The fall was arrested. The pony threw up its head. The man's face, pressed deeper into the mud, disappeared altogether.

The pony was secure, trembling but safe, and Charlotte, in horror and disbelief, found herself making weeping mews and gulps. All her limbs and fingers, her head, her innards, shook. She closed her mouth. She sought control.

'All right? Smudge?' she quavered.

Smudge, aboard the pony still, not having seen the apparition but alarmed enough by her own situation, could only nod.

'Shall we go on?'

They continued.

The mud and stones beneath Charlotte's spoiled shoes were mud and stones once more. There was no body underneath them. There was no corpse's face to step upon, just the sliding makeshift slope of the stairs.

Above, the household craned and stared; around and below, the host of wan visitors watched in dread silence.

A few more steps – the pony could have jumped down now if she'd a mind to – and they had reached the ground.

All four pony legs and two human ones were planted level once more.

'There,' said Charlotte, and swallowed, and gave a laugh that was very like a sob.

The onlookers – even the drained travellers – could not resist a small, weak cheer.

Smudge beamed up at them. She slithered gratefully from Lady's back and into her mother's arms.

Charlotte kissed her head. Smudge thought that it was a good thing her mother's dress was ruined already, so she couldn't spoil it with her dirty embrace.

There was a breath of mildness in the air as Emerald and Ernest led Levi and the relieved pony back to the stables. The groom's quarters were silent and empty still. The moment they released her into her stall, the pony turned away and began to tear hungrily at the hay in her manger, apparently suffering no ill effects at all from her adventure. Emerald kissed Levi on the nose and she and Ernest walked back hand in hand. The smell of the springtime in the dark, after the heavy rain, was like a spell upon them.

On their return to the Old House they entered by the main door and closed it behind themselves, engulfed by the smell of the travellers.

'They must be ready for bed now,' said Emerald, sliding the bolt home.

Above them, on the broad gallery, the others were busily making last-minute adjustments to the makeshift dormitory, but the passengers had – in characteristic precipitation – already started up the stairs, slow but eager.

'Come up!' cried Clovis from the gallery.

They left their belongings behind them as they went, and

heaved their heavy feet from step up to step. The others whispered along behind. One by one they poured onto the leaning gallery above the great hall; their strange bedroom.

Emerald and Ernest pushed through the crowds as politely as they could. They had to hold their breaths against the stench and reached the top breathless.

'Will it do?' asked Clovis, casting an eye about the gallery.

The rows and rows of beds awaited their occupants. Made from sheep hurdles, boxes, planks, but laid over with layers and layers of Sterne's softest bedding, they were padded here with a tapestry cushion, there with a muffler, and draped with shawls of Charlotte's, rugs from the floors of the rooms.

'They are the best we could do for them,' said Patience.

'Just a moment!' cried Emerald, running to straighten a blanket.

'There!' cried Florence, as the last bed was finished. 'I think that's that!'

And the family guided each of the weary travellers towards a bed, taking arms, holding hands, overcoming their natural revulsion at the utterly spent, dirty persons trudging exhaustedly to their rest, limbs buckling, flesh sinking.

'Thank you,' they said.

'Thank you for your kindness.'

'Thank you.'

'Oh, we weren't kind,' said Emerald, thinking of the household's inconvenience and reluctant servitude.

'You were; you were, in the end,' they answered her.

One by one, and bit by bit, the torn and tarnished passengers found places and laid their heads down. Mothers clasped children to their breasts, husbands lay with wives. No more complaining, just a vast and encompassing relief, as each and all, with sighs of blissful calm, found that no feather bed, no prince's couch, no ample mattress of any kind compared with

these hard resting places, these coffin-shaped portals to their longer peace.

Laid out in rows, calmly stretching out their limbs – where they had them – all crossing their hands across their chests and breathing their last and pleasant breaths, they fell into deep, deep oblivion. And were released.

All was utter and human stillness in the Old House, among the living and the dead.

Charlotte, Emerald, Smudge, Patience, Florence, Ernest, Clovis and John stood in a row by the hole in the wall that opened into the little bedroom and watched the bodies laid out. The stench that had filled the house and clung all about them thinned, paled, lifted, and was, quite suddenly, absent. The air was alive and young. Their consciences, which had been leaden since the strange arrivals, lightened and were free. There was nothing more to do.

'I think it's time we rested, too,' said Charlotte, and they all withdrew.

Excited, fevered, believing they would never sleep, each of them was met, one by one, by flat exhaustion – and perhaps the easing of some wakeful spell that had fired them – until, at last, like the sated passengers, they slumbered in oblivion.

Emerald, who was wrapped in a paisley shawl and other scraps, held Smudge in her arms. Their breath was sweet and measured, as all the breathing of the household was sweet and measured, for in the few hours before the dawn, they found the peace of a long night. None of them had the sheets or blankets belonging to their bedrooms – or any sheets or blankets at all. All of them slept haphazardly, in disorganised necessity. Ernest slumbered in his greatcoat, solemn; Clovis with his arm flung out, sprawled across his bed like a puppy,

with the spaniels Nell and Lucy to make up the litter. Patience, tidy even in sleep, had tucked herself into her trunk, like a gold ring in a box. Florence – ah, Florence Trieves – she made a different shape that night. Where once she had slept alert, almost standing, like the animals in the fields, guarded against life, that night she was loose-limbed; deep, deep, deep in trusting, restorative sleep – with John Buchanan beside her, just for warmth.

And Charlotte slept on her window seat, heaped with her underthings and other garments as bedclothes, watching for her husband. The cat Lloyd slept, the horses Levi and Lady in their stalls, the lurcher Forth, the spaniels, Lucy and Nell, Tenterhooks, and even the mice, all, all, all slept.

8

EDWARD SWIFT RETURNS

Night drew back on a mild delightful day. All the elements that represent a spring morning were at their boldest: tumbling birdsong, mist rising from the wet ground; this was a May Day to celebrate.

Sun hurtled through the windows and bathed the extreme filth of the house in its beams. Mud glinted in the heavenly glow. Emerald danced through the debris.

'Good morning, Myrtle! No Pearl Meadows again?' she sang, and did not notice that Myrtle's mood did not match her own. Myrtle was washing up, like a tortoise climbing a mountain.

'Morning, Miss Em,' she said. 'If you don't mind my asking . . .' And she gestured towards the door of the Old House, which stood wide open, revealing the mud-covered stairs and still smoking fire.

Emerald tripped gaily past Myrtle and stepped through. There was a woman in a blue dress, standing with her hands open to the sunlight, as if she were beneath a waterfall.

'Florence?' said Emerald. 'Mrs Trieves?' Florence turned. 'Your dress . . .' said Emerald weakly.

She found she was gawping and failed to rearrange her face.

'Good morning, Miss Em,' said Florence. 'The passengers have all gone!'

'Gone?' Emerald picked up her skirt to climb the muddy

stair. It was true. The beds were there but the passengers had quite disappeared. The air that floated through the front door was scented with hyacinths, narcissi and grass.

'The Railway must have come for them,' said Florence.

'And about time, too,' remarked Emerald.

She crossed to the nearest little nest, one into which she herself had lain a child, and picked up the pillow that lay upon it. The pillow was fresh and crisp, starchy and white as if it had just been taken from the cupboard. Holding it, she looked about. All around her the beds were made, with sheets and fresh cotton, untouched.

Gradually the household emerged, yawning and refreshed, oddly buoyant after their short, disarranged sleep. Walking about the house, converging in rooms that bore the marks of the night's activities – dozens of cups strewn here and there, plates stacked by the fireguard in the morning room, cigars all over the floors – they took delight and pleasure in discovering the proof that what had taken place was real, as if conceivably they could have concocted such events from fantasy. The fact remained, though, that however many little proofs were found – the forty chairs crowded into two small rooms, Clovis's missing collar and tie, every knife, spoon and fork in the house dirtied – it was not the material facts that eluded them, but the feeble imprint they made on their minds. They could not seem to make it stick.

Still, if anyone were to doubt the veracity of their hosting the hoards at Sterne, the harshest of undeniable truths was the mess. No birthday party any of them had known or dreamed of could have produced the like.

The gargantuan task of returning things to a semblance of order was undertaken in an atmosphere of cheerfulness by both family and guests. Mud was the main imposter, and grease

the next. A number of scrubbing brushes were worn to the wood.

'Perhaps we could leave the old stairs to grow grass?' suggested Patience.

'When Pearl Meadows does deign to honour us with her presence she can have sole charge of polishing them,' Myrtle was heard to mutter. She had grumpily risen at dawn, determined to ignore any apology from Florence Trieves that might be forthcoming, following her harridan attack of the night before, but having found the woman in a cotton frock, singing as she went about the place, she had been partially disarmed immediately, and the rest of her defences were laid down when, on seeing her, Florence enveloped her in arms – warm! – and a smile – warmer! – and apologised, not perfunctorily, but generously, not just for having shouted the day before, but for any historical bad temper the girl could summon to memory. Who could bear a grudge then? Not Myrtle, certainly, although she gave Florence a wide berth anyway, in case her good humour was caused by some mental aberration of which violence was the next stage.

Glancing across the morning like a pebble on water, we see Smudge sleeping deeply, in Emerald's bed, until rising, late but happy, to join in the activity; buckets of water heaved and sloshing; oddly chiming clocks marking differently occupied hours as the house emerges into clear day.

As the morning goes by, we see Emerald and Ernest, craving time together to bask in their similarities, excusing themselves for half an hour to find the dusty microscope in the attics.

The attics – ah, what stored dreams and pleasures were there among the stained curtains and wobbly tables, waiting to be mended? They stepped across the beams, through the shafts of sun carefully.

'Do you remember where it is?' asked Ernest.

'Of course. It's over there.'

They did not have to search.

Ernest knelt beside her as she took the heavy wooden box, like a little coffin, from its place. *Click. Click.* Click. She released the familiar brass clasps. He opened the box of slides, removed the card (*with love from your friend, Patience*) and handed her one to unwrap. She slipped it from its tissue paper and slid it beneath the lens, securing it with neat, remembering fingers. He began to rummage about the things nearest to them, looking for a suitable object for their scrutiny, she cleared a space and set the microscope square. They acted naturally, in unison, both conscious of the same practical fascination, the understood sympathy of the other.

'Spider—' he said.

'Large?'

'Not very.'

'Anything else?'

'Feather?' Being with Ernest as they went about the jumbled attic it was as if, looking at the tapestry in the dining room for the millionth time, she had seen a new set of deer emerge from the trees, new trumpets, another scattering of embroidered flowers. She glanced up at him. The light shone on her face, but his was in shadow, looking down at her.

'What colour are your eyes?' she asked.

'I haven't the vaguest notion, why?'

Then they kissed.

They missed each other's mouths at first as neither had ever done it before, but they made a good study of it and progressed marvellously quickly. They kissed until they were breathless, and feared forgetting themselves.

Drawing away, she said a little unsteadily, 'We haven't any

butterfly wings or beetle's legs. Here, give me a strand of your hair.'

Only Charlotte was exempt from the general cheeriness. Not because she did not want to help (although she didn't), but rather because she was more cautious in the piecing together of events in her mind to a pleasing conclusion, and too occupied by questions to forget the discomfort and horror of the night.

When it was the turn of the dining room to be cleared, she went ahead, and stood, staring at the shattered glass and port stain on the damask that shouted out the game of Hinds and Hounds – the game that had undone her . . . And yet, she had emerged unscathed. Wonderingly she picked up a thin shard between her thumb and forefinger, and seemed to hear *pass the glass, pass the glass* ring in the panelling around her. Charlie Traversham-Beechers had defied the natural rules of life and death to ruin her and yet – he loved her. She did not now doubt that she had seen his face beneath the pony's foot upon the stair, she did not doubt he saved them. She shivered. The laughing sounds of her family were distant as a chill surrounded her. Where was he now? she wondered. And, when she banished him, where had he gone? She knew the innocent passengers were released to kind oblivion, but what would release a man like Charlie Traversham-Beechers from the eternal waiting?

As Emerald and Ernest desired time alone with one another, so Charlotte, bruised by her ordeal, needed solitude in which to regain her own equilibrium. She slipped out of the house and walked, as Emerald had done the day before, along the border, now decimated with holes and ground down by tramping feet, until she reached the gate to the yard behind the harness room and stables.

'Good God!' she said out loud, and suddenly, 'Where on earth did Robert and Stanley get to!'

The trees around the glade in which she stood reached pale limbs to the duck-egg sky, fluttering their acid-green leaves in the sunlight. There came, upon the breeze, the sound of hooves and wheels approaching.

'Edward!' She turned and ran back to the drive.

They all ran from the house in a group as the cart arrived; pulled by Ferryman, driven by Robert, with Stanley in the back of it – and Edward, upright and wholesome, next to Robert on the seat. It rolled to a halt by the front door.

'Oh, we are glad to see you!' said Emerald, to all of them, and beamed at the groom and his boy as Robert climbed down to greet them.

Charlotte joined them, nervously patting her hair.

'There wasn't any passengers to be seen,' said Robert.

'Where on earth *were* you all this time?' cried Emerald, as her mother ran to her husband and held up her face for kissing, tugging on his sleeve.

'Well . . .' Robert appeared confused. 'Stanley?'

Stanley was pulling Edward's cases down from the cart. 'It was raining,' he said, pausing. 'We looked where they told us – then—' He stopped, uncertain. 'Da?'

'We were in the woods for some time,' said Robert. 'Mr Edward's train came in on time,' he finished, as if that was an end to it. And both seemed to trail off into a reverie.

Edward had climbed down from the cart and held his wife about the waist, smiling at them all. He had the gladness of a returning soldier, the benign glance of a prince.

'A little unusual to be collected in the cart when we keep a carriage and a car,' he said.

Charlotte clung to him as he greeted the men with hand-shakes and Patience with a respectful raising of his hat.

'I was sorry to miss the birthday,' he said to Emerald. 'How was it?'

'I might have to be thrashed,' said Smudge, emerging from behind her mother's skirts.

'What for?' he asked seriously. 'You know I'll do it.' (He wouldn't.)

'For bringing Lady into the house,' said Charlotte, widening her eyes.

'Up or down?'

'Up,' said Emerald.

'Oh. That's grave. I did that once, when I was a boy, and we had to get Brian Doonan out with his winch. It was a dreadful calamity, but the pony survived.'

'What was your pony's name?' asked Smudge.

'He was Godfrey.'

Smudge nodded.

'It was a Great Undertaking,' she said.

'I don't doubt it,' was his reply.

They all made their way into the house, as the tale of the descent of Lady was told to him.

'Fun and games here,' he said, 'compared to the terrible crash they had down at Whorley.'

At this, every one of them stopped, entirely arrested in the act of walking and leaving Edward to go on alone a step or two before realising it.

'A crash?' said Charlotte faintly. 'A train?'

'Yes, a dire one. Fifty people lost their lives, George at the station was telling me. Men, women and children – all of one carriage, and casualties from the next. They say we're all equal in the eyes of God, but they were all of them from Third

Class. An unfair disadvantage. Except for one unfortunate fellow from First.'

He did not think their silence odd, the news being so shocking. After a moment, Emerald whispered, 'What did the others do?'

'The others?'

'From the train – the *survivors*.'

'They took them on to Whorley, I believe. There's the hotel there and the inn. George said the Railway had to lay on a motorbus and several horse-drawn for the journey, all at short notice. It's a terrible thing. They were all in shocked discombobulation, you can imagine.'

They were standing in the hall, each absorbing the news of the crash, but none moved to discuss their impressions.

'Shall we?' said Charlotte at last, and they continued.

With daylight and their own concrete concerns to occupy them, it's perhaps not so odd that a train crash elsewhere, affecting strangers, bore little significance to Emerald, Charlotte and Clovis, who wanted to know if the house were to be saved, or Ernest, who was only thinking about Emerald, or Patience, who was looking at Clovis . . . Edward had journeyed to Manchester to see about saving Sterne, and the time had come for them to discover if he had succeeded.

'I have news,' he said. 'It's family business, and somewhat delicate, being concerned with financial matters.'

'Then we shall leave you,' said Ernest.

'No, no – we'll leave you. We'll go to the morning room, if you'll forgive us.'

'No, of course,' said John, and as the family left the room, Smudge hung back, knowing she would not be wanted.

'Smudge!' Charlotte called as she left.

Smudge never knew if her name meant 'go away' or 'come here' – but it was usually the former.

'Come!' Charlotte cried, and embraced her as she did so. 'We're going to talk about grown-up things now, but if you wait, shall we find something to do later?'

The gift horse of her mother's attention would not have its mouth peered into by Smudge. She nodded in squashed and surprised delight.

'Yes please, Mother,' she said.

Charlotte continued, 'Patience dear, would you mind taking Imogen with you and finding her a hair ribbon?'

Of course Patience was delighted to be charged with the task, and held out her hand happily. Watching her go, Clovis wondered how he would ever be able to see her cheerfully off to Berkshire on Monday, she had become something of a drug to him.

'Mrs Trieves!' trilled Charlotte. 'You're one of us, surely; do come in!'

And so Florence Trieves, at a respectful distance, followed.

It did seem strange for the family to enter the sunlit morning room after the adventures of the night, with the step-parent Edward Swift at their head once more. They all arranged themselves, Florence the furthest away, behind Charlotte, the others grouped around Edward at the fireplace.

Emerald noticed a blue and white teacup, teetering on a high shelf.

'Your birthday was rather a rum go by all accounts then, Emerald?' he asked, with his back to the fireplace, his arm behind his back.

'Rum's not the word for it,' she told him, and smiled.

Clovis had seated himself on the chaise, with Nell and Lucy at his feet. He found himself eager to show his stepfather his advancement towards maturity, but was unsure how to do it.

'We had a devil of a time getting Ferryman into harness,'

he said, by way of an introduction to civility, and Edward responded in kind.

'So Robert told me, but he behaved himself nicely on the way from the station.'

They smiled at one another, and with that short exchange laid much of their past ill-feeling to rest.

Charlotte sat quite still with her hands in her lap, looking at him expectantly.

The conversation stumbled, faltered and ceased. This was the moment. The fate of Sterne was Edward's to divulge.

'Sterne,' said Charlotte.

'Go on,' whispered Emerald, clenching her fists. 'Tell us what happened.'

'It has turned out very oddly,' said Edward. He seemed momentarily unsure of himself, but then continued. 'As you all know, I went to see Mr Jarvis. And it was much as I thought. He's an unpleasant man and his rejection of my request for a loan was given unpleasantly.'

'He turned you down?'

'Yes.' There was a brief silence as they contemplated the significance of this. 'You know my feelings about Mr Jarvis. I was both disappointed and relieved. Well, it came to nothing; so that's that.'

'Oh!' said Emerald and Charlotte together, while Clovis merely dropped his chin and stared unseeingly at the spaniel Nell's domed head.

So that was that. There was no money; he had failed.

Bad news could be told so quickly. How swift and decisive was the hand of fate.

'But that's not all,' he went on hastily. 'There's a great deal more. I—' He broke off and turned his back to them. He seemed to examine the photograph of Charlotte and Horace that stood on the mantel, while the family behind him waited,

with shallow breaths. 'The fact of the matter is this,' he said quietly, still not turning. 'And if it had not happened to me, if I had not seen the papers and had them verified myself, I wouldn't believe it . . .'

'Believe what?' Charlotte was more frightened now than curious. All three felt a frisson, like a cold wind over a wheat field. The very strange events of the nighttime had reached out, and come to visit them in this cheerful sunny room.

Could it be that Edward Swift, the most solid of men, had himself come across the Insubstantial, and wondered at it, as they had?

He turned to face them once more, but it was Charlotte, and Charlotte alone, he addressed.

'Somebody from your past has taken a hand in our affairs,' he said.

His words were leaden. Clovis sat back at once and looked askance at the empty grate. Emerald felt a lump rise in her throat and her scalp prickle. The spectre of dishonour had again raised itself.

'Oh?' said Charlotte.

She reached a hand blindly behind her, and found it gripped, warmly, by Florence Trieves' strong fingers. They clutched one another as he continued.

'A most extraordinary and wonderful thing has happened.'

'Wonderful?' echoed Charlotte in a whisper.

'When I left Mr Jarvis's office yesterday, it was still very early, so I decided to stop by my chambers on my way to the club for dinner. I hadn't any appointments, and I wasn't expecting anyone to be there – anyone save the porter, you understand.'

'Go on.'

'Well . . . When I got there, when I arrived, the porter – you know him, Hargreaves – wasn't there.'

'Wasn't there?' she whispered.

'No, his cousin – that is, a fellow who claimed to be his cousin – was there.'

'Claimed to be? Did you doubt it?'

'I had no cause to, but it was odd – I don't know why I mention it. He was a queer fellow – very pale, unwell, I think. Anyway, he said he sometimes stands in for Hargreaves when there is no one about, and they hadn't expected me there on a Saturday, of course, but that the gentleman I was expecting was in my chambers, and waiting for me.' He glanced around their faces, as if to make sure they were listening. 'You know, I wasn't expecting any gentleman. The man's name was—' He stopped. 'Well, it was . . . Modkin, or Malcolm, or – Lord, it's not like me to forget a fellow's name. It was Martin then, whatever it was, he was an old man, weak, possibly, distinguished. And he claimed to have business with me, and, what's more, that I had known about it for a fortnight. Am I soft in the head, Charlotte?'

'No, Edward.'

'Emerald?'

'No, of course not: please go on.'

'He said I had known about it, and that he was in Manchester on another matter, but that he had thought it would be more civil and appropriate to speak to me face to face, given the large sum of money.'

'What large sum of money?'

'The one left to Horace – excuse me, Charlotte, for mentioning his name when I know it pains you to hear it – for Horace Torrington's child. Money left by a wealthy and distant relative called—' Again he stopped, perplexed. 'Perhaps I'm tired,' he said. 'It's not like me to forget names.'

'Sit down; go on,' said Charlotte, who was herself as white as the pillows on which the passengers had laid their poor and rotting faces.

He sat and, doing so, he drew a narrow sheaf of papers, tied

with a black ribbon, from his breast pocket. He untied it by tugging the free end neatly with his front teeth as was his habit, opened it, and read. 'A great-aunt named Mabel Eglantine Breeches – that was it! – Mabel Eglantine Breeches, which is a very odd name and no wonder she never married if she was as odd as it was. But as I say, she has bequeathed to the youngest child of Horace Torrington, the sum of – Emerald, see to your mother.' Emerald went and sat by her mother, and took her hand. '– the sum of sixty thousand pounds.'

'The child?' whispered Charlotte. '*Children*, surely?'

'No, it clearly states "child", and it names Smudge, see here: "Imogen Artemis Torrington". "To secure for her, and her mother, who may do with it as she sees fit, a dignified life." Odd wording from an odd woman. A dignified life. See? I can't make head nor tail of it.'

He held the paper out to her. Charlotte did not move to take it, so Emerald took it for her.

'It's all very . . . I can't understand the language very well, Edward,' Charlotte said.

'Trust me, then. This isn't the will, you understand, this is a document drawn up by the gentleman, Mr . . . What was his name? McCloud? He has the will, signed and sealed, in Lincoln's Inn, in London. This Modkin wasn't her lawyer, but simply charged with the delivery of the papers to me. It's all quite legal and respectable, if unconventional.' There was a silence. 'Miss Breeches died some months ago.' Still nobody responded. 'She had no other relatives.'

'Horace had no one,' said Charlotte weakly. 'His family were dead – poor and dead.'

'So you've always told me. You were mistaken.'

'What did you say was her name?'

He checked the paper once more. 'Mabel Eglantine Breeches.'

'And she's dead?'

He was patient. 'Yes, Charlotte, she's dead.'

'I see. Sixty thousand pounds?'

'Yes.'

'And the house is saved?'

'Yes, my dear. And everyone in it.'

'We have a roof?'

'A large one.' (He was not a man to point out that his own respectable salary would have kept them modestly until they died, in a smaller and more sensible house.)

'Dignified,' said Charlotte. 'Dignified.' And then she bowed her head and cried.

'There, Dearest, there . . .' said Edward.

John Buchanan was taking his leave. His gleaming car, restored, seemed about to paw the gravel with its eagerness to be gone, as he followed Robert down the stairs with his luggage. Emerald stood waiting by the newel post, with a fonder look than any she had bestowed upon him before.

'John,' she said. 'I don't know whether to apologise or thank you.'

John paused beside her and let Robert and the trunk get away from them before replying, 'You've nothing to thank me for, Emerald, and certainly no apology to make, either. You are—'

He was lost for words, for the moment, seeing in an instant that having desired Emerald's house, her hair, her dazzling excellence, he now did *not* desire exactly those same attributes. She was a fine example of womanhood, to be sure. He was a fine specimen, too, he thought, but of a different species from Emerald Torrington and they would have made an unhappy hybrid. Unable to articulate any of these rare insights, he made do with smacking her on the arm.

'Happy Birthday,' he said. 'I hope I can persuade you and Clovis into town for some more conventional entertainments. For fun.'

'Fun would be grand. Goodbye, John.'

'Goodbye.'

With that, they joined the others outside.

John glanced back, once, at the sun-bathed, elegant front of Sterne. He swallowed his residual disappointment that, given the news the house was saved, he would not now be its master, by money or marriage. Then he shook hands all round, and grinned and boomed his way out, thumping Ernest on the back and making confident little bows to the ladies. (He had the temerity to wink at Florence; she had the gall to wink back.)

'Goodbye!' called Emerald.

'Goodbye!' called everybody else, and he slapped his thigh with his driving gloves, climbed into his car, made a neat half circle, and sped away between the yews. He waved a hand in farewell to the group assembled on the drive and, with a splutter and a pop, he out-raced the lurcher Forth before reaching the road.

Smudge, encircled by her mother's arm, remarked, 'I like the farmer John Buchanan. He's not bad,' as if somebody had said he was.

The shiny car as it receded did not hold their attention for long, and as Forth galloped back towards them, Emerald looked up at Ernest, and Clovis took Patience's hand and pulled her into the shadow of the porch. He kissed her, briefly, crushing her mouth most adorably.

'I like you, too,' she whispered. 'Now stop that: you're very naughty.'

They emerged onto the driveway like a pair of coy acrobats who've just pulled off a tricky triple somersault.

Observing them, Edward remarked, 'I have only been away for one night, Charlotte; the children are transformed!'

'Yes,' answered she, vaguely, moving closer to him.

He bent to kiss her, but she interrupted him.

'What is that divine smell?' she sang as he noticed his nose, too, was tantalised by something marvellous.

They all turned as Florence Trieves emerged from the house.

'You didn't discover bacon?' said Charlotte to her.

'I did.'

'My God, you're superb.'

The spring morning, a tolerably clean house, fresh clothes, love, and four pounds of bacon were to the Torrington-Swifts and their guests the very pinnacle of bliss.

The dining room was bare of decoration, only themselves, the plates, the huge pile of rashers and jugs of coffee (with a tiny amount of cream between all of them).

Emerald sat close to Ernest, wondering at the way the sunlight touched his cheek and the dazzling deep hues of his hair. His eyes were amber, now she could see them in daylight. It was like eating bacon with a lion; she might sit there forever comparing the glorious tones of him against the tapestry and revelling in his thinking her clever. Ernest himself could not look at Emerald at all, for fear of ravishing her where they sat. Patience licked her fingers neatly like a kitten – the actual kitten Tenterhooks curled up on her lap, and the cat Lloyd on the sideboard, glaring at them.

They had no bread and no eggs either, nothing but the heaped rashers, that were alternately crispy and juicy, wet with hot fat and gorgeously salty.

'We should keep hens,' said Emerald.

Charlotte gave a shrug and said, 'Oh, you know *hens*, they're so small-minded,' to which there was no sensible reply.

CURTAIN

ACKNOWLEDGEMENTS

I consider myself tremendously lucky to have Caroline Wood as an agent; from the first draft manuscript until long after paperback release she is there, a fantastic agent and a great friend.

It is my immense good fortune to be published by Chatto and Windus. Clara Farmer's ability to see what a book *is* and enable it to be more so is a rare talent. She has been each book's closest and kindest friend, and I am in her debt.

The Uninvited Guests took in some ways something of a new direction and I am immensely grateful to Vintage Publishing, Random House, for unstintingly celebrating and supporting it. Not just Clara, but Dan Franklin, Rachel Cugnoni, Juliet Brooke and of course, Gail Rebuck, all have my heartfelt thanks. For their work in promoting the books with me, and the fun we have in doing so, I would like to thank Sue Amaradivakara, Bethan Jones, Lisa Gooding, Fiona Murphy and Claire Wilshaw.

For the US edition, I am grateful to have Terry Karten at Harper Collins, whose enthusiasm and delight in *The Uninvited Guests* has thrilled and encouraged me. Thanks as well to Jonathan Burnham, for taking the book to his heart. Many thanks to Sarah Odell, and to Jane Beirn for all her hard work – and her keenness; it has been a pleasure to work with her again. Also thanks to the wonderful Stephanie Cabot at The Gernert Company.

I should like to thank Christopher Neal for his witty cover illustration for the Chatto edition, and Suzanne Dean for her invaluable design. Thanks, too, to Tomer Hanuka for the gorgeous cover of the US edition.

In Canada, at Knopf, I am tremendously grateful to Louise Dennys for her passion and pleasure in the book, and to Marion Garner for her hard work and generosity. Thanks too, to Adria Iwasutiak.

I should also like to thank Mrs Beeton, very much.

Sadie Jones, December 2011